Contents Table

Section 6: Advanced Routing Techniques

Section 7: Network Automation and Scripting

Section 8: High Availability and Scalability

Section 9: Performance Optimization

Section 10: Monitoring and Troubleshooting

Section 11: Virtualization and Cloud Integration

Section 12: Case Studies and Best Practices

Section 13: Emerging Trends and Future Directions

Appendices

- **Appendix A: Glossary of Networking Terms**
- **Appendix B: Juniper Certification Paths**
- **Appendix C: Resources for Further Learning**

~ Conclusion

Welcome & What You'll Learn

Welcome to *Juniper Networks Unveiled: A Guide to Junos OS and Network Implementation*. This book is your comprehensive resource to mastering Juniper Networks, one of the most advanced and robust networking solutions in the industry. Whether you're a seasoned network engineer or just beginning your journey, this guide has been meticulously designed to provide you with the knowledge and insights you need to navigate and excel in the world of Junos OS and Juniper's powerful networking capabilities.

Why This Book?

The networking landscape is evolving rapidly, with organizations demanding faster, more secure, and highly scalable solutions. Juniper Networks has consistently delivered cutting-edge tools and technologies to meet these demands. From its flagship Junos OS to its hardware and virtualized platforms, Juniper's offerings are trusted worldwide for their reliability, innovation, and performance.

This book is not just a technical manual but a step-by-step guide to understanding, configuring, and optimizing Juniper Networks' solutions. With a structured and practical approach, it bridges the gap between theory and real-world implementation, enabling you to harness the full potential of Juniper's ecosystem.

Who Is This Book For?

This book caters to a broad audience, including:

- **Network Engineers and Architects** looking to expand their expertise in Juniper solutions.
- **IT Professionals** aiming to enhance their knowledge of networking technologies.
- **Students and Beginners** eager to develop foundational skills in network design and management.
- **Certification Aspirants** preparing for Juniper Networks certifications like JNCIA, JNCIS, or JNCIP.

Regardless of your current skill level, this book will guide you step by step, ensuring you build both confidence and competence in managing Juniper Networks.

What You'll Learn

In this book, we will delve into a wide range of topics, from fundamental concepts to advanced networking techniques. Here's a glimpse of what you can expect:

1. **Introduction to Juniper Networks**
   Gain insights into the history and evolution of Juniper Networks, explore the core features of Junos OS, and understand why Juniper is a preferred choice for modern networking solutions.
2. **Junos OS Essentials**
   Learn the installation, configuration, and management of Junos OS. Master the Command Line Interface (CLI) and the J-Web graphical interface for efficient network management.
3. **Routing and Switching Fundamentals**
   Explore static and dynamic routing protocols, VLANs, spanning tree protocols, and advanced Layer 2 and Layer 3 switching capabilities.
4. **Security and Advanced Routing**
   Discover how Juniper Networks secures your infrastructure with SRX firewalls, VPNs, and intrusion detection, while mastering advanced routing techniques like MPLS and traffic engineering.
5. **Network Automation and High Availability**
   Dive into automation using tools like NETCONF, SLAX, and Python, and learn high-availability configurations for resilient networks.

6. **Performance Optimization and Troubleshooting**
   Optimize network performance with QoS and CoS configurations, and develop troubleshooting skills using Junos monitoring tools and debugging techniques.
7. **Virtualization and Cloud Integration**
   Understand Juniper's virtualization solutions and learn how to integrate cloud architectures using SD-WAN and Contrail.
8. **Case Studies and Best Practices**
   Apply your knowledge through real-world case studies and proven best practices to design scalable and secure networks.
9. **Emerging Trends in Networking**
   Stay ahead of the curve with insights into the future of networking, including AI, machine learning, Zero Trust security, and 5G deployments.

How to Use This Book

Each section and chapter is crafted with clear objectives, detailed explanations, and practical examples. You'll find hands-on exercises, configuration steps, and troubleshooting tips to reinforce your learning. For quick reference, the appendices include common Junos OS commands, a glossary of networking terms, and resources to deepen your knowledge.

What You'll Gain

By the end of this book, you will:

- Understand the architecture and capabilities of Junos OS.
- Be able to configure, manage, and troubleshoot Juniper Networks devices effectively.
- Develop advanced networking skills, from routing and switching to security and automation.
- Gain insights into designing and optimizing scalable, secure, and high-performing networks.
- Be prepared to tackle real-world challenges and certification exams with confidence.

A Journey of Expertise

Embarking on this journey will not only expand your technical expertise but also position you as a sought-after professional in the networking industry. Juniper Networks is at the forefront of innovation, and by mastering its tools and technologies, you will be equipped to drive success in any networking environment.

Let's get started and unveil the world of Juniper Networks together!

Section 1:
Introduction to Juniper Networks

The Evolution of Juniper Networks

Juniper Networks, founded in 1996, emerged as a transformative force in the networking industry, challenging established players and pioneering innovations that continue to define modern networking solutions. The journey of Juniper Networks is one of vision, growth, and unwavering commitment to excellence in building scalable, secure, and high-performance networks.

The Early Years: A Vision for Innovation

Juniper Networks was the brainchild of Pradeep Sindhu, who recognized the need for a new kind of networking solution in the mid-1990s. At the time, internet traffic was rapidly increasing, but the infrastructure to support it was lagging behind. Recognizing this gap, Juniper focused on developing routers capable of handling high-speed data traffic more efficiently than existing solutions.

The company's first major breakthrough came in 1998 with the launch of the M40 router. Built on the custom-designed Junos OS, the M40 was revolutionary, offering unmatched scalability, reliability, and performance. It quickly gained traction among major internet service providers, establishing Juniper as a serious contender in the networking space.

Pioneering Junos OS

The development of Junos OS, Juniper's proprietary network operating system, was a defining moment in the company's history. Unlike competing systems, Junos was built with modularity and a unified architecture in mind. This design allowed for consistent performance across various device types, simplifying network management and reducing operational complexity.

Junos OS became the foundation of all Juniper products, providing a unified platform for routers, switches, and security devices. Its robust architecture, combined with a focus on innovation, enabled Juniper to rapidly expand its product offerings while maintaining the reliability and efficiency that customers had come to expect.

Expansion and Diversification

Juniper Networks didn't stop with routers. The company diversified its product portfolio to address the growing needs of enterprises, service providers, and data centers. This included:

- **Switching Solutions**: The EX Series switches brought enterprise-grade Layer 2 and Layer 3 capabilities to organizations worldwide.
- **Security Solutions**: With the acquisition of NetScreen Technologies in 2004, Juniper entered the security market, introducing firewalls, VPNs, and intrusion prevention systems.
- **Virtualized Networking**: Juniper embraced the virtualization trend early, offering solutions like vSRX and vMX to support cloud and virtualized environments.

Through these expansions, Juniper positioned itself as a one-stop solution for networking infrastructure, catering to diverse industries and use cases.

Strategic Acquisitions and Partnerships

Over the years, Juniper has strategically acquired companies and formed partnerships to enhance its technological capabilities. Notable acquisitions include:

- **Netscreen Technologies (2004)**: Strengthened Juniper's security portfolio.
- **Mist Systems (2019)**: Brought AI-driven networking solutions to Juniper, marking its entry into AI-powered network management.
- **128 Technology (2020)**: Enhanced Juniper's SD-WAN capabilities with advanced session-based routing technology.

These acquisitions have not only expanded Juniper's product offerings but have also reinforced its reputation as a leader in innovation and cutting-edge technology.

Driving Industry Standards

Juniper Networks has played a key role in shaping the standards and protocols that define modern networking. From MPLS (Multiprotocol Label Switching) to advanced routing and security protocols, Juniper has been at the forefront of technology development. The company's commitment to open standards and interoperability has made its solutions widely compatible and adaptable across diverse network environments.

Juniper Today: A Trusted Global Leader

Today, Juniper Networks is a trusted name in networking, serving enterprises, service providers, and government organizations around the globe. With a strong focus on automation, AI, and cloud integration, Juniper continues to push the boundaries of what's possible in networking.

Key milestones in Juniper's recent evolution include:

- **AI-Driven Networking**: Integration of AI and machine learning through Mist Systems for proactive network management and enhanced user experiences.
- **Cloud-Ready Solutions**: Products like Contrail Networking support seamless integration with public and private cloud environments.
- **5G and Beyond**: Juniper is actively involved in building the infrastructure required for 5G networks, ensuring scalable and efficient connectivity for the next generation of devices and applications.

Commitment to the Future

Juniper Networks remains committed to driving the next wave of networking innovations. Its focus on sustainability, automation, and intelligent networking solutions positions the company to address the challenges of an increasingly connected world.

As you delve deeper into this book, you will uncover the technologies, strategies, and tools that make Juniper Networks a global leader in networking. From its humble beginnings to its current role as a cornerstone of modern networking, Juniper's journey is a testament to the power of vision, innovation, and relentless pursuit of excellence.

Overview of Junos OS

Junos OS is the cornerstone of Juniper Networks' product offerings, designed to deliver robust, scalable, and high-performance networking solutions. As a purpose-built operating system, Junos OS powers Juniper's routers, switches, and security devices, providing a unified and efficient platform for managing complex network infrastructures. This chapter offers an in-depth overview of Junos OS, highlighting its architecture, functionality, and unique features that set it apart from other network operating systems.

The Foundation of Junos OS

Developed as a single, modular operating system, Junos OS was introduced alongside Juniper's first product, the M40 router, in 1998. The operating system was designed with three key principles: simplicity, reliability, and innovation. These principles remain central to its architecture, making Junos OS a trusted choice for service providers, enterprises, and data centers worldwide.

Core Philosophy:

- **Unified Code Base**: Unlike many network operating systems that have disparate versions for different platforms, Junos OS operates on a single code base. This means the same OS runs across all Juniper devices, simplifying updates, feature integration, and troubleshooting.
- **Operational Consistency**: A standardized interface and configuration structure ensure a consistent user experience across devices, reducing operational complexity and the learning curve for network administrators.

Key Components of Junos OS

Junos OS is built on a modular architecture, separating its functions into distinct components. This design enhances its stability, security, and scalability.

1. **Control Plane:**
   The control plane manages the system's routing protocols and network management functions. Running on the Routing Engine (RE), it handles tasks such as route calculation and network policy implementation.
2. **Forwarding Plane:**
   The forwarding plane, managed by the Packet Forwarding Engine (PFE), is responsible for processing and forwarding network traffic at high speeds. By isolating the control and forwarding planes, Junos OS ensures that data forwarding remains unaffected even during control plane failures or updates.
3. **Management Plane:**
   This layer handles administrative tasks such as device configuration, monitoring, and management. It includes the Junos CLI and J-Web interface, providing flexibility for administrators to interact with the system.
4. **Network Services:**
   Junos OS integrates advanced services like MPLS, VPNs, and firewall capabilities, enabling comprehensive and secure network deployments.

Design and Features

Junos OS offers a range of features that make it a preferred choice for modern networking environments.

1. Modularity and Stability

The modular design of Junos OS allows individual components to operate independently. For example, a failure or update in one module, such as a routing protocol, does not affect the rest of the system. This reduces downtime and enhances network reliability.

2. Scalability

From small-scale networks to global infrastructures, Junos OS can scale seamlessly. Its robust architecture supports the demands of large data centers, service providers, and enterprise networks.

3. Ease of Use

- **CLI Simplicity**: The Junos CLI is intuitive and user-friendly, offering structured commands and context-sensitive help to simplify configuration and management.
- **J-Web Interface**: For users who prefer a graphical interface, J-Web provides an accessible alternative for managing Junos OS devices.

4. Integrated Security

Junos OS includes built-in security features such as firewall filters, intrusion prevention systems, and VPN support. These capabilities ensure that network traffic is both optimized and protected against evolving threats.

5. Automation and APIs

Junos OS supports advanced automation features, including:

- **NETCONF and REST APIs** for programmatic configuration and management.
- **Python and SLAX scripting** for automating repetitive tasks.
  These tools help organizations streamline operations and reduce manual intervention.

6. Regular Updates and Support

Juniper Networks provides frequent updates to Junos OS, ensuring compatibility with the latest technologies and standards. Security patches and performance enhancements are regularly rolled out, keeping systems optimized and secure.

Supported Platforms

Junos OS is the operating system for a wide range of Juniper devices, including:

- **Routers**: MX Series, PTX Series, ACX Series
- **Switches**: EX Series, QFX Series
- **Security Devices**: SRX Series, vSRX for virtual environments

This versatility enables organizations to deploy Juniper solutions across different network layers, from access and aggregation to the core and edge.

Why Junos OS Stands Out

Junos OS has been instrumental in distinguishing Juniper Networks from its competitors. Its focus on simplicity, efficiency, and innovation provides the following benefits:

1. **Reduced Operational Costs**: A consistent operating system across devices minimizes training and operational overhead.
2. **Enhanced Network Performance**: Optimized forwarding and routing processes ensure low latency and high throughput.
3. **Future-Ready Design**: Built to adapt to emerging technologies, Junos OS supports features like SDN (Software-Defined Networking) and cloud integration.

Conclusion

Junos OS is much more than a network operating system; it is the backbone of Juniper Networks' success and a key enabler of modern networking. By combining modularity, scalability, and ease of use, Junos OS delivers unmatched reliability and performance for organizations of all sizes.

As we move forward, the subsequent chapters will delve deeper into the unique features of Junos OS, its configuration, and its application in various networking scenarios. By mastering Junos OS, you will unlock the full potential of Juniper Networks, setting the stage for efficient, secure, and scalable network deployments.

Key Features of Junos OS

Junos OS stands at the heart of Juniper Networks' success, offering a robust and flexible foundation for managing networking devices across diverse environments. Its design reflects a commitment to simplicity, scalability, and innovation, making it a powerful tool for organizations seeking efficient and reliable network operations. This chapter explores the key features that distinguish Junos OS from other network operating systems and highlight its value in modern networking.

1. Unified Operating System Across All Platforms

One of the most significant features of Junos OS is its unified architecture. Unlike many competitors that deploy multiple operating systems for different device types, Junos OS is designed as a single code base running across all Juniper routers, switches, and security devices.

Benefits of a Unified OS:

- **Consistency**: Simplifies device management by ensuring the same commands, interface, and workflows across all devices.
- **Reduced Complexity**: Minimizes the learning curve for network administrators and reduces errors.
- **Streamlined Updates**: Rolling out updates and patches is straightforward, ensuring consistency across the network.

2. Modular Architecture

Junos OS is built on a modular design, where different functions and processes are isolated into independent modules. This architecture enhances reliability, performance, and scalability.

Key Advantages:

- **Fault Isolation**: Failures in one module (e.g., routing protocols) do not impact others, ensuring system stability.
- **Ease of Upgrades**: Individual modules can be updated or patched without affecting the entire operating system.
- **Improved Security**: Modular isolation helps contain vulnerabilities and prevents them from spreading across the system.

3. Separation of Control and Forwarding Planes

Junos OS separates the control plane, which handles routing and management, from the forwarding plane, which processes and forwards traffic. This design provides several operational advantages:

- **Increased Reliability**: Forwarding continues uninterrupted even if the control plane is under heavy load or undergoing updates.
- **Optimized Performance**: Traffic forwarding is streamlined for low latency and high throughput.
- **Simplified Troubleshooting**: Issues in one plane are easier to diagnose and resolve without affecting the other.

4. Powerful and Intuitive Command Line Interface (CLI)

The Junos OS CLI is widely regarded as one of the most user-friendly and efficient interfaces in the networking world.

Features of the CLI:

- **Hierarchical Structure**: The CLI uses a tree-like structure, mirroring the configuration hierarchy of the device. This makes navigation intuitive and logical.
- **Contextual Help**: Command suggestions and syntax guidance reduce errors and assist administrators in crafting configurations.
- **Rollbacks and Commit Confirmations**: Changes to configurations can be rolled back instantly, and commit confirmations ensure safe deployments.

5. J-Web Interface for Web-Based Management

For users who prefer a graphical interface, Junos OS includes the J-Web Interface, providing a visual approach to managing and configuring devices.

Highlights of J-Web:

- **User-Friendly Dashboard**: Displays real-time device status and performance metrics.
- **Visual Configuration Tools**: Simplifies tasks like interface management and security rule creation.
- **Accessibility**: Allows remote device management through a web browser.

6. Integrated Security Features

Security is a core component of Junos OS, with built-in capabilities that protect networks from a wide range of threats.

Key Security Features:

- **Firewall Filters**: Enforce traffic policies and protect against unauthorized access.
- **Intrusion Detection and Prevention (IDP)**: Detects and blocks malicious traffic in real-time.
- **VPN Support**: Enables secure communication across untrusted networks.
- **Event Logging**: Monitors and records security events for analysis and compliance.

7. Automation and Programmability

Junos OS is designed to support automation, enabling organizations to streamline operations and reduce manual effort.

Automation Tools and Features:

- **NETCONF and REST APIs**: Allow programmatic access for configuration and monitoring tasks.
- **Scripting Support**: Supports Python, SLAX, and event-driven scripts to automate repetitive tasks and respond to network events.
- **Junos PyEZ**: A Python library that simplifies device interaction and automation workflows.

8. High Availability Features

In mission-critical environments, high availability is essential. Junos OS incorporates features that ensure network uptime and reliability.

High Availability Capabilities:

- **Graceful Routing Protocol Restart**: Prevents disruptions during routing protocol updates.
- **Redundant Routing Engines**: Ensures seamless failover in case of hardware failure.
- **Virtual Router Redundancy Protocol (VRRP)**: Provides redundancy for default gateways.

9. Advanced Monitoring and Troubleshooting Tools

Junos OS includes a range of tools for monitoring network performance and diagnosing issues.

Monitoring Tools:

- **Real-Time Performance Monitoring (RPM)**: Tracks metrics such as latency, jitter, and packet loss.
- **Telemetry Streaming**: Provides detailed analytics for proactive network management.
- **SNMP Support**: Enables integration with third-party monitoring solutions.

Troubleshooting Utilities:

- **Packet Capture**: Captures and analyzes live network traffic.
- **Diagnostics Commands**: Quickly identify and resolve issues at the protocol or hardware level.

10. Regular Updates and Support

Juniper Networks provides continuous updates for Junos OS, ensuring devices remain secure and compatible with evolving technologies. This includes:

- **Feature Enhancements**: New features and protocols are introduced to address modern networking needs.
- **Security Patches**: Protect against emerging threats and vulnerabilities.
- **Comprehensive Support**: Juniper offers extensive documentation, community forums, and professional support services.

Conclusion

Junos OS stands out as a robust, versatile, and user-friendly operating system that addresses the challenges of modern networking. Its modular architecture, unified code base, and advanced features make it an ideal choice for managing networks of all sizes and complexities.

In the following chapters, we will explore how these features translate into practical configurations, routing strategies, and security implementations. Understanding and leveraging these key features will enable you to maximize the potential of your Juniper Networks infrastructure.

Benefits of Choosing Juniper Networks

In today's fast-paced, interconnected world, businesses and organizations demand reliable, scalable, and secure networking solutions. Juniper Networks has earned its reputation as a trusted leader in the networking industry by providing innovative, high-performance products and services that meet these needs. This chapter highlights the key benefits of choosing Juniper Networks, exploring how its technologies empower businesses to build robust and future-ready networks.

1. Unparalleled Performance

At the core of Juniper Networks' offerings is the commitment to delivering high-performance networking solutions. Whether it's powering service provider backbones or enterprise networks, Juniper's hardware and software are engineered to handle high data volumes with minimal latency.

Performance Highlights:

- **Custom Silicon Chips:** Juniper's proprietary Application-Specific Integrated Circuits (ASICs) provide exceptional data processing speeds.
- **Optimized Traffic Management:** Advanced traffic engineering ensures efficient resource utilization even in high-demand environments.
- **Scalability:** Juniper solutions support networks of all sizes, from small enterprises to global service providers.

2. Consistent Operating System Across Platforms

Junos OS, Juniper's unified operating system, is a standout feature of the company's product portfolio. By offering a single operating system across routers, switches, and security devices, Juniper eliminates many challenges associated with managing heterogeneous networks.

Benefits of Junos OS:

- **Simplified Management:** Administrators use the same interface and commands across all devices, reducing complexity.
- **Streamlined Updates:** A single code base makes it easier to deploy patches and feature updates across the network.
- **Reduced Training Costs:** Teams only need to learn one operating system, accelerating the onboarding process and reducing training expenses.

3. Advanced Security Features

As cyber threats become increasingly sophisticated, securing networks is more critical than ever. Juniper Networks places a strong emphasis on integrated security, providing robust solutions that protect against a wide range of threats.

Key Security Advantages:

- **Integrated Security in Junos OS:** Features like firewall filters, intrusion detection, and VPN capabilities are built directly into Junos OS.
- **SRX Series Firewalls:** These high-performance devices deliver advanced threat protection, including intrusion prevention, URL filtering, and antivirus capabilities.

- **Zero Trust Networking:** Juniper supports Zero Trust architectures, ensuring strict access control and verification across the network.

---

4. Future Ready Innovations

Juniper Networks has always been at the forefront of technological advancements, providing solutions that adapt to emerging trends and technologies.

Innovative Features:

- **5G and IoT Support:** Juniper's infrastructure is designed to handle the increased demands of 5G networks and the growing number of IoT devices.
- **Cloud-Ready Solutions:** Products like Contrail Networking simplify cloud integration and hybrid cloud deployments.
- **AI-Driven Networking:** With the acquisition of Mist Systems, Juniper has integrated AI-powered features for network optimization and user experience enhancement.

---

5. Automation and Simplified Operations

Managing complex networks can be time-consuming and error-prone. Juniper Networks addresses this challenge with advanced automation tools and features that simplify routine tasks.

Automation Benefits:

- **NETCONF and REST APIs:** Enable programmatic access for configuration and monitoring.
- **Junos PyEZ Library:** Allows administrators to automate tasks using Python scripts.
- **AI and Machine Learning:** Predictive analytics and AI-powered insights reduce downtime and optimize performance.

---

6. Cost Efficiency

While Juniper Networks offers premium products, it delivers significant cost savings over time by reducing operational expenses and improving network efficiency.

Cost-Saving Features:

- **Energy-Efficient Devices:** Many Juniper products are designed to consume less power without compromising performance.
- **Modular Upgrades:** Devices can often be upgraded with new features or components, extending their lifespan and reducing replacement costs.
- **Fewer Downtime Costs:** High availability and robust performance minimize outages, which can be costly for businesses.

---

7. Comprehensive Product Portfolio

Juniper Networks provides an end-to-end portfolio of solutions that cater to diverse networking needs. From data centers to branch offices, Juniper offers products that integrate seamlessly to create a cohesive infrastructure.

Product Categories:

- **Routing:** High-performance routers like the MX Series and PTX Series.
- **Switching:** Enterprise-grade switches such as the EX Series and QFX Series.
- **Security:** SRX Series firewalls and virtualized security solutions like vSRX.
- **Automation and Orchestration:** Tools like NorthStar Controller and AppFormix for managing complex networks.

8. Industry-Leading Support and Certification Programs

Juniper Networks is committed to customer success, offering extensive support and training programs to ensure the best possible experience.

Support Services:

- **Juniper Care Services:** Provides 24/7 support and proactive monitoring for critical issues.
- **Documentation and Knowledge Base:** Comprehensive resources are available for troubleshooting and learning.

Certification Programs:

- **Juniper Networks Certification Program (JNCP):** Includes certifications like JNCIA, JNCIS, and JNCIP, which validate expertise and enhance career prospects.

9. Proven Track Record

With over two decades of experience, Juniper Networks has built a reputation for reliability, innovation, and excellence. Its solutions are trusted by enterprises, service providers, and governments worldwide.

Key Milestones:

- Pioneering high-performance routing with the M40 router.
- Leading the way in MPLS, SDN, and cloud integration technologies.
- Supporting critical infrastructure in industries such as telecommunications, finance, and healthcare.

Conclusion

Choosing Juniper Networks means investing in a proven, reliable, and future-ready networking partner. With its high-performance products, robust security, and innovative features, Juniper empowers organizations to build networks that are efficient, scalable, and secure.

Understanding Network Architecture Basics

A solid understanding of network architecture is the foundation for building and managing reliable, efficient, and scalable networks. Network architecture defines the structure, components, and operational principles of a network, enabling effective data flow between devices and systems. This chapter explores the fundamental concepts of network architecture, providing a baseline for the deeper discussions on Juniper Networks solutions and Junos OS in subsequent chapters.

---

1. What is Network Architecture?

Network architecture refers to the framework that outlines how a network's components—such as routers, switches, servers, and endpoints—interact to facilitate communication and data transfer. It encompasses:

- **Design Principles**: How the network is planned to meet performance, scalability, and reliability requirements.
- **Infrastructure Components**: Physical and virtual devices that form the backbone of the network.
- **Protocols and Standards**: Rules governing data transmission and interoperability.

A well-designed network architecture ensures:

- **Efficient Data Flow**: Minimizing latency and maximizing throughput.
- **Scalability**: Supporting growth without significant reconfiguration.
- **Resilience**: Maintaining performance during failures or traffic surges.

---

2. Core Components of Network Architecture

To understand Juniper Networks' role in network design, it's essential to grasp the core components of a network architecture.

a. Physical Components

- **Routers**: Devices that direct data packets between networks. Juniper's MX Series excels in high-speed routing and scalability.
- **Switches**: Devices that connect devices within a local area network (LAN), such as the EX and QFX Series from Juniper.
- **Servers and Endpoints**: These include physical and virtual machines, IoT devices, and user devices that send and receive data.

b. Logical Components

- **IP Addressing**: Defines unique identifiers for devices within a network.
- **Subnets**: Segments of an IP network that improve traffic management and security.
- **Routing Tables**: Guide data packet movement through the most efficient paths.

c. Software-Defined Components

- **Software-Defined Networking (SDN)**: Centralized management of network resources, often implemented using tools like Juniper's Contrail Networking.
- **Network Virtualization**: Virtual instances of routers or switches, such as Juniper's vMX and vSRX, reduce the reliance on physical hardware.

---

3. Layers of Network Architecture

Network architecture is commonly organized into layers, each serving specific functions to ensure smooth data communication. The Open Systems Interconnection (OSI) model and the TCP/IP model are standard frameworks used to describe these layers.

The OSI Model (Seven Layers):

1. **Physical Layer**: Transmits raw data bits via cables or wireless.
2. **Data Link Layer**: Manages data transfer between directly connected devices (e.g., Ethernet).
3. **Network Layer**: Handles routing and IP addressing (e.g., IPv4, IPv6).
4. **Transport Layer**: Ensures reliable data delivery through protocols like TCP/UDP.
5. **Session Layer**: Manages connections between devices.
6. **Presentation Layer**: Converts data for compatibility between systems.
7. **Application Layer**: Interfaces with end-user applications (e.g., HTTP, FTP).

The TCP/IP Model (Four Layers):

1. **Network Access**: Combines OSI's physical and data link layers.
2. **Internet**: Focuses on IP addressing and routing.
3. **Transport**: Ensures end-to-end communication integrity.
4. **Application**: Provides protocols for specific applications.

Juniper Networks' products and solutions operate across these layers, with a strong emphasis on the network and transport layers to ensure high-performance routing and switching.

---

4. Network Architectures in Practice

Networks are often categorized based on their scale and purpose.

a. Local Area Network (LAN)

- A LAN connects devices within a small geographical area, such as an office.
- Juniper's EX Series switches are ideal for high-performance LAN setups.

b. Wide Area Network (WAN)

- WANs span large geographic areas, often connecting multiple LANs.
- Juniper's MX Series routers enable efficient data routing across WANs.

c. Data Center Networks

- Designed to handle high volumes of traffic and storage, data centers use specialized architectures like spine-leaf designs.
- Juniper's QFX Series switches and Contrail Networking are widely used in data center environments.

d. Cloud Networks

- These architectures leverage virtualization to connect resources hosted on public or private clouds.
- Juniper's vMX and vSRX platforms support cloud integration with ease.

---

5. Key Design Principles of Network Architecture

A successful network architecture follows certain principles to meet organizational goals.

a. Scalability

- The ability to grow without significant redesign. Juniper's modular hardware and SDN solutions make scalability seamless.

b. Redundancy

- Redundancy ensures network availability even during failures. Features like Virtual Router Redundancy Protocol (VRRP) in Junos OS support this principle.

c. Security

- Protecting data and infrastructure is crucial. Juniper integrates security into every layer of its solutions, from firewalls to Zero Trust architectures.

d. Performance Optimization

- Techniques like Quality of Service (QoS) and traffic shaping ensure optimal performance. These features are native to Junos OS.

e. Automation

- Automated tools reduce operational complexity and errors. Juniper's automation capabilities include scripting, APIs, and AI-driven networking.

---

6. The Role of Juniper Networks in Modern Architectures

Juniper Networks excels in delivering solutions that align with modern network architecture requirements.

Key Contributions:

- **Unified Operating System:** Junos OS simplifies operations across all devices.
- **Cutting-Edge Hardware:** High-performance routers, switches, and security devices power networks of all scales.
- **Advanced Features:** Support for MPLS, SDN, and cloud integration ensures future readiness.
- **Automation and AI:** Tools like Juniper Mist enhance efficiency and user experiences.

Conclusion

Understanding network architecture basics is essential for designing and managing efficient networks. Juniper Networks provides the tools and technologies to implement these architectures effectively, ensuring scalability, reliability, and security.

Section 2:
Getting Started with Junos OS

Installation and Setup of Junos OS

Setting up Junos OS is the first step to leveraging the powerful capabilities of Juniper Networks devices. This chapter provides a comprehensive guide to installing and configuring Junos OS, ensuring a smooth transition from initial setup to operational readiness. Whether you're deploying Junos OS on a physical device or a virtual platform, the principles and processes outlined here will prepare you to effectively manage your Juniper infrastructure.

1. Prerequisites for Installation

Before starting the installation process, ensure that the following prerequisites are met:

a. Hardware Requirements

- Verify compatibility of your Juniper device with the specific Junos OS version you plan to install.
- Ensure sufficient hardware resources, such as memory and storage.
- Physical devices like MX Series, EX Series, and SRX Series require proper rack installation and power connections.

b. Software Requirements

- Obtain the correct Junos OS software image from Juniper's official support site.
- Ensure you have a valid license for the software image, especially for advanced features.

c. Tools and Access

- A serial console cable or SSH client for CLI access.
- A terminal emulator like PuTTY or SecureCRT for serial or SSH connectivity.
- Network access to the Juniper device for remote setup.

d. Backup Plan

- Back up existing configurations if you are upgrading or reinstalling Junos OS.
- Ensure a recovery plan is in place in case of installation errors.

2. Installing Junos OS on Physical Devices

a. Accessing the Device

1. **Connect via Console**:
   - Use a console cable to connect your PC to the Juniper device.
   - Launch a terminal emulator with the appropriate settings (9600 baud rate, 8 data bits, no parity, 1 stop bit).
2. **Power On the Device**:
   - Turn on the device and wait for the boot process to complete.

○ Access the CLI when prompted.

b. Loading the Junos OS Image

1. **Upload the Software Image**:
   ○ Transfer the Junos OS image to the device using SCP, FTP, or a USB drive. Example SCP command:

   ```
   scp junos-image.tgz user@<device_ip>:/var/tmp
   ```

2. **Install the Image**:
   ○ Use the request `system software add` command to install the image. For example:

   ```
   request system software add /var/tmp/junos-image.tgz
   ```

   ○ Confirm the installation prompts and let the process complete.
3. **Reboot the Device**:
   ○ After installation, reboot the device with:

   ```
   request system reboot
   ```

c. Verifying Installation

- Once the device restarts, log in and check the OS version using:

```
show version
```

- Confirm that the desired Junos OS version is active.

---

3. Installing Junos OS on Virtual Platforms

Juniper offers virtualized instances like **vMX** and **vSRX**, which require installation on hypervisors or cloud platforms.

a. Supported Platforms

- VMware ESXi
- KVM
- AWS, Azure, and other cloud platforms

b. Steps for Installation

1. **Download the Virtual Image**:
   ○ Obtain the appropriate virtual image (e.g., `.qcow2` for KVM, `.ova` for VMware).
2. **Deploy the Image**:
   ○ For VMware:
     ■ Import the `.ova` file into the ESXi environment.
   ○ For KVM:
     ■ Use `virt-manager` or command-line tools to create a virtual machine and attach the `.qcow2` image.
3. **Allocate Resources**:
   ○ Assign CPU, memory, and storage as recommended for the virtual instance.
   ○ Configure network interfaces for management and data planes.
4. **Power On and Configure**:
   ○ Start the virtual machine and access the CLI via a console or SSH.

c. Initial Configuration for Virtual Instances

- Set the root password and configure management interfaces for remote access.
- Example commands:

```
configure
set system root-authentication plain-text-password
set interfaces ge-0/0/0 unit 0 family inet address <mgmt_ip>/<subnet>
commit
```

---

4. Performing Initial Setup

a. Setting Up the Device

After Junos OS is installed, follow these steps to prepare the device for use:

1. **Login**:
   - Default username: root
   - No default password; set one during the first login.
2. **Set Hostname**:
   - Example:

   ```
   configure
   set system host-name MyJuniperDevice
   commit
   ```

3. **Configure Management Access**:
   - Assign an IP address to the management interface and enable SSH:

   ```
   set interfaces fxp0 unit 0 family inet address <mgmt_ip>/<subnet>
   set system services ssh
   commit
   ```

4. **Enable DNS and NTP**:
   - Configure DNS and time synchronization:

   ```
   set system name-server <dns_ip>
   set system ntp server <ntp_server>
   commit
   ```

---

5. Upgrading or Downgrading Junos OS

a. When to Upgrade

- To access new features, bug fixes, or security patches.

b. Process

1. Backup the current configuration:

   ```
   save /var/tmp/config-backup.conf
   ```

2. Follow the same steps for installing a new OS image.

c. Downgrade Steps

- If compatibility issues arise, you can roll back to a previous version using:

```
request system software rollback
```

---

6. Troubleshooting Installation Issues

a. Common Errors

- **Insufficient Disk Space**: Clear unused files in /var/tmp.
- **Corrupted Image File**: Re-download the software image.
- **Boot Failure**: Use the recovery mode to reinstall Junos OS.

b. Recovery Mode

- Access the recovery shell during boot by pressing <space> when prompted.
- Reinstall Junos OS using a USB or SCP.

Conclusion

The successful installation and setup of Junos OS is the foundation for building an efficient and secure network. Whether you're working with physical devices or virtualized instances, following the outlined steps ensures a smooth deployment.

Navigating the Junos CLI

The Junos Command Line Interface (CLI) is a powerful tool that enables network administrators to configure, manage, and troubleshoot Juniper devices. Its intuitive structure and logical design make it one of the most user-friendly CLIs in the networking world. In this chapter, we'll explore the basics of navigating the Junos CLI, providing you with the skills necessary to interact efficiently with your Juniper devices.

1. Overview of the Junos CLI

The Junos CLI is a text-based interface that allows you to perform tasks such as:

- Configuring device settings.
- Monitoring network performance.
- Diagnosing and troubleshooting issues.

The CLI operates in a hierarchical structure, with distinct modes for operational commands and configuration tasks. This design simplifies navigation and ensures that commands are context-specific.

2. Accessing the Junos CLI

You can access the CLI using the following methods:

a. Console Access

- Connect your PC to the Juniper device using a serial console cable.
- Use a terminal emulator (e.g., PuTTY, SecureCRT) with settings:
  - **Baud Rate:** 9600
  - **Data Bits:** 8
  - **Parity:** None
  - **Stop Bits:** 1
  - **Flow Control:** None

b. Remote Access (SSH)

- Connect remotely using an SSH client. Example:

```
ssh root@<device_ip>
```

- Ensure SSH is enabled on the device's management interface.

c. Out-of-Band Management

- Use the dedicated management port (fxp0) for secure access to the CLI.

3. Modes in the Junos CLI

The Junos CLI has two primary modes:

a. Operational Mode

- Used for monitoring, troubleshooting, and viewing system information.
- Prompts with the > symbol.
- Examples of commands:

```
show interfaces
show configuration
ping <ip_address>
```

b. Configuration Mode

- Used for modifying device settings.
- Entered by typing configure in operational mode. Prompts with the # symbol.
- Examples of commands:

```
set system host-name MyDevice
commit
```

- Exit configuration mode with:

```
exit
```

4. Navigating the CLI Hierarchy

Junos CLI uses a hierarchical structure for organizing configuration settings. Each level represents a specific feature or component of the device.

a. Moving Through the Hierarchy

- Use edit to navigate to a specific section. Example:

```
edit interfaces
```

- To move back up:

```
up
```

- To return to the top level:

```
top
```

b. Viewing the Hierarchy

- Use show to display the current configuration or settings at any level.

```
show
```

5. Common CLI Commands

a. Viewing System Information

- Show device hostname and software version:

```
show system information
```

- Display hardware details:

  ```
  show chassis hardware
  ```

b. Monitoring Interfaces

- View the status of all interfaces:

  ```
  show interfaces terse
  ```

- Check traffic statistics:

  ```
  show interfaces statistics
  ```

c. Performing Basic Troubleshooting

- Ping a remote host:

  ```
  ping <ip_address>
  ```

- Trace a network route:

  ```
  traceroute <ip_address>
  ```

- View system logs:

  ```
  show log messages
  ```

d. Managing Files

- List files in a directory:

  ```
  file list
  ```

- View the contents of a file:

  ```
  file show /var/tmp/filename
  ```

---

6. Making Configuration Changes

a. Setting Parameters

- To set a configuration parameter, use the set command. Example:

  ```
  set system services ssh
  ```

b. Deleting Parameters

- To remove a parameter, use the delete command. Example:

  ```
  delete system services ssh
  ```

c. Committing Changes

- Save changes to the device with the commit command.

- Use `commit confirmed` to apply changes temporarily, reverting them if not confirmed within 10 minutes:

```
commit confirmed
```

d. Rolling Back Changes

- Roll back to a previous configuration using:

```
rollback <number>
```

- Example:

```
rollback 1
```

---

7. Using CLI Shortcuts

a. Auto-Completion

- Press <Tab> to auto-complete commands and options.

b. Abbreviating Commands

- Use the shortest unique abbreviation for commands. Example:

```
sho ver
```

- is equivalent to:

```
show version
```

c. Searching Command History

- Use the up and down arrow keys to scroll through previous commands.

d. Filtering Output

- Pipe output through filters to narrow down results:

```
show interfaces | match ge-0/0/0
```

---

8. Viewing and Saving Configuration

a. Viewing the Current Configuration

- Display the full configuration:

```
show configuration
```

- Display only active configuration lines:

```
show configuration | display set
```

b. Saving the Configuration

- Save the current configuration to a file:

```
save /var/tmp/myconfig.conf
```

Conclusion

The Junos CLI is a versatile and intuitive tool for managing Juniper devices. By understanding its structure and mastering key commands, you can efficiently configure, monitor, and troubleshoot your network.

Understanding Junos Configuration Hierarchy

The Junos OS configuration hierarchy is one of its most powerful and user-friendly features. It organizes configuration settings in a structured, logical tree format, enabling administrators to efficiently manage and customize device settings. By understanding the configuration hierarchy, you can easily navigate, modify, and maintain the settings of your Juniper devices. This chapter provides a detailed overview of the Junos configuration hierarchy, including its structure, navigation methods, and best practices.

1. Overview of the Configuration Hierarchy

The Junos OS configuration is organized into a hierarchical tree structure, where each level represents specific device settings or features. This design simplifies configuration management by grouping related settings together.

Key Concepts

- **Parent and Child Nodes**:
  The hierarchy is composed of parent nodes (categories) and child nodes (specific settings).
  For example:
  - Parent Node: `interfaces`
  - Child Node: `ge-0/0/0` (specific interface settings)
- **Levels of Configuration**:
  Each level in the hierarchy represents a layer of specificity, starting from global settings at the top and narrowing down to granular options.

2. Navigating the Configuration Hierarchy

a. Viewing the Current Configuration

To display the current configuration, use the `show configuration` command. This provides a complete overview of all active settings in the hierarchy.

Example:

```
show configuration
```

Output:

```
system {
    host-name MyDevice;
    root-authentication {
        encrypted-password "$1$abc123...";
    }
}
interfaces {
    ge-0/0/0 {
        unit 0 {
            family inet {
                address 192.168.1.1/24;
            }
        }
    }
}
```

b. Exploring Specific Sections

Use the `edit` command to move to a specific section of the hierarchy.

Example:
To edit the `interfaces` section:

```
edit interfaces
```

c. Returning to Higher Levels

- Move up one level:

  ```
  up
  ```

- Return to the top of the hierarchy:

  ```
  top
  ```

d. Viewing Configuration at a Specific Level

Use show to display configuration details for the current or specific hierarchy level.

Example:

```
show
```

3. Common Configuration Hierarchy Categories

a. System Settings

This section includes global settings like hostname, time zone, and user authentication.

Example:

```
system {
    host-name MyDevice;
    time-zone UTC;
    root-authentication {
        encrypted-password "$1$abc123...";
    }
}
```

b. Interfaces

Defines the configuration for network interfaces, including IP addresses and protocols.

Example:

```
interfaces {
    ge-0/0/0 {
        unit 0 {
            family inet {
                address 192.168.1.1/24;
            }
        }
```

```
    }
}
```

c. Protocols

Configures routing protocols such as OSPF, BGP, and IS-IS.

Example:

```
protocols {
    ospf {
        area 0.0.0.0 {
            interface ge-0/0/0.0;
        }
    }
}
```

d. Security

Includes settings for firewalls, intrusion prevention, and VPNs.

Example:

```
security {
    policies {
        from-zone trust to-zone untrust {
            policy allow-all {
                match {
                    source-address any;
                    destination-address any;
                    application any;
                }
                then {
                    permit;
                }
            }
        }
    }
}
```

---

4. Making Changes to the Configuration

a. Adding Configuration Settings

Use the set command to add new settings at the current level or specify the full path to the setting.

Example:
To set a hostname:

```
set system host-name MyDevice
```

b. Modifying Existing Settings

Simply use the set command with the new value.

Example:
To change an interface IP address:

```
set interfaces ge-0/0/0 unit 0 family inet address 192.168.2.1/24
```

c. Deleting Configuration Settings

Use the `delete` command to remove specific settings.

Example:
To delete an interface IP address:

```
delete interfaces ge-0/0/0 unit 0 family inet address 192.168.1.1/24
```

d. Committing Changes

Save changes to the device configuration with the `commit` command.

Example:

```
commit
```

e. Rolling Back Changes

To revert to a previous configuration version, use the `rollback` command.

Example:

```
rollback 1
commit
```

---

5. Best Practices for Working with the Configuration Hierarchy

1. **Plan Before You Configure**
   - Understand the hierarchy and required settings before making changes.
2. **Use Commit Confirm**
   - When making significant changes, use `commit confirmed` to allow automatic rollback if the changes cause issues.

   Example:

   ```
   commit confirmed
   ```

3. **Backup Configurations**
   - Save configurations regularly to prevent data loss.

   Example:

   ```
   save /var/tmp/backup.conf
   ```

4. **Use Display Options**
   - Use `| display set` to view the configuration in a script-friendly format.

   Example:

   ```
   show configuration | display set
   ```

5. **Document Changes**
   - Maintain a log of configuration changes for future reference.

Conclusion

Understanding the Junos configuration hierarchy is essential for efficient network management. By leveraging its structured design, you can easily navigate, configure, and maintain Juniper devices. As you practice these concepts, you'll gain confidence in managing even the most complex network environments.

Initial System Configuration

The initial system configuration of a Junos OS device is a critical step in preparing it for production use. This process involves setting up essential system parameters, securing the device, and ensuring it is ready to be integrated into the network. This chapter provides a step-by-step guide to configuring a Junos OS device for the first time, covering fundamental tasks such as user authentication, interface setup, and system services.

1. Accessing the Device for Initial Configuration

Before you can configure the device, establish access through one of the following methods:

a. Console Access

- Connect your PC to the device using a console cable.
- Use a terminal emulator (e.g., PuTTY or SecureCRT) with these settings:
  - Baud rate: **9600**
  - Data bits: **8**
  - Parity: **None**
  - Stop bits: **1**

b. Remote Access via SSH

- If the device has a pre-configured management IP address, use an SSH client to connect:

```
ssh root@<management_ip>
```

2. Initial Login and Configuration Mode

When accessing the device for the first time:

1. Log in as the default user:
   - **Username**: root
   - **Password**: No password by default.
2. Enter configuration mode:

```
configure
```

The prompt changes to indicate you are in configuration mode:

```
[edit]
```

3. Setting the Hostname

The hostname identifies the device within the network. Set it using the following command:

```
set system host-name <hostname>
```

Example:

```
set system host-name Juniper-Edge-Router
commit
```

Verify the hostname with:

```
show system information
```

---

4. Configuring User Authentication

a. Setting the Root Password

To secure the device, set a root password:

```
set system root-authentication plain-text-password
```

You will be prompted to enter and confirm the password.

b. Adding User Accounts

To create additional user accounts:

```
set system login user <username> class <user-class> authentication
plain-text-password
```

Example:

```
set system login user admin class super-user authentication plain-text-password
```

---

5. Configuring Interfaces

Interfaces are the primary means of communication for the device. Configure the management and operational interfaces as follows:

a. Management Interface

Assign an IP address to the management interface (e.g., fxp0):

```
set interfaces fxp0 unit 0 family inet address <ip_address>/<subnet_mask>
commit
```

Example:

```
set interfaces fxp0 unit 0 family inet address 192.168.1.1/24
commit
```

b. Operational Interfaces

For general interfaces (e.g., ge-0/0/0):

```
set interfaces ge-0/0/0 unit 0 family inet address <ip_address>/<subnet_mask>
commit
```

Example:

```
set interfaces ge-0/0/0 unit 0 family inet address 10.0.0.1/24
commit
```

6. Configuring System Services

a. Enabling SSH

SSH provides secure remote access to the device:

```
set system services ssh
commit
```

b. Enabling Telnet (if required)

Telnet is not recommended due to security concerns but can be enabled for specific use cases:

```
set system services telnet
commit
```

c. Configuring DNS

Set DNS servers to resolve domain names:

```
set system name-server <dns_server_ip>
commit
```

Example:

```
set system name-server 8.8.8.8
commit
```

d. Configuring NTP

Ensure accurate time synchronization by configuring an NTP server:

```
set system ntp server <ntp_server_ip>
commit
```

Example:

```
set system ntp server 192.168.2.100
commit
```

7. Configuring Static Routes

Static routes ensure traffic reaches its destination. To add a route:

```
set routing-options static route <destination_network>/<subnet_mask> next-hop
<next_hop_ip>
commit
```

Example:

```
set routing-options static route 0.0.0.0/0 next-hop 192.168.1.254
commit
```

8. Saving and Verifying the Configuration

a. Committing Changes

After making changes, save them with:

```
commit
```

b. Reviewing the Configuration

View the current configuration:

```
show configuration
```

c. Saving the Configuration to a File

Save the configuration for backup purposes:

```
save /var/tmp/initial-config.conf
```

---

9. Rolling Back Changes

If recent changes cause issues, you can revert to a previous configuration:

```
rollback <version_number>
commit
```

Example:

```
rollback 1
commit
```

List available rollback versions with:

```
show system rollback
```

---

10. Best Practices for Initial Configuration

1. **Secure Access**: Always set a root password and use SSH for remote access.
2. **Document Changes**: Maintain records of configuration settings for troubleshooting and future reference.
3. **Test Connectivity**: Verify interface configurations with `ping` and `traceroute` commands.
4. **Backup Configurations**: Save configurations regularly to avoid data loss.
5. **Apply Changes Incrementally**: Commit changes in small batches to simplify troubleshooting.

Conclusion

The initial system configuration lays the foundation for a stable and secure Junos OS deployment. By following the steps outlined in this chapter, you can ensure that your Juniper device is ready for integration into the network.

Using J-Web Interface for Configuration

The J-Web interface provides a graphical user interface (GUI) for configuring and managing Juniper Networks devices. It is an excellent alternative for users who prefer a visual approach over the Command Line Interface (CLI). The J-Web interface simplifies tasks like initial setup, system monitoring, and troubleshooting, making it an invaluable tool for administrators. This chapter walks you through accessing, navigating, and using the J-Web interface to configure your Junos OS device.

1. Overview of the J-Web Interface

The J-Web interface is a web-based management tool built into Junos OS devices. It offers:

- **User-Friendly Navigation**: Visual menus and wizards for configuration tasks.
- **Real-Time Monitoring**: Live dashboards for network and device status.
- **Integrated Tools**: Options for diagnostics, log viewing, and troubleshooting.

Key Features

- Configure system settings, interfaces, and protocols.
- Manage security policies and firewall filters.
- Monitor traffic and device health metrics.
- Perform software upgrades and manage system files.

2. Accessing the J-Web Interface

To use the J-Web interface, you need to access the device via a web browser.

a. Pre-Requisites

- **IP Address**: Ensure the device's management interface (e.g., fxp0) has an IP address configured.
- **Browser Compatibility**: Use a modern browser (e.g., Chrome, Firefox, or Edge).
- **Credentials**: Have the username and password for device login.

b. Steps to Access J-Web

1. Open a web browser.
2. Enter the management IP address of the device in the address bar.
   Example:

   ```
   https://192.168.1.1
   ```

3. Accept any security certificate warnings, as the default certificate may not be trusted.
4. Log in with your Junos OS credentials (e.g., root username and configured password).

3. Navigating the J-Web Interface

After logging in, the main dashboard appears, offering an overview of the device's status and quick access to configuration and monitoring tools.

a. Key Sections of the Dashboard

- **System Overview**: Displays hostname, software version, and uptime.
- **Interface Summary**: Provides status and statistics for all interfaces.
- **System Alarms**: Highlights critical and warning alerts.
- **Resource Usage**: Shows CPU and memory utilization.

b. Main Menu Options

The navigation menu is typically divided into the following sections:

- **Monitor**: Real-time statistics and logs.
- **Configure**: System, interfaces, security, and protocols configuration.
- **Diagnostics**: Tools for troubleshooting and testing.
- **Maintenance**: Software upgrades and backups.

---

4. Configuring the Device Using J-Web

a. Setting the Hostname

1. Go to `Configure > System Properties`.
2. Enter the desired hostname in the **Hostname** field.
3. Click **Apply** to save the changes.

b. Configuring Interfaces

1. Navigate to `Configure > Interfaces`.
2. Select the desired interface (e.g., `ge-0/0/0`).
3. Assign an IP address, subnet mask, and other settings.
4. Click **Apply** to activate the configuration.

c. Setting Up Routing

1. Go to `Configure > Routing`.
2. Add static routes by specifying the destination network and next-hop IP.
3. Save the changes by clicking **Apply**.

d. Enabling Services

1. Navigate to `Configure > Services`.
2. Enable or disable SSH, Telnet, or FTP as required.
3. Click **Apply** to confirm changes.

---

5. Monitoring and Diagnostics

The J-Web interface provides powerful tools to monitor and troubleshoot your network.

a. Real-Time Monitoring

- View interface statistics under `Monitor > Interfaces`.
- Check CPU and memory usage in `Monitor > System Overview`.

b. System Logs

1. Navigate to `Monitor > Logs`.

2. Filter logs based on severity or keywords for detailed troubleshooting.

c. Ping and Traceroute

- Perform connectivity tests under `Diagnostics > Tools`.

d. Alarm Management

- Check critical system alerts in `Monitor > Alarms`.
- Resolve issues by following suggested corrective actions.

---

6. Maintenance Tasks

The J-Web interface simplifies routine maintenance tasks.

a. Software Upgrades

1. Navigate to `Maintenance > Software Upgrade`.
2. Upload the new Junos OS image.
3. Follow the on-screen instructions to install and reboot the device.

b. Backups and Rollbacks

- Save the current configuration under `Maintenance > Configuration > Save`.
- Roll back to a previous configuration if needed.

---

7. Best Practices for Using J-Web

1. **Secure Access**: Use HTTPS and configure strong passwords for user accounts.
2. **Regular Backups**: Always save configurations before making significant changes.
3. **Monitor Regularly**: Use dashboards to keep track of system health and resource usage.
4. **Combine with CLI**: Use J-Web for quick tasks and the CLI for advanced configurations.

Conclusion

The J-Web interface offers a convenient and efficient way to configure and manage Juniper devices. Its graphical approach simplifies complex tasks, making it ideal for administrators who prefer a visual interface.

Section 3:
Routing Fundamentals in Junos OS

Understanding Routing Protocols in Junos OS

Routing protocols are the backbone of any network, enabling devices to dynamically discover and exchange route information to ensure data reaches its intended destination efficiently. Junos OS, with its robust architecture and support for a wide range of routing protocols, provides unparalleled flexibility and scalability for routing in modern networks. This chapter introduces the fundamental concepts of routing protocols and their implementation within Junos OS.

1. What are Routing Protocols?

Routing protocols are mechanisms that routers use to dynamically share and learn routes within a network. They determine the best path for data packets to travel from source to destination.

Key Functions of Routing Protocols

- **Path Discovery**: Discovering all available routes to a destination.
- **Path Selection**: Choosing the optimal route based on metrics like cost, bandwidth, and delay.
- **Route Maintenance**: Keeping routing tables updated as network conditions change.

Routing protocols fall into two main categories:

- **Interior Gateway Protocols (IGPs)**: Operate within an autonomous system (e.g., OSPF, IS-IS).
- **Exterior Gateway Protocols (EGPs)**: Operate between autonomous systems (e.g., BGP).

2. Types of Routing Protocols in Junos OS

a. Static Routing

Static routes are manually configured by network administrators and remain constant unless explicitly changed.

Benefits:

- Simple and predictable.
- No overhead from protocol traffic.

Limitations:

- Not scalable for large networks.
- Does not adapt to network changes automatically.

b. Dynamic Routing

Dynamic routing protocols automatically discover and adjust routes based on network conditions.

Benefits:

- Adaptable to changes in topology.
- Scales well for large networks.

Types of Dynamic Routing Protocols Supported by Junos OS:

1. **OSPF (Open Shortest Path First)**:
   - A link-state IGP designed for scalability and efficiency.
   - Uses areas to optimize large network deployments.
2. **BGP (Border Gateway Protocol)**:
   - An EGP used for internet routing and large-scale enterprise networks.
   - Capable of policy-based routing.
3. **IS-IS (Intermediate System to Intermediate System)**:
   - A link-state IGP similar to OSPF, often used in service provider networks.
4. **RIP (Routing Information Protocol)**:
   - A distance-vector protocol suitable for small networks.
5. **Multicast Routing Protocols**:
   - Include PIM (Protocol Independent Multicast) for efficient delivery of multicast traffic.

3. Routing in Junos OS

Junos OS uses a modular routing architecture, separating routing decisions from packet forwarding.

a. Routing Table

The routing table contains all known routes and is used to determine the best path for packet delivery.

- View the routing table with:

```
show route
```

b. Routing Instances

Junos OS supports multiple routing instances, allowing logical separation of routing tables.

- **Default Instance**: Handles standard routing.
- **Virtual Routing Instances**: Used for multi-tenancy or advanced network segmentation.

Configure a routing instance:

```
set routing-instances <instance_name> instance-type virtual-router
```

4. Routing Protocol Metrics

Routing protocols use metrics to evaluate and compare paths. Metrics vary by protocol:

- **OSPF**: Uses cost, based on bandwidth.
- **BGP**: Employs path attributes like AS-path, local preference, and MED.
- **RIP**: Uses hop count.

Protocols with lower metrics are preferred for routing decisions.

5. Configuring Routing Protocols in Junos OS

a. Enabling a Routing Protocol

Routing protocols are enabled in the `protocols` section of the configuration hierarchy.

b. Example: Configuring OSPF

1. Enter configuration mode:

```
configure
```

2. Enable OSPF and configure an area:

```
set protocols ospf area 0.0.0.0 interface ge-0/0/0.0
commit
```

c. Example: Configuring BGP

1. Set the BGP local AS number:

```
set protocols bgp group external type external
set protocols bgp group external local-as 65001
```

2. Configure a neighbor:

```
set protocols bgp group external neighbor 192.168.1.2
commit
```

d. Viewing Protocol Status

- OSPF neighbors:

```
show ospf neighbor
```

- BGP sessions:

```
show bgp summary
```

6. Best Practices for Routing Protocols

1. **Use Authentication**: Secure routing protocols using MD5 or IPsec to prevent unauthorized updates.
2. **Summarize Routes**: Reduce routing table size by summarizing routes where possible.
3. **Monitor Protocol Health**: Regularly check protocol neighbors and adjacencies.
4. **Plan and Document**: Plan the routing topology carefully and document all configurations.

7. Troubleshooting Routing Protocols

a. Verify Routing Tables

Check the routing table for missing or incorrect routes:

```
show route
```

b. Diagnose Protocol Issues

- For OSPF:

```
show ospf interface
```

- For BGP:

```
show bgp neighbor
```

c. Check Logs

Examine system logs for protocol errors:

```
show log messages | match <protocol_name>
```

Conclusion

Routing protocols in Junos OS provide the flexibility and scalability required for modern networks. By understanding their principles and configurations, you can design efficient and reliable routing infrastructures.

Static Routing Configuration

Static routing is one of the simplest forms of routing, where routes are manually configured by the network administrator. While it lacks the dynamic adaptability of routing protocols, static routing is highly predictable and efficient in smaller or less complex network environments. This chapter explores static routing, its use cases, and how to configure it in Junos OS.

1. What is Static Routing?

Static routing involves manually defining paths that data packets must follow to reach their destinations. Unlike dynamic routing, static routes do not automatically adjust to network changes or failures.

Key Characteristics of Static Routing

- **Manual Configuration**: Routes must be manually created and updated.
- **No Protocol Overhead**: Unlike dynamic routing, static routing does not generate control traffic.
- **High Control**: Network administrators have full control over routing paths.
- **Low Scalability**: Not suitable for large or frequently changing networks.

2. When to Use Static Routing

Static routing is best suited for the following scenarios:

- **Small Networks**: Networks with few routers and minimal complexity.
- **Stub Networks**: Networks with only one route in and out, where dynamic routing is unnecessary.
- **Backup Routes**: As a fallback for dynamic routes in case of failure.
- **Security and Predictability**: When precise control over traffic flow is required.

3. Configuring Static Routes in Junos OS

Configuring static routes in Junos OS involves defining the destination network and specifying the next-hop address.

Basic Syntax

```
set routing-options static route <destination_network>/<subnet_mask> next-hop
<next_hop_ip>
```

a. Example Configuration

1. Enter configuration mode:

   ```
   configure
   ```

2. Add a static route:

   ```
   set routing-options static route 192.168.2.0/24 next-hop 10.0.0.1
   ```

3. Commit the configuration:

   ```
   commit
   ```

b. Viewing Configured Static Routes

To display the current static routes:

```
show configuration routing-options
```

Output:

```
routing-options {
    static {
        route 192.168.2.0/24 {
            next-hop 10.0.0.1;
        }
    }
}
```

4. Verifying Static Routes

Once configured, verify that the static route is active and reachable in the routing table.

a. Check the Routing Table

Use the show route command:

```
show route 192.168.2.0/24
```

Output:

```
inet.0: 10 destinations, 10 routes (10 active, 0 holddown, 0 hidden)
+ = Active Route, - = Last Active, * = Both

192.168.2.0/24     *[Static/5] 00:00:03
                      > to 10.0.0.1 via ge-0/0/0.0
```

b. Test Connectivity

Ping the destination network to confirm reachability:

```
ping 192.168.2.1
```

5. Advanced Static Route Options

a. Configuring Multiple Next-Hops

For load balancing or redundancy, configure multiple next-hops for a static route:

```
set routing-options static route 192.168.3.0/24 next-hop [10.0.0.1 10.0.0.2]
```

b. Configuring Static Route Preferences

To prioritize static routes over other routes, set a preference value (lower is preferred):

```
set routing-options static route 192.168.4.0/24 next-hop 10.0.0.1 preference 5
```

c. Using Reject or Discard Actions

Static routes can be configured to reject or discard traffic for specific destinations:

- **Reject**: Sends an ICMP unreachable message:

```
set routing-options static route 192.168.5.0/24 reject
```

- **Discard**: Silently drops traffic:

```
set routing-options static route 192.168.6.0/24 discard
```

---

6. Best Practices for Static Routing

1. **Keep It Simple**: Use static routing for small or simple networks. Avoid overcomplicating configurations.
2. **Document Routes**: Maintain records of all static routes for troubleshooting and audits.
3. **Test Configurations**: Verify routes and connectivity after every change.
4. **Use Backup Routes**: Combine static and dynamic routing for fault tolerance.
5. **Monitor and Update**: Regularly review and update static routes to reflect network changes.

---

7. Troubleshooting Static Routes

a. Verify Next-Hop Reachability

Ensure the next-hop address is reachable:

```
ping <next_hop_ip>
```

b. Check Interface Status

Verify the status of the interface associated with the next-hop address:

```
show interfaces terse
```

c. Analyze Logs

Check logs for routing issues:

```
show log messages | match "static"
```

d. Debug Route Installation

Use the following command to debug route issues:

```
show route extensive 192.168.2.0/24
```

Conclusion

Static routing is a fundamental networking skill and a key feature of Junos OS. By mastering static routing, you can build predictable and efficient networks, especially in smaller or simpler environments.

Dynamic Routing Overview

Dynamic routing plays a pivotal role in modern networks, enabling routers to adapt to changing network conditions without manual intervention. By automatically discovering and maintaining routing information, dynamic routing protocols provide scalability, flexibility, and resilience for complex networks. This chapter provides an overview of dynamic routing concepts and highlights the routing protocols supported by Junos OS.

1. What is Dynamic Routing?

Dynamic routing involves the use of protocols that enable routers to exchange routing information and adjust their routing tables based on changes in the network. Unlike static routing, dynamic routing eliminates the need for manual updates, making it ideal for large and evolving networks.

Key Characteristics of Dynamic Routing

- **Automated Route Discovery**: Automatically learns routes and adapts to topology changes.
- **Scalability**: Easily handles large and complex networks.
- **Fault Tolerance**: Reacts to link failures and reroutes traffic dynamically.
- **Protocol Overhead**: Generates control traffic to maintain routing tables.

2. Benefits of Dynamic Routing

Dynamic routing provides significant advantages for managing modern networks:

- **Flexibility**: Adapts to topology changes, ensuring continuous connectivity.
- **Simplified Management**: Reduces administrative overhead in large networks.
- **Optimized Paths**: Automatically selects the best paths based on protocol-specific metrics.
- **Load Balancing**: Distributes traffic across multiple links for improved performance.

3. Dynamic Routing Protocol Types

Dynamic routing protocols are categorized based on their operation and the scope of their routing domain.

a. Interior Gateway Protocols (IGPs)

IGPs operate within a single autonomous system (AS) and are commonly used for internal routing.

Examples:

1. **OSPF (Open Shortest Path First)**
   - A link-state protocol that uses areas to optimize routing in large networks.
   - Metric: Cost (based on bandwidth).
2. **IS-IS (Intermediate System to Intermediate System)**
   - A link-state protocol designed for scalability, often used in service provider networks.
3. **RIP (Routing Information Protocol)**
   - A distance-vector protocol suitable for small networks.
   - Metric: Hop count (limited to 15 hops).

b. Exterior Gateway Protocols (EGPs)

EGPs operate between different autonomous systems and are essential for internet routing.

Example:

1. **BGP (Border Gateway Protocol)**
   - The de facto standard for internet routing.
   - Capable of policy-based routing and managing large-scale networks.

c. Hybrid Protocols

Combine features of both link-state and distance-vector protocols.

Example:

1. **EIGRP (Enhanced Interior Gateway Routing Protocol)**
   - A Cisco proprietary protocol, not natively supported by Junos OS.

---

4. Routing Metrics

Dynamic routing protocols use metrics to evaluate and compare paths. Metrics vary by protocol and include:

- **Hop Count**: Number of routers between the source and destination (used by RIP).
- **Cost**: A metric based on bandwidth or other factors (used by OSPF).
- **Latency**: Time taken for data to traverse the path.
- **AS Path Length**: The number of autonomous systems a route traverses (used by BGP).

---

5. How Dynamic Routing Works in Junos OS

Junos OS supports a wide range of dynamic routing protocols, making it a versatile platform for network deployments.

a. Routing Information Exchange

Routers running dynamic protocols exchange information using protocol-specific messages. For example:

- **OSPF**: Sends Link-State Advertisements (LSAs).
- **BGP**: Exchanges route updates through peers.

b. Route Calculation

Each protocol uses its algorithm to calculate the best paths:

- **OSPF**: Uses Dijkstra's algorithm.
- **RIP**: Employs Bellman-Ford algorithm.

c. Updating the Routing Table

The Routing Engine in Junos OS updates the routing table with the best paths based on metrics and policies.

---

6. Configuring Dynamic Routing in Junos OS

Dynamic routing protocols are configured in the `protocols` hierarchy. The basic steps include enabling the protocol, specifying interfaces, and configuring protocol-specific parameters.

a. Enabling OSPF

1. Enter configuration mode:

```
configure
```

2. Enable OSPF and specify the area and interface:

```
set protocols ospf area 0.0.0.0 interface ge-0/0/0.0
commit
```

b. Enabling BGP

1. Set the local AS number:

```
set protocols bgp group external type external
set protocols bgp group external local-as 65001
```

2. Configure a neighbor:

```
set protocols bgp group external neighbor 192.168.1.2 commit
```

7. Monitoring Dynamic Routing Protocols

Junos OS provides tools to monitor and troubleshoot dynamic routing protocols.

a. Checking Protocol Status

- For OSPF:

```
show ospf neighbor
```

- For BGP:

```
show bgp summary
```

b. Viewing the Routing Table

Display active routes:

```
show route
```

8. Challenges of Dynamic Routing

While dynamic routing offers significant benefits, it also has some challenges:

- **Protocol Complexity**: Configuration and troubleshooting require expertise.
- **Control Traffic Overhead**: Protocol messages consume bandwidth and resources.
- **Convergence Time**: Some protocols may take time to converge after topology changes.

9. Best Practices for Dynamic Routing

1. **Use Authentication**: Secure routing protocols to prevent unauthorized route updates.
2. **Limit Protocol Scope**: Use route summarization and area design to reduce complexity.
3. **Monitor Protocol Performance**: Regularly check protocol metrics and neighbor relationships.
4. **Combine with Static Routing**: Use static routes for predictable paths or as backups.

Conclusion

Dynamic routing is essential for managing large and complex networks, enabling routers to automatically discover and adapt to changes in topology. By understanding the fundamentals of dynamic routing and the protocols supported by Junos OS, you can design scalable and resilient networks.

OSPF Configuration in Junos

Open Shortest Path First (OSPF) is one of the most widely used dynamic routing protocols, known for its scalability, reliability, and efficiency. Designed as a link-state protocol, OSPF is ideal for large and complex network environments. This chapter provides a comprehensive guide to configuring OSPF on Junos OS, from basic setup to advanced features.

1. Overview of OSPF

What is OSPF?

OSPF is an Interior Gateway Protocol (IGP) that operates within a single autonomous system. It determines the best path for data based on the shortest path first (SPF) algorithm.

Key Characteristics of OSPF:

- **Link-State Protocol**: Each router maintains a database of the network's topology.
- **Hierarchical Design**: Supports areas to optimize large networks.
- **Fast Convergence**: Quickly adapts to topology changes.
- **Classless Routing**: Supports variable-length subnet masks (VLSM).

2. OSPF Areas and Design

OSPF organizes networks into areas to reduce the size of the link-state database (LSDB) and improve scalability.

Common Area Types:

- **Backbone Area (Area 0)**: The central hub for OSPF routing; all other areas connect to it.
- **Stub Area**: Does not allow external routes, reducing routing table size.
- **Totally Stubby Area**: A Cisco extension, supported by Junos, that blocks all external and inter-area routes except a default route.
- **Not-So-Stubby Area (NSSA)**: Allows limited external routes.

Best Practices for Area Design:

1. Always include Area 0 as the backbone.
2. Limit the number of routers in an area to improve performance.
3. Use stub or NSSA areas to minimize resource consumption in smaller segments.

3. Enabling OSPF on Junos OS

Basic OSPF Configuration Steps:

1. Define OSPF areas.
2. Assign interfaces to the appropriate areas.
3. Configure network types if necessary (broadcast, point-to-point, etc.).

a. Enabling OSPF on an Interface

To enable OSPF on an interface and assign it to Area 0:

```
configure
set protocols ospf area 0.0.0.0 interface ge-0/0/0.0
commit
```

b. Verifying the Configuration

Check the OSPF configuration:

```
show configuration protocols ospf
```

Output:

```
protocols {
    ospf {
        area 0.0.0.0 {
            interface ge-0/0/0.0;
        }
    }
}
```

---

4. Advanced OSPF Configuration

a. Specifying Router ID

OSPF uses a router ID (RID) to uniquely identify routers. If not manually set, Junos selects the highest IP address.

To configure a router ID:

```
set routing-options router-id 192.168.1.1
commit
```

b. Adjusting OSPF Metrics

OSPF uses a cost metric based on interface bandwidth. You can manually adjust the cost:

```
set protocols ospf area 0.0.0.0 interface ge-0/0/0.0 metric 20
commit
```

c. Configuring Authentication

OSPF supports authentication to secure route exchanges.

Plaintext Authentication:

```
set protocols ospf area 0.0.0.0 interface ge-0/0/0.0 authentication simple
"password"
commit
```

MD5 Authentication:

```
set protocols ospf area 0.0.0.0 interface ge-0/0/0.0 authentication md5 1 key
"securekey"
commit
```

---

5. OSPF Neighbor Relationships

OSPF routers form neighbor relationships to exchange routing information. Neighbors must share the same:

- Area ID
- Hello and dead intervals
- Authentication settings

Viewing OSPF Neighbors:

```
show ospf neighbor
```

Output:

```
Address          Interface     State     ID              Pri  Dead
192.168.1.2      ge-0/0/0.0    Full      192.168.1.2     1    33
```

Troubleshooting Neighbor Issues:

- Ensure interfaces are in the same subnet.
- Verify OSPF settings (area, authentication, timers).

---

6. Monitoring OSPF

Junos OS provides several commands to monitor OSPF operations.

a. Viewing the OSPF Database

Check the link-state database (LSDB):

```
show ospf database
```

b. Checking OSPF Routes

Display routes learned via OSPF:

```
show route protocol ospf
```

c. Viewing Interface Status

Inspect OSPF-specific interface settings:

```
show ospf interface
```

---

7. Configuring OSPF for Stub and NSSA Areas

a. Stub Area Configuration

To create a stub area:

```
set protocols ospf area 1 stub
commit
```

b. NSSA Configuration

To create an NSSA:

```
set protocols ospf area 2 nssa
commit
```

8. Best Practices for OSPF Deployment

1. **Optimize Area Design**: Keep area sizes manageable and use stub areas where applicable.
2. **Secure OSPF**: Always enable authentication to prevent unauthorized route updates.
3. **Monitor Continuously**: Use show ospf commands to ensure OSPF operates as expected.
4. **Document Configurations**: Maintain clear records of OSPF settings and area assignments.
5. **Plan for Scalability**: Consider future growth when designing OSPF networks.

9. Troubleshooting OSPF

a. Common Issues

- **Neighbor Not Forming**: Check timers, authentication, and subnet configurations.
- **Route Missing from Table**: Ensure LSDB is synchronized and SPF algorithm runs correctly.

b. Debugging Commands

- View detailed OSPF logs:

```
show log messages | match ospf
```

- Analyze OSPF neighbor relationships:

```
show ospf neighbor detail
```

Conclusion

OSPF is a powerful and flexible routing protocol, making it a staple in enterprise and service provider networks. By understanding its configuration and best practices in Junos OS, you can effectively deploy and manage OSPF in your network.

BGP Configuration Essentials

The Border Gateway Protocol (BGP) is the backbone of the internet and plays a critical role in large-scale enterprise and service provider networks. Unlike IGPs like OSPF or IS-IS, BGP is an Exterior Gateway Protocol (EGP) that focuses on interdomain routing between autonomous systems (AS). This chapter provides an essential guide to configuring BGP in Junos OS, covering the basics, key concepts, and advanced configurations.

1. Overview of BGP

What is BGP?

BGP is a path-vector routing protocol that exchanges routing information between autonomous systems. It is used for:

- **Internet Routing**: Managing IP prefixes across the global internet.
- **Policy-Based Routing**: Controlling traffic flow using routing policies.
- **Scalable Networks**: Handling large routing tables and complex topologies.

Key Features of BGP

- **Path Attributes**: Influences route selection with attributes like AS path, MED, and local preference.
- **Reliability**: Uses TCP (port 179) for reliable route exchange.
- **Scalability**: Designed for large-scale networks with thousands of routes.

2. Types of BGP

a. Internal BGP (IBGP)

- Operates within a single AS.
- Requires a full-mesh topology or route reflectors to avoid routing loops.

b. External BGP (EBGP)

- Operates between different ASes.
- Typically used for internet or interdomain routing.

3. BGP Configuration Basics

a. Prerequisites

1. Assign unique AS numbers to participating networks.
2. Ensure IP connectivity between BGP peers (IBGP or EBGP).
3. Define routing policies if needed.

b. Basic Configuration Syntax

BGP configuration in Junos OS is done in the `protocols bgp` hierarchy:

```
set protocols bgp group <group_name> type [internal|external]
set protocols bgp group <group_name> local-as <local_as>
```

```
set protocols bgp group <group_name> neighbor <neighbor_ip>
```

4. Step-by-Step BGP Configuration

a. Configuring EBGP

1. Enter configuration mode:

   ```
   configure
   ```

2. Define the BGP group and specify it as external:

   ```
   set protocols bgp group EBGP-Group type external
   ```

3. Set the local AS number:

   ```
   set protocols bgp group EBGP-Group local-as 65001
   ```

4. Define the EBGP peer:

   ```
   set protocols bgp group EBGP-Group neighbor 192.168.1.2 peer-as 65002
   ```

5. Commit the configuration:

   ```
   commit
   ```

b. Configuring IBGP

1. Define the IBGP group:

   ```
   set protocols bgp group IBGP-Group type internal
   ```

2. Specify the local AS number:

   ```
   set protocols bgp group IBGP-Group local-as 65001
   ```

3. Add IBGP neighbors:

   ```
   set protocols bgp group IBGP-Group neighbor 192.168.1.3
   set protocols bgp group IBGP-Group neighbor 192.168.1.4
   ```

4. Commit the configuration:

   ```
   commit
   ```

5. Verifying BGP Configuration

a. Check BGP Neighbor Status

Use the following command to verify neighbor relationships:

```
show bgp neighbor
```

```
Peer: 192.168.1.2+179 Local: 192.168.1.1+179
  Type: External    State: Established
  Local AS: 65001   Peer AS: 65002
```

b. View BGP Routes

Display routes learned via BGP:

```
show route protocol bgp
```

c. Monitor BGP Session Summary

Get a summary of BGP sessions:

```
show bgp summary
```

Output:

```
Peer AS      InPkt   OutPkt   State      PrefRcv
192.168.1.2  65002   100      100        Established   25
```

---

6. Advanced BGP Configuration

a. Configuring Route Reflectors

To reduce the need for IBGP full-mesh topology:

1. Configure a router as a route reflector:

   ```
   set protocols bgp group IBGP-Group cluster 192.168.1.1
   ```

2. Specify clients:

   ```
   set protocols bgp group IBGP-Group neighbor 192.168.1.3 route-reflector-client
   set protocols bgp group IBGP-Group neighbor 192.168.1.4 route-reflector-client
   ```

3. Commit the configuration:

   ```
   commit
   ```

b. Configuring BGP Authentication

Secure BGP sessions with MD5 authentication:

```
set protocols bgp group EBGP-Group authentication-key "SecureKey123"
commit
```

c. Applying Routing Policies

Control route advertisement and acceptance using policies:

1. Define a policy:

   ```
   set policy-options policy-statement Export-Policy term 1 from route-filter
   10.0.0.0/24 exact
   ```

```
set policy-options policy-statement Export-Policy term 1 then accept
```

2. Apply the policy to a BGP group:

```
set protocols bgp group EBGP-Group export Export-Policy
commit
```

7. Troubleshooting BGP

a. Common Issues

- **Neighbor Not Established**: Check IP connectivity and AS numbers.
- **Missing Routes**: Verify routing policies and prefix advertisements.
- **Flapping Sessions**: Check link stability and keepalive timers.

b. Useful Debugging Commands

- Check detailed BGP neighbor information:

```
show bgp neighbor detail
```

- View advertised and received routes:

```
show route advertising-protocol bgp <neighbor_ip>
show route receive-protocol bgp <neighbor_ip>
```

- Check logs for BGP-related messages:

```
show log messages | match bgp
```

8. Best Practices for BGP Configuration

1. **Secure Sessions**: Always use MD5 authentication for BGP peers.
2. **Use Route Summarization**: Reduce routing table size and improve performance.
3. **Monitor Regularly**: Use show bgp commands to monitor sessions and routes.
4. **Document Policies**: Maintain clear documentation for routing policies.
5. **Plan for Scalability**: Use route reflectors or confederations for large networks.

Conclusion

BGP is an essential protocol for large-scale networks, providing the flexibility and scalability required for interdomain routing. By mastering the basics and leveraging advanced configurations, you can effectively implement BGP in your Juniper-based networks.

IS-IS Implementation

Intermediate System to Intermediate System (IS-IS) is a dynamic, link-state routing protocol commonly used in service provider and large enterprise networks. Known for its scalability, efficiency, and robust design, IS-IS plays a crucial role in maintaining optimal routing in complex networks. This chapter provides a detailed guide to understanding and implementing IS-IS in Junos OS.

1. Overview of IS-IS

What is IS-IS?

IS-IS is a link-state Interior Gateway Protocol (IGP) that routes data within a single autonomous system (AS). It uses the Dijkstra algorithm to calculate the shortest path to a destination.

Key Characteristics of IS-IS:

- **Layer 2 Protocol**: Operates directly over the data link layer, independent of IP.
- **Scalability**: Suitable for large and hierarchical network designs.
- **Flexibility**: Supports IPv4, IPv6, and multi-topology routing.
- **Efficient Convergence**: Quickly adapts to topology changes.

2. IS-IS Network Architecture

a. Levels of IS-IS

IS-IS operates at two levels to provide hierarchical routing:

- **Level 1 (L1)**: Intra-area routing within a single area.
- **Level 2 (L2)**: Inter-area routing between areas.

Devices can function as:

- **L1 Routers**: Route traffic within an area.
- **L2 Routers**: Route traffic between areas.
- **L1/L2 Routers**: Operate at both levels.

b. Addressing in IS-IS

IS-IS uses Network Entity Titles (NETs) for identification, consisting of:

- **Area ID**: Identifies the area.
- **System ID**: Unique identifier for the router.
- **NSEL**: Always set to 00 for routing.

Example NET:

49.0001.1921.6801.1001.00

3. Configuring IS-IS on Junos OS

a. Basic Configuration Steps

1. Enable IS-IS on the device.
2. Assign IS-IS interfaces to the desired level (L1, L2, or L1/L2).
3. Configure the NET address.

b. Configuring the NET Address

The NET address must be unique within the network. Set it in the routing-options hierarchy:

```
configure
set routing-options router-id 192.168.1.1
set protocols isis level 2 network-entity 49.0001.1921.6801.1001.00
commit
```

c. Enabling IS-IS on Interfaces

Assign IS-IS to the appropriate interfaces:

```
set protocols isis interface ge-0/0/0.0 level 2
set protocols isis interface ge-0/0/1.0 level 1
commit
```

d. Configuring IS-IS Levels

To configure a router as L1, L2, or L1/L2:

- L1 only:

  ```
  set protocols isis level 1
  ```

- L2 only:

  ```
  set protocols isis level 2
  ```

- L1/L2:

  ```
  set protocols isis level 1
  set protocols isis level 2
  ```

---

4. Verifying IS-IS Configuration

a. Check IS-IS Status

View IS-IS configuration and operational status:

```
show isis overview
```

b. Check IS-IS Neighbors

Verify neighbor relationships:

```
show isis adjacency
```

Output:

```
Interface        System       L State    Hold Timer  SNPA
ge-0/0/0.0       RouterA      2 Up        27          00:00:5e:00:53:01
```

c. View the IS-IS Database

Inspect the link-state database:

```
show isis database
```

d. Check Routes

Display routes learned via IS-IS:

```
show route protocol isis
```

---

5. Advanced IS-IS Configuration

a. Configuring Metrics

Adjust IS-IS metrics to influence route selection:

```
set protocols isis interface ge-0/0/0.0 metric 10
commit
```

b. Enabling Authentication

Secure IS-IS routing with authentication:

- Configure an area-wide password:

  ```
  set protocols isis area-authentication-type simple-password "SecurePass"
  commit
  ```

- Configure an interface-specific password:

  ```
  set protocols isis interface ge-0/0/0.0 authentication simple-password
  "InterfacePass"
  commit
  ```

c. Multi-Topology Routing

Enable multi-topology IS-IS for IPv4 and IPv6:

```
set protocols isis ipv6-topology
commit
```

---

6. Troubleshooting IS-IS

a. Common Issues

- **Adjacency Not Forming**:
  - Verify that both routers are in the same level (L1 or L2).
  - Check IP connectivity and MTU settings.
- **Routes Missing**:
  - Ensure the IS-IS metric is not higher than expected.
  - Verify the link-state database synchronization.

b. Debugging Commands

- View IS-IS logs:

```
show log messages | match isis
```

- Check detailed adjacency information:

```
show isis adjacency detail
```

- Analyze LSPs in the database:

```
show isis database detail
```

---

7. Best Practices for IS-IS Implementation

1. **Use Hierarchical Design**: Implement L1 and L2 areas for scalability.
2. **Secure IS-IS**: Always enable authentication to prevent unauthorized updates.
3. **Optimize Metrics**: Adjust metrics to control traffic flow effectively.
4. **Monitor Continuously**: Use IS-IS monitoring tools to ensure stable operation.
5. **Document NETs and Areas**: Maintain clear documentation of addressing and topology.

Conclusion

IS-IS is a robust and efficient routing protocol well-suited for large-scale networks. By understanding its hierarchical design, configuration options, and best practices, you can deploy IS-IS to achieve optimal routing performance in Junos OS.

Multicast Routing Fundamentals

Multicast routing is a technique used to efficiently deliver data packets to multiple destinations simultaneously. Unlike unicast (one-to-one) or broadcast (one-to-all) communication, multicast allows one-to-many data delivery, making it ideal for applications such as video conferencing, IPTV, and real-time data distribution. In this chapter, we'll explore the fundamentals of multicast routing and its implementation in Junos OS.

1. What is Multicast Routing?

Multicast routing enables the transmission of data from a single source to multiple receivers in a network. It reduces network bandwidth usage by sending data only once over shared links and replicating it only when necessary.

Key Concepts of Multicast

- **Multicast Group**: A set of receivers interested in a specific data stream, identified by a multicast IP address (e.g., 224.0.0.0 to 239.255.255.255).
- **Source**: The device sending multicast traffic.
- **Receivers**: Devices that join a multicast group to receive data.
- **Multicast Distribution Tree**: A structure used by routers to forward multicast traffic to receivers.

2. Multicast Routing Protocols

Multicast routing relies on protocols to manage group memberships and route traffic efficiently.

a. Internet Group Management Protocol (IGMP)

- Used by hosts to communicate multicast group memberships to routers.
- Versions:
    - **IGMPv1**: Basic group join and leave functionality.
    - **IGMPv2**: Adds leave messages for quicker group departure.
    - **IGMPv3**: Supports source-specific multicast (SSM).

b. Protocol Independent Multicast (PIM)

PIM builds multicast distribution trees and forwards traffic. It operates in two main modes:

- **PIM Sparse Mode (PIM-SM)**: Constructs a tree only when receivers explicitly join a group. Ideal for networks with sparse multicast receivers.
- **PIM Dense Mode (PIM-DM)**: Floods traffic to all routers and prunes unwanted paths. Suitable for networks with dense receiver populations.

c. Multicast Listener Discovery (MLD)

- The IPv6 equivalent of IGMP.

3. Multicast Distribution Trees

Multicast routers build and maintain distribution trees for efficient data delivery.

a. Source Tree

- Also known as the shortest path tree (SPT).
- Built using the source IP address as the root.

b. Shared Tree

- Uses a rendezvous point (RP) as the root, regardless of the source.

---

4. Configuring Multicast Routing in Junos OS

To implement multicast routing, you need to enable IGMP and PIM on the relevant interfaces and configure additional settings such as the RP if required.

Step 1: Enabling IGMP

1. Enter configuration mode:

```
configure
```

2. Enable IGMP on the desired interface:

```
set protocols igmp interface ge-0/0/0.0
commit
```

Step 2: Enabling PIM

1. Configure PIM sparse mode on the interface:

```
set protocols pim interface ge-0/0/0.0 mode sparse
commit
```

Step 3: Configuring the RP (Rendezvous Point)

1. Define the RP for the multicast group:

```
set protocols pim rp static address 192.168.1.1 group 224.0.0.0/4
commit
```

Step 4: Verifying Multicast Routes

View the multicast routing table:

```
show route protocol multicast
```

---

5. Monitoring and Troubleshooting Multicast

Junos OS provides several tools to monitor and troubleshoot multicast routing.

a. Viewing IGMP Memberships

Check group memberships on interfaces:

```
show igmp group
```

b. Checking PIM Neighbors

Display PIM neighbor relationships:

```
show pim neighbors
```

c. Inspecting Multicast Forwarding State

Verify the multicast forwarding state:

```
show pim join
```

d. Troubleshooting Commands

- Check multicast traffic flow:

```
show multicast forwarding
```

- View multicast logs:

```
show log messages | match multicast
```

6. Multicast Security

Secure multicast routing to prevent unauthorized access and misuse.

a. Filter Multicast Traffic

Apply firewall filters to control multicast group memberships:

```
set firewall family inet filter multicast-filter term 1 from source-address
224.0.0.0/4
set firewall family inet filter multicast-filter term 1 then accept
commit
```

b. Enable PIM Authentication

Use MD5 authentication for PIM neighbors:

```
set protocols pim interface ge-0/0/0.0 authentication md5-key "SecureKey123"
commit
```

7. Best Practices for Multicast Routing

1. **Plan the Multicast Design**: Use PIM-SM for sparse receivers and PIM-DM for dense environments.
2. **Secure Multicast Groups**: Limit access to multicast groups with filters and authentication.
3. **Monitor Continuously**: Use IGMP and PIM monitoring commands to ensure proper operation.
4. **Optimize RP Placement**: Position RPs centrally to minimize tree complexity and latency.
5. **Document Configurations**: Maintain clear records of multicast configurations and group assignments.

Conclusion

Multicast routing is an essential technology for efficient data distribution in modern networks. By understanding multicast concepts, protocols, and configurations in Junos OS, you can implement scalable and reliable multicast solutions.

Section 4:
Switching Essentials with Junos OS

Layer 2 Switching Basics

Layer 2 switching is a fundamental aspect of networking, responsible for forwarding data within a local area network (LAN) based on MAC addresses. In Junos OS, Layer 2 switching enables efficient traffic management, providing robust features for modern network infrastructures. This chapter delves into the principles of Layer 2 switching, its benefits, and how it is implemented in Juniper Networks.

1. What is Layer 2 Switching?

Layer 2 switching operates at the data link layer of the OSI model, forwarding Ethernet frames based on the destination MAC address. Unlike Layer 3 routing, which deals with IP addresses, Layer 2 switching is concerned with physical addressing and is confined to the same broadcast domain.

Key Functions of Layer 2 Switching

- **Frame Forwarding**: Determines the frame's destination based on MAC address lookups.
- **MAC Address Learning**: Dynamically learns and updates the MAC address table.
- **Broadcast Control**: Manages broadcast traffic within the LAN.

2. Benefits of Layer 2 Switching

Layer 2 switching offers several advantages for LAN environments:

- **High Performance**: Provides low-latency, high-speed communication.
- **Scalability**: Supports the addition of devices without complex configurations.
- **Efficient Resource Use**: Reduces unnecessary traffic by forwarding frames only to the destination.
- **Ease of Management**: Simple configuration and monitoring for small to medium-sized networks.

3. Switching Fundamentals in Junos OS

a. Forwarding Process

1. **MAC Address Table Lookup**: The switch checks the MAC address table for the destination address.
2. **Frame Forwarding**: If the address is found, the frame is forwarded to the corresponding port.
3. **Flooding**: If the address is unknown, the frame is flooded to all ports except the source.

b. Learning Process

Junos OS dynamically learns MAC addresses by examining the source address of incoming frames. These addresses are stored in the MAC address table, associating each MAC address with a specific switch port.

c. Aging Process

Unused MAC addresses are periodically removed from the MAC address table to free resources and maintain efficiency.

---

4. Configuring Layer 2 Switching in Junos OS

a. Setting Up a Switch

To enable Layer 2 switching on Junos OS, configure the interfaces as part of a bridge domain.

1. Enter configuration mode:

   ```
   configure
   ```

2. Create a bridge domain:

   ```
   set bridge-domains LAN1 vlan-id 10
   ```

3. Assign interfaces to the bridge domain:

   ```
   set bridge-domains LAN1 interface ge-0/0/0.0
   set bridge-domains LAN1 interface ge-0/0/1.0
   ```

4. Commit the configuration:

   ```
   commit
   ```

b. Configuring VLANs

Virtual LANs (VLANs) enhance Layer 2 switching by segmenting traffic. To assign a VLAN to a bridge domain:

```
set bridge-domains LAN1 vlan-id 10
```

---

5. Verifying Layer 2 Switching

a. View MAC Address Table

Check the dynamically learned MAC addresses:

```
show ethernet-switching table
```

Output:

```
MAC address          VLAN    Interface
00:1a:2b:3c:4d:5e    10      ge-0/0/0.0
```

b. Monitor VLAN Configuration

Verify VLAN membership:

```
show bridge-domains
```

c. Inspect Traffic Statistics

Monitor traffic on interfaces:

```
show interfaces statistics
```

---

6. Advanced Layer 2 Features

a. Spanning Tree Protocol (STP)

STP prevents network loops in Layer 2 topologies by blocking redundant paths.

Enable STP on an interface:

```
set protocols stp interface ge-0/0/0.0
commit
```

b. Port Security

Port security limits the number of MAC addresses learned on an interface to enhance security:

```
set ethernet-switching-options secure-access-port interface ge-0/0/0 maximum-mac 10
commit
```

c. Link Aggregation

Combine multiple physical links into a single logical link for redundancy and increased bandwidth:

```
set chassis aggregated-devices ethernet device-count 2
set interfaces ae0 aggregated-ether-options link-speed 1g
set interfaces ae0 unit 0 family ethernet-switching vlan members 10
commit
```

---

7. Best Practices for Layer 2 Switching

1. **Plan VLAN Design**: Segment traffic logically using VLANs for better traffic management.
2. **Implement STP**: Avoid network loops and ensure redundancy.
3. **Secure Access Ports**: Limit the number of MAC addresses on access ports to prevent unauthorized devices.
4. **Monitor Regularly**: Use Junos monitoring tools to ensure network health and performance.
5. **Document Configurations**: Maintain clear records of bridge domains, VLANs, and interfaces.

Conclusion

Layer 2 switching is a critical component of any LAN, providing the foundation for efficient and scalable communication. By leveraging Junos OS's robust switching features, you can build and manage networks that meet modern demands.

VLAN Configuration and Management

Virtual Local Area Networks (VLANs) are a crucial component of modern network design, providing segmentation, security, and efficient traffic management within a Layer 2 network. In Junos OS, VLANs are managed through bridge domains and VLAN tagging, offering flexibility and scalability for both enterprise and service provider environments. This chapter provides a comprehensive guide to VLAN configuration and management in Junos OS.

---

1. What is a VLAN?

A VLAN is a logical grouping of devices within a physical network. It allows devices to communicate as if they were in the same broadcast domain, regardless of their physical location.

Key Benefits of VLANs:

- **Traffic Segmentation**: Isolates traffic between groups of devices.
- **Improved Security**: Limits access to sensitive resources.
- **Enhanced Performance**: Reduces broadcast traffic within each VLAN.
- **Simplified Network Management**: Logical segmentation allows better organization and troubleshooting.

---

2. VLAN Concepts

a. VLAN ID

Each VLAN is identified by a unique VLAN ID, ranging from 1 to 4094.

b. VLAN Tagging

VLAN tagging uses the IEEE 802.1Q standard to insert VLAN IDs into Ethernet frames.

- **Tagged Frames**: Used on trunk ports to carry traffic for multiple VLANs.
- **Untagged Frames**: Used on access ports for a single VLAN.

c. VLAN Membership

Devices are assigned to VLANs either statically (based on port) or dynamically (based on MAC address or protocols).

---

3. Configuring VLANs in Junos OS

VLANs are configured using bridge domains, which represent Layer 2 broadcast domains in Junos OS.

Step 1: Creating a VLAN

1. Enter configuration mode:

   ```
   configure
   ```

2. Define a VLAN and assign a VLAN ID:

```
set bridge-domains VLAN10 vlan-id 10
```

3. Commit the configuration:

```
commit
```

Step 2: Assigning Interfaces to a VLAN

Assign interfaces to a VLAN as access or trunk ports.

Access Port:

```
set bridge-domains VLAN10 interface ge-0/0/0.0
commit
```

Trunk Port:

```
set interfaces ge-0/0/1.0 unit 0 family ethernet-switching port-mode trunk
set interfaces ge-0/0/1.0 unit 0 family ethernet-switching vlan members [10 20]
commit
```

4. VLAN Trunking

a. What is VLAN Trunking?

VLAN trunking allows multiple VLANs to be transmitted over a single physical link. Trunk ports are typically used between switches or between a switch and a router.

b. Configuring a Trunk Port

1. Set the port to trunk mode:

```
set interfaces ge-0/0/1.0 unit 0 family ethernet-switching port-mode trunk
```

2. Add VLANs to the trunk:

```
set interfaces ge-0/0/1.0 unit 0 family ethernet-switching vlan members [10
20]
commit
```

5. Verifying VLAN Configuration

a. View VLAN Details

Check VLAN and interface configuration:

```
show bridge-domains
```

Output:

```
Bridge Domain    VLAN ID    Interfaces
VLAN10           10         ge-0/0/0.0
```

b. Inspect VLAN Membership

Display VLAN membership for a specific interface:

```
show ethernet-switching interfaces
```

c. Monitor VLAN Traffic

Check traffic statistics for a VLAN:

```
show interfaces statistics
```

---

6. Managing VLANs

a. Adding or Removing Interfaces

Add a new interface to an existing VLAN:

```
set bridge-domains VLAN10 interface ge-0/0/2.0
commit
```

Remove an interface from a VLAN:

```
delete bridge-domains VLAN10 interface ge-0/0/0.0
commit
```

b. Deleting a VLAN

To delete a VLAN:

```
delete bridge-domains VLAN10
commit
```

c. Configuring Native VLANs

A native VLAN handles untagged traffic on trunk ports.

```
set interfaces ge-0/0/1.0 unit 0 family ethernet-switching native-vlan-id 10
commit
```

---

7. Best Practices for VLAN Management

1. **Use Consistent VLAN IDs**: Maintain consistent VLAN IDs across switches to avoid configuration errors.
2. **Document VLAN Configurations**: Clearly document VLAN IDs, names, and associated devices.
3. **Secure Trunk Ports**: Disable unused VLANs on trunk ports to prevent unauthorized access.
4. **Monitor VLAN Usage**: Regularly review traffic and membership to optimize network performance.
5. **Implement VLAN Segmentation**: Group devices logically to enhance security and reduce broadcast traffic.

VLANs are a powerful tool for segmenting and managing network traffic, providing both security and efficiency. Junos OS simplifies VLAN configuration and management with robust tools and clear commands.

Spanning Tree Protocols (STP and RSTP)

The Spanning Tree Protocol (STP) and its faster iteration, Rapid Spanning Tree Protocol (RSTP), are essential mechanisms for ensuring loop-free and stable Layer 2 network topologies. These protocols detect and block redundant paths in a network while maintaining redundancy for failover scenarios. In this chapter, we explore the fundamentals of STP and RSTP, their configuration in Junos OS, and best practices for their deployment.

1. Introduction to Spanning Tree Protocol

STP, defined in IEEE 802.1D, prevents Layer 2 loops by logically blocking redundant links in a switched network. Loops can cause broadcast storms, MAC address table instability, and network congestion.

Key Functions of STP:

1. **Root Bridge Selection**: A single switch is elected as the root bridge for the spanning tree.
2. **Path Selection**: All switches calculate the shortest path to the root bridge.
3. **Loop Prevention**: Redundant links are placed into a blocking state.

2. Rapid Spanning Tree Protocol (RSTP)

RSTP, defined in IEEE 802.1w, is an enhancement of STP that provides faster convergence. It introduces new port roles and states to reduce the time required to adapt to topology changes.

Improvements of RSTP:

- **Faster Convergence**: Reduced transition time for port states.
- **Port Roles**: Introduces alternate and backup port roles for faster recovery.
- **Backward Compatibility**: Interoperable with STP.

3. STP and RSTP Port States

Ports in STP and RSTP transition through several states:

1. **Disabled**: The port is administratively shut down.
2. **Blocking**: Prevents loops by not forwarding traffic.
3. **Listening (STP Only)**: Listens for BPDUs but does not forward frames.
4. **Learning**: Learns MAC addresses but does not forward frames.
5. **Forwarding**: Actively forwards traffic.

4. Configuring STP and RSTP in Junos OS

a. Enabling STP

To enable STP globally:

```
configure
set protocols stp
commit
```

Assign interfaces to STP:

```
set protocols stp interface ge-0/0/0.0
commit
```

b. Enabling RSTP

To enable RSTP globally:

```
configure
set protocols rstp
commit
```

Assign interfaces to RSTP:

```
set protocols rstp interface ge-0/0/1.0
commit
```

c. Configuring Bridge Priority

The switch with the lowest bridge priority becomes the root bridge. Lower the priority to increase the likelihood of root bridge election:

```
set protocols rstp bridge-priority 4096
commit
```

---

5. Verifying and Monitoring STP/RSTP

a. Check STP Status

View the operational status of STP:

```
show spanning-tree bridge
```

Output:

```
Bridge ID        Priority 4096   Address 00:11:22:33:44:55
Root ID          Priority 0      Address 00:11:22:33:44:56
Root Path Cost   0
```

b. Inspect RSTP Interfaces

View RSTP interface status:

```
show spanning-tree interface
```

c. Display BPDU Information

Monitor BPDUs (Bridge Protocol Data Units):

```
show spanning-tree statistics
```

---

6. Advanced Configuration

a. Configuring Edge Ports

Edge ports are directly connected to end devices and do not participate in spanning tree calculations. Enable edge mode to avoid delays:

```
set protocols rstp interface ge-0/0/2.0 edge
commit
```

b. Enabling BPDU Protection

BPDU protection disables edge ports if BPDUs are received, preventing loops caused by accidental switch connections:

```
set protocols rstp bpdu-block
commit
```

c. Adjusting Timers

Modify timers for faster convergence if necessary:

- **Hello Timer**: Frequency of BPDU transmission.

  ```
  set protocols rstp hello-time 2
  ```

- **Forward Delay**: Time spent in listening and learning states.

  ```
  set protocols rstp forward-delay 10
  ```

- **Max Age**: Time a BPDU is valid before being discarded.

  ```
  set protocols rstp max-age 20
  ```

Commit the changes:

```
commit
```

---

7. Troubleshooting STP/RSTP

a. Common Issues

1. **Root Bridge Misconfiguration**: Ensure the correct device is the root bridge.
2. **Loops Persisting**: Verify blocked ports and BPDU transmissions.
3. **Convergence Delays**: Adjust timers or investigate high network traffic.

b. Useful Commands

- **Check root bridge status**:

  ```
  show spanning-tree root
  ```

- **View port roles and states**:

  ```
  show spanning-tree interface detail
  ```

- **Monitor BPDU flow**:

  ```
  show log messages | match spanning-tree
  ```

8. Best Practices for Spanning Tree Protocols

1. **Use RSTP Over STP**: Leverage faster convergence for improved network performance.
2. **Optimize Root Bridge Selection**: Set bridge priorities to ensure the intended switch is the root bridge.
3. **Enable DPDU Protection**: Prevent unauthorized devices from participating in spanning tree.
4. **Design with Redundancy**: Use multiple paths to ensure failover capabilities.
5. **Monitor Continuously**: Regularly check spanning tree status and logs to prevent issues.

Conclusion

Spanning Tree Protocols (STP and RSTP) are critical for ensuring stable, loop-free Layer 2 networks while maintaining redundancy. By configuring and monitoring these protocols in Junos OS, network administrators can optimize performance and maintain reliable connectivity.

Virtual Chassis Configuration

Virtual Chassis technology is a unique feature in Juniper Networks that allows multiple switches to operate as a single logical device. This configuration simplifies network management, improves scalability, and enables high availability. This chapter explores the fundamentals of Virtual Chassis and provides a step-by-step guide to configuring it in Junos OS.

1. What is Virtual Chassis?

Virtual Chassis technology enables multiple physical switches to connect and operate as a single logical unit. These switches share a single control plane and behave as one switch in the network.

Key Benefits of Virtual Chassis:

- **Simplified Management**: Manage multiple switches as one device.
- **High Availability**: Redundant control planes ensure network stability.
- **Scalability**: Easily add or remove switches in the chassis.
- **Cost-Effective Redundancy**: Eliminates the need for additional hardware like stacking modules.

2. Virtual Chassis Components

a. Master and Backup Roles

- **Master**: The switch controlling the Virtual Chassis, responsible for all management and configuration tasks.
- **Backup**: Takes over if the master fails, ensuring seamless operation.

b. Linecard Members

These are the additional switches in the Virtual Chassis that forward traffic based on the master's instructions.

c. Virtual Chassis Ports (VCPs)

Designated physical ports used to interconnect member switches.

3. Configuring Virtual Chassis

a. Prerequisites

- Ensure all member switches run compatible Junos OS versions.
- Physically connect the switches using supported ports or cables.

b. Step-by-Step Configuration

Step 1: Enable Virtual Chassis Mode
On each member switch:

```
request virtual-chassis mode enable
commit
```

Step 2: Set Member IDs
Assign unique member IDs to each switch:

```
set virtual-chassis member 0 role master
set virtual-chassis member 1 role backup
set virtual-chassis member 2 role linecard
commit
```

Step 3: Configure Virtual Chassis Ports (VCPs)
Designate ports as VCPs to link switches:

```
set interfaces ge-0/0/0 gigether-options vcp
set interfaces ge-1/0/0 gigether-options vcp
commit
```

Step 4: Verify the Configuration
Check the Virtual Chassis status:

```
show virtual-chassis status
```

Example output:

```
Member ID   Role      Status    Priority
0           Master    Online    128
1           Backup    Online    128
2           Linecard  Online    128
```

4. Managing Virtual Chassis

a. Adding a New Member

1. Physically connect the new switch to the existing chassis.
2. Assign a member ID and role:

   ```
   set virtual-chassis member 3 role linecard
   commit
   ```

b. Removing a Member

1. Remove the switch from the configuration:

   ```
   delete virtual-chassis member 2
   commit
   ```

2. Physically disconnect the switch.

c. Changing the Master Role

1. Assign a new master:

   ```
   set virtual-chassis member 1 role master
   commit
   ```

2. Reboot the current master for the change to take effect.

5. Verifying and Monitoring Virtual Chassis

a. Check Virtual Chassis Status

Display overall status:

```
show virtual-chassis
```

b. Inspect Member Details

View detailed information about each member:

```
show virtual-chassis member
```

c. Monitor VCPs

Check the status of Virtual Chassis Ports:

```
show virtual-chassis vc-port
```

d. Synchronization Status

Ensure configuration synchronization across members:

```
show configuration | compare rollback 0
```

---

6. Troubleshooting Virtual Chassis

a. Common Issues

- **Mastership Conflicts**: Occurs when multiple switches are configured as master.
- **VCP Failures**: Caused by cable or port issues.
- **Member Inconsistencies**: Arises when members run different Junos OS versions.

b. Useful Commands

- View detailed logs for Virtual Chassis events:

  ```
  show log messages | match "virtual-chassis"
  ```

- Check for member conflicts:

  ```
  show virtual-chassis status
  ```

c. Resolving Mastership Conflicts

Manually assign the master role:

```
set virtual-chassis member 0 role master
commit
```

---

7. Best Practices for Virtual Chassis Configuration

1. **Standardize Configurations**: Use consistent configurations across all members.
2. **Test VCP Connections**: Verify all Virtual Chassis Ports are operational.
3. **Monitor Regularly**: Use monitoring tools to track the health of the Virtual Chassis.

4. **Plan Redundancy**: Ensure a backup member is available to take over the master role.
5. **Upgrade Carefully**: Perform synchronized upgrades to avoid version mismatches.

Conclusion

Virtual Chassis technology simplifies network management and enhances scalability in modern networks. By leveraging this feature in Junos OS, administrators can create robust, efficient, and easily managed switch infrastructures.

Link Aggregation Control Protocol (LACP)

Link Aggregation Control Protocol (LACP) is a vital technology for enhancing network performance, redundancy, and fault tolerance. By bundling multiple physical links into a single logical link, LACP improves bandwidth utilization and ensures network resilience. This chapter explores the principles of LACP, its configuration in Junos OS, and best practices for its implementation in Juniper Networks.

1. What is LACP?

LACP, defined in IEEE 802.3ad/802.1AX, is a dynamic protocol used for link aggregation. It allows multiple Ethernet interfaces to operate as a single logical link, referred to as an aggregated Ethernet (AE) interface or LAG (Link Aggregation Group).

Key Benefits of LACP:

- **Increased Bandwidth**: Combines the capacity of multiple links.
- **Redundancy**: Automatically re-routes traffic in case of link failure.
- **Dynamic Negotiation**: Automatically detects and configures link aggregation.
- **Load Balancing**: Distributes traffic across available links based on algorithms.

2. LACP Components

a. Actor and Partner

- **Actor**: The local device participating in LACP.
- **Partner**: The remote device participating in LACP.

b. LAG

A Link Aggregation Group (LAG) is the logical entity comprising multiple physical links.

c. Modes of LACP Operation

- **Active Mode**: Actively initiates LACP negotiation with the partner.
- **Passive Mode**: Responds to LACP negotiation requests but does not initiate them.

3. Configuring LACP in Junos OS

a. Prerequisites

- Ensure the physical links are operational and use the same speed and duplex settings.
- Verify compatibility between devices in the LAG.

b. Step-by-Step Configuration

Step 1: Create an Aggregated Ethernet Interface

1. Enter configuration mode:

```
configure
```

2. Define the aggregated Ethernet interface (e.g., ae0):

```
set interfaces ae0 aggregated-ether-options lacp active
```

Step 2: Add Member Interfaces to the LAG

Assign physical interfaces to the aggregated Ethernet interface:

```
set interfaces ge-0/0/0 ether-options 802.3ad ae0
set interfaces ge-0/0/1 ether-options 802.3ad ae0
commit
```

Step 3: Configure LACP Parameters

Set the LACP mode and system priority:

```
set interfaces ae0 aggregated-ether-options lacp active
set interfaces ae0 aggregated-ether-options lacp system-priority 100
commit
```

Step 4: Assign VLANs to the Aggregated Interface

For Layer 2 switching:

```
set interfaces ae0 unit 0 family ethernet-switching vlan members 10
commit
```

For Layer 3 routing:

```
set interfaces ae0 unit 0 family inet address 192.168.1.1/24
commit
```

---

4. Verifying LACP Configuration

a. Check LAG Status

Display the status of the LAG and its member links:

```
show interfaces ae0 extensive
```

Output:

```
Aggregated Ethernet interface: ae0
LACP state: Active
Member links: ge-0/0/0, ge-0/0/1
```

b. View LACP Protocol Information

Inspect LACP protocol status:

```
show lacp interfaces
```

Output:

```
Interface     Actor State     Partner State
ge-0/0/0      Active          Active
ge-0/0/1      Active          Passive
```

---

5. Managing and Tuning LACP

a. Changing LACP Modes

To configure an interface in passive mode:

```
set interfaces ae0 aggregated-ether-options lacp passive
commit
```

b. Adjusting LACP Timer

The LACP timer determines how often LACP packets are sent. Configure the fast timer (1 second):

```
set interfaces ae0 aggregated-ether-options lacp periodic fast
commit
```

c. Monitoring LACP Health

Monitor the health and performance of LACP links:

```
show lacp statistics
```

6. Troubleshooting LACP

a. Common Issues

1. **LAG Not Forming**:
   - Verify LACP mode on both ends.
   - Ensure all physical interfaces have the same settings.
2. **Link Imbalance**:
   - Check the load-balancing algorithm.
   - Verify traffic distribution across links.

b. Useful Commands

- Check LACP neighbors:

  ```
  show lacp neighbors
  ```

- Inspect individual link status:

  ```
  show interfaces extensive
  ```

7. Best Practices for LACP

1. **Use Active Mode**: Configure at least one side of the LAG in active mode for dynamic negotiation.
2. **Enable Redundancy**: Always include at least two physical links in a LAG for fault tolerance.
3. **Monitor Regularly**: Use monitoring tools to ensure LAG health and performance.
4. **Optimize Load Balancing**: Select an appropriate hashing algorithm based on traffic patterns.
5. **Document Configurations**: Clearly document member links, LAG settings, and VLAN assignments.

Conclusion

LACP is a critical technology for enhancing the performance and reliability of network connections. By implementing LACP in Junos OS, network administrators can achieve efficient link aggregation and improved fault tolerance.

Section 5:
Security in Juniper Networks

Juniper's Approach to Network Security

In today's interconnected world, robust network security is paramount. Juniper Networks adopts a comprehensive approach to safeguarding networks by combining advanced technologies, policy-driven frameworks, and an extensive suite of security features. This chapter delves into Juniper's security philosophy, its key technologies, and how they integrate with Junos OS to provide a strong defense against evolving threats.

1. Juniper's Security Philosophy

a. End-to-End Protection

Juniper emphasizes securing every aspect of the network—from the core infrastructure to the edge, ensuring holistic defense.

b. Policy-Driven Security

By implementing centralized policies, Juniper simplifies the management of complex network environments while maintaining flexibility and scalability.

c. Zero Trust Architecture (ZTA)

Juniper's security solutions align with Zero Trust principles, emphasizing "never trust, always verify." This ensures that all network traffic, internal or external, undergoes rigorous authentication and validation.

d. AI-Driven Insights

Juniper integrates AI and machine learning to proactively identify, mitigate, and adapt to security threats in real time.

2. Key Security Technologies in Juniper Networks

a. Unified Threat Management (UTM)

Juniper's UTM consolidates multiple security functions into a single solution, including:

- **Antivirus**: Protects against malware and viruses.
- **Intrusion Prevention System (IPS)**: Identifies and blocks malicious traffic.
- **Content Filtering**: Restricts access to harmful or inappropriate web content.

b. Juniper Advanced Threat Prevention (ATP)

A cloud-based solution that leverages AI to detect and mitigate sophisticated threats like zero-day vulnerabilities.

c. Security Intelligence (SecIntel)

Real-time threat intelligence feeds that provide actionable insights to block malicious traffic before it impacts the network.

d. Juniper SRX Series Firewalls

High-performance, next-generation firewalls that provide stateful inspection, intrusion prevention, and application-layer security.

---

3. Core Features of Junos OS Security

a. Zone-Based Security Architecture

Junos OS organizes the network into security zones, each with specific policies controlling traffic flow between zones.

b. Stateful Firewall

The firewall in Junos OS monitors the state of active connections, ensuring secure and efficient traffic management.

c. Intrusion Detection and Prevention (IDP)

Built-in IDP capabilities protect against known and unknown threats by analyzing traffic patterns and signatures.

d. Virtual Private Network (VPN) Support

Junos OS supports site-to-site and remote access VPNs using IPsec for secure communication over public networks.

---

4. Configuring Security Features in Junos OS

a. Creating Security Zones

1. Define zones and associate them with interfaces:

```
set security zones security-zone trust interfaces ge-0/0/0.0
set security zones security-zone untrust interfaces ge-0/0/1.0
commit
```

b. Configuring Policies

Define policies to control traffic between zones:

```
set security policies from-zone trust to-zone untrust policy allow-http match
source-address any
set security policies from-zone trust to-zone untrust policy allow-http match
destination-address any
set security policies from-zone trust to-zone untrust policy allow-http match
application junos-http
set security policies from-zone trust to-zone untrust policy allow-http then permit
commit
```

c. Enabling IDP

1. Configure IDP policies:

```
set security idp active-policy my-idp-policy
set security idp sensor-configuration recommended-profile
commit
```

d. Configuring VPNs

1. Define the IPsec VPN settings:

```
set security ipsec vpn my-vpn ike gateway my-gateway
set security ipsec vpn my-vpn ike policy my-policy
set security ipsec vpn my-vpn bind-interface st0.0
commit
```

---

5. Monitoring and Troubleshooting Security

a. Monitoring Security Zones

Verify zone statistics and traffic:

```
show security zones detail
```

b. Checking Firewall Policies

Inspect active policies and their hit counts:

```
show security policies
```

c. Monitoring IDP Activity

View intrusion detection logs:

```
show security idp attack detail
```

d. Troubleshooting VPNs

Debug VPN connections:

```
show security ipsec statistics
```

---

6. Best Practices for Network Security

1. **Implement Defense-in-Depth**: Use multiple layers of security, including firewalls, IDP, and UTM.
2. **Regularly Update Policies**: Adapt policies to address emerging threats and changing business needs.
3. **Leverage Threat Intelligence**: Integrate SecIntel feeds to proactively block known threats.
4. **Enable Logging and Monitoring**: Continuously monitor security events and maintain logs for forensic analysis.
5. **Educate Users**: Train staff on security best practices, such as avoiding phishing attacks.

---

7. Future Directions in Juniper's Security Approach

Juniper Networks continues to innovate in network security with a focus on:

- **AI-Driven Threat Detection**: Leveraging AI to predict and mitigate threats before they occur.
- **Zero Trust Enhancements**: Expanding Zero Trust principles across all network layers.
- **Cloud-Native Security**: Providing scalable security solutions for multi-cloud and hybrid environments.

Conclusion

Juniper's approach to network security combines advanced technologies, a policy-driven framework, and cutting-edge tools to protect modern networks. By leveraging these solutions in Junos OS, organizations can ensure robust and scalable security.

Firewall Filters in Junos OS

Firewall filters in Junos OS are a versatile tool for managing and securing network traffic. Unlike traditional firewalls, which typically operate at the network edge, Junos firewall filters can be applied to interfaces across the network, providing granular control over traffic flow. This chapter explores the structure, configuration, and best practices for implementing firewall filters in Junos OS.

1. What Are Firewall Filters in Junos OS?

Firewall filters are rules or access control lists (ACLs) applied to network interfaces to define how packets should be handled. These filters are highly flexible and can be used to:

- **Permit or deny traffic** based on various criteria.
- **Prioritize specific traffic** for better performance.
- **Log packets** for monitoring and troubleshooting.
- **Apply rate-limiting** to prevent traffic overloads.

2. Components of a Firewall Filter

a. Terms

Each firewall filter consists of one or more **terms**, which define the conditions and actions for specific types of traffic.

b. Match Conditions

Match conditions specify the criteria for identifying packets, such as:

- **Source and destination IP addresses**
- **Protocol type** (TCP, UDP, ICMP, etc.)
- **Port numbers**
- **Packet size or TTL**

c. Actions

Actions define what to do with packets that match the criteria, including:

- **Accept**: Allow the packet through.
- **Discard**: Drop the packet silently.
- **Reject**: Drop the packet and send an ICMP message.
- **Log**: Record details about the packet.

3. Configuring Firewall Filters

a. Creating a Firewall Filter

1. Enter configuration mode:

   ```
   configure
   ```

2. Define the filter and its terms:

```
set firewall family inet filter example-filter term allow-ssh from protocol
tcp
set firewall family inet filter example-filter term allow-ssh from
destination-port 22
set firewall family inet filter example-filter term allow-ssh then accept
```

3. Add a default discard rule to catch unmatched packets:

```
set firewall family inet filter example-filter term default then discard
```

b. Applying the Filter to an Interface

1. Assign the filter to an interface:

```
set interfaces ge-0/0/0 unit 0 family inet filter input example-filter
commit
```

---

4. Advanced Firewall Filter Features

a. Rate Limiting

To limit the rate of packets:

```
set firewall family inet filter rate-limit term limit-icmp from protocol icmp
set firewall family inet filter rate-limit term limit-icmp then policer icmp-policer
set firewall policer icmp-policer if-exceeding bandwidth-limit 1m burst-size-limit 15k
set firewall policer icmp-policer then discard
commit
```

b. Logging Packets

To log packets that match a specific condition:

```
set firewall family inet filter log-http term log-http-traffic from protocol tcp
set firewall family inet filter log-http term log-http-traffic from destination-port 80
set firewall family inet filter log-http term log-http-traffic then log
set firewall family inet filter log-http term log-http-traffic then accept
commit
```

c. Applying Multiple Filters

You can assign separate filters to inbound and outbound traffic:

```
set interfaces ge-0/0/0 unit 0 family inet filter input inbound-filter
set interfaces ge-0/0/0 unit 0 family inet filter output outbound-filter
commit
```

---

5. Monitoring and Verifying Firewall Filters

a. Viewing Filter Statistics

Check how often each term in a filter has been matched:

```
show firewall
```

Example output:

```
Filter: example-filter
Term: allow-ssh
    Count: 12345
Term: default
    Count: 5678
```

b. Checking Filter Application

Verify which filters are applied to an interface:

```
show configuration interfaces ge-0/0/0
```

c. Logging Analysis

Review logged packets:

```
show log messages | match "firewall"
```

---

6. Troubleshooting Firewall Filters

a. Common Issues

- **No Matches**: Ensure the filter criteria accurately match the intended traffic.
- **Unintended Blocking**: Verify the order of terms, as filters are processed sequentially.
- **Performance Impact**: Optimize filters to avoid excessive resource usage.

b. Useful Commands

- Inspect the firewall filter configuration:

  ```
  show configuration firewall
  ```

- Test the filter with specific traffic:

  ```
  ping <destination> source <source> routing-instance <instance>
  ```

---

7. Best Practices for Firewall Filters

1. **Use Explicit Policies**: Clearly define policies to minimize unintended traffic blocks.
2. **Log Strategically**: Log critical traffic events but avoid excessive logging.
3. **Apply Default Deny Policies**: Always include a catch-all discard term for unmatched traffic.
4. **Test Filters**: Test configurations in a staging environment before deployment.
5. **Document Rules**: Maintain detailed documentation of each filter and its terms.

Conclusion

Firewall filters in Junos OS provide powerful and flexible traffic management capabilities. By mastering their configuration and monitoring, network administrators can secure their networks against a wide range of threats.

Configuring Junos SRX Firewalls

Junos SRX firewalls are a cornerstone of Juniper Networks' security offerings, providing robust protection with advanced features such as stateful inspection, intrusion prevention, and application-layer security. This chapter delves into the key aspects of configuring Junos SRX firewalls, covering the basic setup, zone-based policies, NAT configuration, and integration with advanced security features.

1. Overview of SRX Firewalls

The SRX series combines routing, switching, and security in a single platform, making it ideal for enterprise and service provider environments. Key features include:

- **Stateful Firewall**: Monitors the state of active connections to allow or block traffic.
- **Zone-Based Security**: Applies policies to traffic moving between defined zones.
- **Unified Threat Management (UTM)**: Consolidates features like antivirus, web filtering, and intrusion prevention.
- **Scalability**: Available in models suitable for small businesses to large enterprises.

2. Basic Configuration of SRX Firewalls

a. Initial Setup

1. Connect to the SRX device via the console or SSH.
2. Enter configuration mode:

```
configure
```

3. Set the root authentication:

```
set system root-authentication plain-text-password
commit
```

4. Configure the hostname and basic system parameters:

```
set system host-name srx-firewall
set system domain-name example.com
set system time-zone UTC
commit
```

3. Configuring Security Zones

Security zones are logical groupings that define how traffic is handled between interfaces.

a. Create Zones and Assign Interfaces

1. Define zones and assign interfaces:

```
set security zones security-zone trust interfaces ge-0/0/0.0
set security zones security-zone untrust interfaces ge-0/0/1.0
commit
```

b. Configure Host-Inbound Traffic

Enable protocols and services for inbound traffic on each zone:

```
set security zones security-zone trust host-inbound-traffic system-services ssh
set security zones security-zone untrust host-inbound-traffic system-services ping
commit
```

4. Configuring Security Policies

Security policies control traffic flow between zones based on specified conditions.

a. Define a Policy

1. Allow traffic from the trust zone to the untrust zone:

```
set security policies from-zone trust to-zone untrust policy allow-http match
source-address any
set security policies from-zone trust to-zone untrust policy allow-http match
destination-address any
set security policies from-zone trust to-zone untrust policy allow-http match
application junos-http
set security policies from-zone trust to-zone untrust policy allow-http then
permit
commit
```

2. Add a deny-all policy for unmatched traffic:

```
set security policies from-zone trust to-zone untrust policy deny-all then
deny
commit
```

5. Configuring Network Address Translation (NAT)

NAT translates private IP addresses to public IP addresses for communication over the internet.

a. Configure Source NAT

1. Define a source NAT pool:

```
set security nat source pool src-nat-pool address 192.0.2.10/32
```

2. Apply the NAT rule:

```
set security nat source rule-set src-nat-rule-set from zone trust
set security nat source rule-set src-nat-rule-set to zone untrust
set security nat source rule-set src-nat-rule-set rule src-nat-rule match
source-address 192.168.1.0/24
set security nat source rule-set src-nat-rule-set rule src-nat-rule then
source-nat pool src-nat-pool
commit
```

b. Configure Destination NAT

1. Define a destination NAT pool:

```
set security nat destination pool dst-nat-pool address 192.168.1.100/32
```

2. Apply the NAT rule:

```
set security nat destination rule-set dst-nat-rule-set from zone untrust
set security nat destination rule-set dst-nat-rule-set rule dst-nat-rule match
destination-address 203.0.113.10/32
set security nat destination rule-set dst-nat-rule-set rule dst-nat-rule then
destination-nat pool dst-nat-pool
commit
```

6. Configuring Unified Threat Management (UTM)

a. Enable UTM

1. Configure UTM profiles for antivirus and web filtering:

```
set security utm feature-profile web-filtering juniper-enhanced server
ip-address 192.0.2.1
set security utm feature-profile antivirus default-action permit
commit
```

b. Apply UTM to a Policy

1. Attach the UTM profile to a security policy:

```
set security policies from-zone trust to-zone untrust policy allow-http then
permit utm web-filtering-profile
commit
```

7. Monitoring and Verifying Firewall Configuration

a. View Security Policy Hits

Check the number of times each policy has been matched:

```
show security policies
```

b. Monitor Active Sessions

List active sessions passing through the firewall:

```
show security flow session
```

c. Check NAT Statistics

Verify NAT translations:

```
show security nat source summary
show security nat destination summary
```

8. Troubleshooting Junos SRX Firewalls

a. Common Issues

- **Policy Misconfiguration**: Ensure policies have correct match conditions and actions.
- **NAT Translation Failures**: Verify NAT rules and address pools.
- **High CPU Usage**: Check for traffic spikes or inefficient policies.

b. Useful Commands

- Review logs for debugging:

```
show log messages | match "security"
```

- Test connectivity between zones:

```
ping <destination> source <source>
```

9. Best Practices for SRX Firewalls

1. **Follow Principle of Least Privilege**: Allow only necessary traffic through security policies.
2. **Log Critical Traffic**: Enable logging for important policies to monitor traffic flow.
3. **Review Regularly**: Periodically audit firewall rules and policies to ensure they align with business needs.
4. **Implement Redundancy**: Use HA (High Availability) configurations for critical deployments.
5. **Keep Firmware Updated**: Regularly update the SRX firmware to ensure access to the latest features and security patches.

Conclusion

Configuring Junos SRX firewalls effectively is critical for ensuring a secure and resilient network. With powerful features such as zone-based policies, NAT, and UTM, SRX firewalls provide comprehensive protection for modern networks.

Intrusion Detection and Prevention (IDP)

In today's sophisticated threat landscape, intrusion detection and prevention systems (IDP) are vital for maintaining network integrity. Juniper Networks' IDP solution, integrated into Junos OS, provides robust security by detecting, blocking, and mitigating known and emerging threats in real time. This chapter explores the principles of IDP, its implementation in Junos OS, and the best practices for configuring and managing IDP effectively.

---

1. What Is Intrusion Detection and Prevention?

a. Intrusion Detection System (IDS)

IDS monitors network traffic for suspicious activity and generates alerts. It is a passive security mechanism that does not actively block threats.

b. Intrusion Prevention System (IPS)

IPS goes a step further by actively preventing malicious activity. It can block traffic based on predefined policies and real-time analysis.

c. Combined IDP in Junos OS

Juniper's IDP offers both detection and prevention capabilities, providing a comprehensive security solution. It uses advanced algorithms and signatures to identify threats across multiple layers of the network.

---

2. Key Features of Juniper's IDP

- **Protocol Anomaly Detection**: Identifies deviations from standard protocol behavior.
- **Signature-Based Detection**: Matches traffic patterns against a database of known attack signatures.
- **Behavior-Based Detection**: Monitors unusual patterns indicative of zero-day threats.
- **Integrated Threat Intelligence**: Leverages feeds like Juniper's Security Intelligence (SecIntel) to stay updated with the latest threats.
- **Granular Policy Control**: Allows tailored policies for specific traffic types or network segments.
- **High Performance**: Optimized for minimal latency, ensuring high throughput even during deep packet inspection.

---

3. Configuring IDP in Junos OS

a. Prerequisites

1. Ensure the SRX device has an IDP license.
2. Update the IDP signature database:

```
request security idp security-package download
request security idp security-package install
```

b. Enabling IDP

1. Set up the IDP policy:

```
set security idp idp-policy my-idp-policy rulebase-ips rule 1 match
source-zone trust
set security idp idp-policy my-idp-policy rulebase-ips rule 1 match
destination-zone untrust
set security idp idp-policy my-idp-policy rulebase-ips rule 1 match
application any
set security idp idp-policy my-idp-policy rulebase-ips rule 1 then action
recommended
commit
```

2. Enable the IDP policy:

```
set security idp active-policy my-idp-policy
commit
```

c. Monitoring IDP

1. View active IDP policy:

```
show security idp active-policy
```

2. Check recent IDP events:

```
show security idp attack detail
```

---

4. Fine-Tuning IDP Policies

a. Configuring Custom Rules

Create rules to address specific threats or network requirements:

```
set security idp idp-policy my-idp-policy rulebase-ips rule custom-rule match
source-address 192.168.1.0/24
set security idp idp-policy my-idp-policy rulebase-ips rule custom-rule then action
close-client
commit
```

b. Setting Thresholds

Adjust thresholds for sensitive detection:

```
set security idp sensor-configuration recommended-profile
set security idp sensor-configuration log-session-initiate
commit
```

c. Avoiding False Positives

- Review alerts to identify patterns of benign activity flagged as threats.
- Adjust rules to exclude known safe traffic.

---

5. Best Practices for IDP Implementation

1. **Keep Signatures Updated**: Regularly update the signature database to protect against new threats.

2. **Start with Detection Mode**: Run IDP in detection-only mode initially to analyze traffic without blocking it.
3. **Use Granular Policies**: Apply specific policies to sensitive zones or critical applications.
4. **Monitor Regularly**: Use logs and reports to identify patterns and optimize IDP settings.
5. **Test Changes**: Test new rules in a staging environment before deployment to production.

6. Advanced IDP Features

a. Integration with UTM

Combine IDP with Unified Threat Management (UTM) features like antivirus and web filtering for a layered defense.

b. Application Awareness

Leverage application-layer signatures to detect threats targeting specific protocols or services.

c. Rate Limiting

Limit the rate of connections or sessions to mitigate DDoS attacks:

```
set security idp sensor-configuration rate-limit-policy my-policy
set security idp sensor-configuration rate-limit-policy my-policy max-connections 1000
commit
```

7. Troubleshooting IDP

a. Common Issues

- **High CPU Usage**: Optimize rules and disable unnecessary signatures.
- **Missed Attacks**: Verify that the signature database is updated and the policy is correctly applied.
- **Excessive False Positives**: Refine rules and tune thresholds.

b. Useful Commands

- Check IDP performance:

  ```
  show security idp statistics
  ```

- Verify traffic matches:

  ```
  show security idp session-traffic
  ```

Conclusion

Juniper's IDP system is a powerful tool for detecting and preventing network intrusions. By combining advanced detection techniques with granular policy control, Junos OS ensures a secure network environment. With proper configuration and ongoing monitoring, administrators can effectively protect their networks against both known and emerging threats.

Virtual Private Network (VPN) Implementation

Virtual Private Networks (VPNs) are a cornerstone of secure communication, enabling organizations to establish encrypted connections over public or untrusted networks. Junos OS supports various VPN implementations, providing flexibility, scalability, and security to meet diverse networking needs. This chapter focuses on VPN concepts, configuration methods, and best practices for implementing VPNs on Juniper devices.

1. Overview of VPNs in Junos OS

a. Types of VPNs Supported

1. **IPsec VPNs**: Secure point-to-point connections for site-to-site or remote access.
2. **Layer 2 VPNs (L2VPN)**: Extend Layer 2 connectivity over MPLS.
3. **Layer 3 VPNs (L3VPN)**: Provide MPLS-based virtualized Layer 3 networks.
4. **Dynamic VPNs**: Allow secure, dynamic remote access for end-users.
5. **SSL VPNs**: Encrypt web-based access without requiring client-side software.

b. Key Features of Junos VPNs

- Strong encryption using protocols like AES and 3DES.
- Support for IKE (Internet Key Exchange) protocols for secure key management.
- Scalability for small to large enterprise deployments.
- Integration with Juniper Security Intelligence (SecIntel) for threat prevention.

2. Configuring Site-to-Site IPsec VPN

a. Configuration Workflow

1. **Phase 1 (IKE) Configuration**:
    - Establishes a secure channel for negotiating Phase 2.
    - Configure the IKE proposal:

      ```
      set security ike proposal ike-proposal-1 authentication-method
      pre-shared-keys
      set security ike proposal ike-proposal-1 dh-group group2
      set security ike proposal ike-proposal-1 encryption-algorithm
      aes-256-cbc
      set security ike proposal ike-proposal-1 lifetime-seconds 3600
      commit
      ```

    - Define the IKE policy:

      ```
      set security ike policy ike-policy-1 proposals ike-proposal-1
      set security ike policy ike-policy-1 pre-shared-key ascii-text
      mysharedkey
      commit
      ```

    - Configure the IKE gateway:

      ```
      set security ike gateway ike-gateway-1 address 203.0.113.1
      set security ike gateway ike-gateway-1 external-interface ge-0/0/0.0
      set security ike gateway ike-gateway-1 ike-policy ike-policy-1
      ```

```
commit
```

2. **Phase 2 (IPsec) Configuration**:
   - Define the IPsec proposal:

   ```
   set security ipsec proposal ipsec-proposal-1 protocol esp
   set security ipsec proposal ipsec-proposal 1 authentication-algorithm
   hmac-sha-256
   set security ipsec proposal ipsec-proposal-1 encryption-algorithm
   aes-256-cbc
   commit
   ```

   - Create the IPsec policy:

   ```
   set security ipsec policy ipsec-policy-1 proposals ipsec-proposal-1
   commit
   ```

   - Configure the VPN tunnel:

   ```
   set security ipsec vpn vpn-1 ike gateway ike-gateway-1
   set security ipsec vpn vpn-1 ike ipsec-policy ipsec-policy-1
   set security ipsec vpn vpn-1 bind-interface st0.0
   commit
   ```

3. **Create Secure Tunnel Interface**:

   ```
   set interfaces st0 unit 0 family inet
   commit
   ```

4. **Routing Configuration**: Add static or dynamic routing to direct traffic through the VPN:

   ```
   set routing-options static route 192.168.2.0/24 next-hop st0.0
   commit
   ```

---

3. Configuring Dynamic VPNs

Dynamic VPNs provide secure, on-demand remote access to users.

a. Key Configuration Steps

1. Enable dynamic VPN on the SRX device:

   ```
   set security dynamic-vpn clients user1 remote-access
   set access profile remote-access authentication-order password
   set access profile remote-access client user1
   set security ipsec vpn dynamic-vpn ike gateway ike-gateway-1
   commit
   ```

2. Configure a secure user authentication mechanism:

   ```
   set access profile remote-access authentication-order radius
   commit
   ```

3. Ensure NAT traversal (NAT-T) is enabled if clients are behind NAT devices.

4. Monitoring and Verifying VPNs

a. Verifying IKE Status

```
show security ike security-associations
```

b. Checking IPsec Statistics

```
show security ipsec security-associations
```

c. Viewing Active Tunnels

```
show interfaces st0 detail
```

d. Testing Connectivity

Use `ping` or `traceroute` to verify traffic is routed through the tunnel.

---

5. Best Practices for VPN Implementation

1. **Use Strong Encryption**: Always use modern algorithms like AES-256 for encryption and HMAC-SHA-256 for authentication.
2. **Leverage Certificate-Based Authentication**: Use certificates instead of pre-shared keys for enhanced security.
3. **Enable NAT-T**: Ensure compatibility with NAT devices.
4. **Monitor VPN Performance**: Regularly check tunnel status and throughput.
5. **Backup Configurations**: Maintain backups of all VPN configurations for quick recovery.
6. **Test Before Deployment**: Validate configurations in a test environment before production.

---

6. Troubleshooting VPN Issues

a. Common Issues

- **Tunnel Fails to Establish**: Verify Phase 1 and Phase 2 configurations, including pre-shared keys and proposals.
- **Traffic Does Not Pass**: Check routing, NAT policies, and firewall filters.
- **Latency or Performance Issues**: Monitor network health and adjust MTU settings if necessary.

b. Useful Commands

- Review IKE logs:

  ```
  show log kmd
  ```

- Debug IPsec issues:

  ```
  show log messages | match ipsec
  ```

Conclusion

VPN implementation is a critical component of network security, enabling secure communication across untrusted networks. Junos OS provides a comprehensive suite of tools to configure and manage various types of VPNs, ensuring flexibility and scalability for diverse deployment scenarios.

Advanced Security Policies

Security policies are fundamental to network defense, acting as the gatekeepers that control traffic flow. In Junos OS, advanced security policies provide enhanced granularity and dynamic capabilities for protecting complex network environments. This chapter explores the configuration and optimization of advanced security policies in Junos OS, focusing on achieving a robust, adaptive, and scalable security posture.

1. Overview of Advanced Security Policies

a. What Are Security Policies?

Security policies in Junos OS are rules that define how traffic is permitted or denied between zones or interfaces. Advanced policies enhance traditional configurations by incorporating dynamic criteria, application awareness, and integration with threat intelligence.

b. Key Features

- **Application-Aware Policies**: Control traffic based on application type rather than just ports and protocols.
- **User-Based Policies**: Enforce rules based on user identity through integration with authentication services.
- **Dynamic Addressing**: Use address groups that automatically update based on threat intelligence or network changes.
- **Logging and Auditing**: Provide detailed insights for traffic analysis and policy optimization.

2. Creating and Managing Security Policies

a. Basic Policy Structure

Security policies typically include:

- **Match Conditions**: Define source, destination, applications, and users.
- **Action**: Permit, deny, or reject traffic.
- **Logging**: Enable logging for detailed visibility.

b. Configuring a Basic Policy

To allow web traffic from the trust zone to the untrust zone:

```
set security policies from-zone trust to-zone untrust policy allow-web match
source-address any
set security policies from-zone trust to-zone untrust policy allow-web match
destination-address any
set security policies from-zone trust to-zone untrust policy allow-web match
application junos-http
set security policies from-zone trust to-zone untrust policy allow-web then permit
commit
```

3. Application-Aware Policies

a. Why Use Application-Aware Policies?

Traditional security policies often rely on ports and protocols, which can be insufficient in identifying modern applications. Application-aware policies identify and control traffic at the application layer, offering granular control.

b. Configuring Application-Aware Policies

To allow only specific applications like Gmail and block social media:

```
set applications application gmail term 1 protocol tcp destination-port 443
set security policies from-zone trust to-zone untrust policy restrict-apps match
application gmail
set security policies from-zone trust to-zone untrust policy restrict-apps then
permit
set security policies from-zone trust to-zone untrust policy restrict-apps match
application facebook
set security policies from-zone trust to-zone untrust policy restrict-apps then
deny
commit
```

4. User-Based Policies

a. Enabling User-Based Security

Integrate with Active Directory or an authentication server to enforce rules based on user roles.

b. Example Configuration

To allow only the "Admin" group access to specific resources:

```
set access-profile user-authentication authentication-order radius
set security policies from-zone trust to-zone data-center policy admin-access match
source-address any
set security policies from-zone trust to-zone data-center policy admin-access match
source-identity admin
set security policies from-zone trust to-zone data-center policy admin-access then
permit
commit
```

5. Dynamic Policies with Address Groups

a. Using Dynamic Address Groups

Dynamic address groups automatically update based on real-time data, such as threat intelligence feeds or IP reputation lists.

b. Example Configuration

To block traffic from malicious IPs:

```
set security dynamic-address-set blocklist-feed address feed-url
http://threatintel.example.com/blocklist
set security policies from-zone untrust to-zone trust policy block-malicious match
source-address dynamic-address-set blocklist-feed
```

```
set security policies from-zone untrust to-zone trust policy block-malicious then
deny
commit
```

---

6. Logging and Monitoring

a. Enabling Logging

Enable logging to analyze policy performance and traffic patterns:

```
set security policies from-zone trust to-zone untrust policy allow-web then permit
log session-init
commit
```

b. Viewing Logs

Monitor policy logs:

```
show log security-policy
```

c. Analyzing Traffic

Use security reports and dashboards to identify trends and refine policies:

```
show security flow session summary
```

---

7. Policy Optimization and Best Practices

a. Simplify Rules

- Consolidate redundant rules to improve readability and performance.
- Use address groups and application sets for common patterns.

b. Enable Threat Detection

Integrate policies with Juniper's Security Intelligence (SecIntel) for automated threat mitigation:

```
set security intelligence policy threat-policy match category malware
set security intelligence policy threat-policy then deny
commit
```

c. Test and Audit Policies

- Test policies in a staging environment before deployment.
- Regularly audit rules to identify unused or outdated configurations.

---

8. Troubleshooting Advanced Policies

a. Common Issues

- **Policy Mismatch**: Incorrect source/destination zones or addresses.
- **Application Misidentification**: Ensure the application signature database is up-to-date.
- **Performance Impact**: Too many rules can degrade performance; optimize policies where possible.

b. Useful Commands

- Verify active policies:

```
show security policies
```

- Debug policy enforcement:

```
show security flow session
```

Conclusion

Advanced security policies in Junos OS offer unparalleled control over traffic, allowing organizations to enforce granular, dynamic, and adaptive rules. By leveraging features like application awareness, user-based controls, and dynamic addressing, administrators can effectively secure their networks against evolving threats.

Section 6:
Advanced Routing Techniques

MPLS Configuration Essentials

MPLS (Multiprotocol Label Switching) is a high-performance network technique that directs data from one node to another based on short path labels rather than long network addresses. It is widely used in Juniper Networks to enhance routing efficiency and enable advanced services such as VPNs, traffic engineering, and QoS. This chapter provides a step-by-step guide to configuring MPLS in Junos OS, ensuring optimized and scalable network performance.

1. Introduction to MPLS

a. What is MPLS?

MPLS is a data-forwarding technology that uses labels for routing decisions, bypassing traditional IP-based routing. This allows for faster and more efficient data delivery.

b. Benefits of MPLS

- **Improved Performance**: Reduces latency by streamlining routing decisions.
- **Scalability**: Easily integrates with existing network infrastructures.
- **Traffic Engineering**: Provides control over traffic paths, optimizing bandwidth utilization.
- **Enhanced VPN Services**: Supports Layer 2 and Layer 3 VPNs with high security and reliability.

2. Prerequisites for MPLS Configuration

Before configuring MPLS, ensure the following:

1. **Enable MPLS on Interfaces**: MPLS must be activated on the interfaces participating in the MPLS network.
2. **Routing Protocols**: OSPF or IS-IS should be configured to exchange label information via LDP (Label Distribution Protocol) or RSVP-TE (Resource Reservation Protocol - Traffic Engineering).
3. **IP Connectivity**: Ensure proper IP connectivity between MPLS nodes.

3. Enabling MPLS on Junos OS

a. Configuring MPLS on Interfaces

To enable MPLS on an interface:

```
set protocols mpls interface ge-0/0/0
set protocols mpls interface ge-0/0/1
commit
```

b. Activating LDP

LDP is used for label distribution in MPLS networks:

```
set protocols ldp interface ge-0/0/0
set protocols ldp interface ge-0/0/1
commit
```

4. Verifying MPLS Configuration

After enabling MPLS, verify the setup using the following commands:

- Check MPLS interface status:

```
show mpls interface
```

- Verify LDP neighbors:

```
show ldp neighbor
```

- Display MPLS label bindings:

```
show mpls ldp database
```

5. Configuring Traffic Engineering with RSVP-TE

RSVP-TE enhances MPLS by enabling traffic engineering capabilities.

a. Enable RSVP-TE

To activate RSVP-TE on interfaces:

```
set protocols rsvp interface ge-0/0/0
set protocols rsvp interface ge-0/0/1
commit
```

b. Configure MPLS Traffic Engineering

Define LSPs (Label Switched Paths) to direct traffic:

```
set protocols mpls label-switched-path LSP1 to 192.168.1.2
set protocols mpls label-switched-path LSP1 primary path1
set protocols mpls path path1 192.168.1.3 192.168.1.4
commit
```

c. Verify LSP Status

Ensure the LSP is active:

```
show mpls lsp
```

6. Quality of Service (QoS) in MPLS

a. Configuring EXP Bits

Use EXP bits to classify and prioritize MPLS traffic:

```
set class-of-service rewrite-rules exp default forwarding-class best-effort
set class-of-service rewrite-rules exp default loss-priority low
commit
```

b. Assigning Queues

Map traffic to appropriate queues.

```
set forwarding-options enhanced-hashing level-1
commit
```

---

7. Troubleshooting MPLS

a. Common Issues

- **Label Mismatches**: Verify label bindings between routers.
- **RSVP Errors**: Ensure RSVP is enabled on all participating interfaces.
- **Connectivity Problems**: Check routing protocol configurations.

b. Diagnostic Commands

- Verify MPLS forwarding:

  ```
  show mpls forwarding-table
  ```

- Check RSVP sessions:

  ```
  show rsvp session
  ```

---

8. Real-World Use Cases for MPLS

a. MPLS VPNs

MPLS is widely used for implementing Layer 3 VPNs, offering secure and scalable connectivity between multiple sites.

b. Bandwidth Optimization

Traffic engineering with MPLS ensures efficient bandwidth utilization by dynamically allocating resources based on network demand.

c. High Availability

MPLS provides robust failover capabilities with minimal downtime through mechanisms like Fast Reroute (FRR).

Conclusion

MPLS is a cornerstone of modern networking, enabling high-speed, efficient, and scalable data forwarding. By mastering MPLS configuration essentials in Junos OS, network administrators can leverage advanced services such as traffic engineering, QoS, and VPNs to optimize their network infrastructure.

Traffic Engineering with RSVP-TE

Traffic engineering is a critical aspect of modern networking, enabling the optimization of resource utilization and improved performance. Junos OS leverages RSVP-TE (Resource Reservation Protocol - Traffic Engineering) as a robust mechanism to define explicit routes, optimize bandwidth utilization, and ensure reliability in large-scale networks. This chapter explores the fundamentals of RSVP-TE in Junos OS, its configuration, and its role in building efficient and resilient networks.

1. Introduction to RSVP-TE

a. What is RSVP-TE?

RSVP-TE extends the RSVP protocol by enabling bandwidth reservation and explicit routing in MPLS (Multiprotocol Label Switching) networks. It allows network administrators to:

- Define explicit label-switched paths (LSPs) for specific traffic flows.
- Allocate bandwidth resources dynamically.
- Ensure high availability through backup paths and fast reroute mechanisms.

b. Benefits of RSVP-TE

- **Traffic Optimization**: Provides better traffic distribution by directing flows through predefined paths.
- **Improved Reliability**: Supports backup LSPs and fast reroute to minimize downtime.
- **Scalability**: Accommodates growing network demands by efficiently managing resources.
- **Quality of Service (QoS)**: Ensures consistent performance by reserving bandwidth for critical traffic.

2. Prerequisites for Configuring RSVP-TE

To implement RSVP-TE in Junos OS, ensure the following:

1. **MPLS is Enabled**: RSVP-TE relies on MPLS for label distribution.
2. **IP Connectivity**: Ensure IP reachability between all RSVP-enabled routers.
3. **LSP Planning**: Define the primary and backup paths for traffic engineering.

3. Configuring RSVP-TE in Junos OS

a. Enabling RSVP-TE on Interfaces

To activate RSVP-TE on specific interfaces:

```
set protocols rsvp interface ge-0/0/0
set protocols rsvp interface ge-0/0/1
commit
```

b. Configuring MPLS Traffic Engineering

Define LSPs to control traffic flows:

```
set protocols mpls label-switched-path LSP1 to 192.168.1.2
set protocols mpls label-switched-path LSP1 primary path1
```

```
set protocols mpls path path1 192.168.1.3 192.168.1.4
commit
```

c. Allocating Bandwidth for LSPs

Reserve bandwidth for specific LSPs:

```
set protocols rsvp interface ge-0/0/0 bandwidth 100m
set protocols mpls label-switched-path LSP1 bandwidth 50m
commit
```

d. Configuring Fast Reroute (FRR)

Enable FRR to minimize downtime during failures:

```
set protocols mpls label-switched-path LSP1 fast-reroute
commit
```

---

4. Verifying RSVP-TE Configuration

After configuring RSVP-TE, use the following commands to validate the setup:

a. Verify LSP Status

```
show mpls lsp
```

b. Check RSVP Sessions

```
show rsvp session
```

c. Monitor Bandwidth Utilization

```
show rsvp bandwidth
```

---

5. Advanced RSVP-TE Features

a. Explicit Path Configuration

Define exact paths for LSPs to optimize traffic flow:

```
set protocols mpls path path1 192.168.1.3 strict 192.168.1.4 strict
commit
```

b. Backup LSPs

Configure secondary paths for failover scenarios:

```
set protocols mpls label-switched-path LSP1 secondary path2
set protocols mpls path path2 192.168.1.5 192.168.1.6
commit
```

c. Shared Risk Link Groups (SRLGs)

Minimize risks by avoiding links with shared failure potential:

```
set protocols mpls label-switched-path LSP1 srlg 10
```

```
commit
```

6. Troubleshooting RSVP-TE

a. Common Issues

- **LSP Failures**: Verify the explicit path and IP connectivity.
- **Bandwidth Allocation Errors**: Ensure sufficient bandwidth is available on RSVP-enabled interfaces.
- **RSVP Session Timeouts**: Check for misconfigurations or packet loss.

b. Diagnostic Commands

- Verify RSVP neighbor relationships:

```
show rsvp neighbor
```

- Check RSVP statistics:

```
show rsvp statistics
```

- Display MPLS forwarding table:

```
show mpls forwarding-table
```

7. Use Cases for RSVP-TE

a. Traffic Distribution

RSVP-TE enables fine-grained control over traffic flow, ensuring balanced utilization of network links.

b. Network Redundancy

With backup LSPs and FRR, RSVP-TE enhances reliability and minimizes service disruption during link or node failures.

c. Bandwidth Optimization

Efficient resource allocation with RSVP-TE ensures critical traffic receives priority, preventing congestion.

Conclusion

RSVP-TE is a powerful tool for traffic engineering in MPLS networks, providing granular control over traffic flows, optimized resource utilization, and enhanced network reliability. By mastering RSVP-TE configuration in Junos OS, network administrators can create resilient and efficient infrastructures that adapt to evolving demands.

BGP Route Reflectors and Confederations

Border Gateway Protocol (BGP) plays a critical role in managing inter-domain routing in large-scale networks. However, as networks grow, scaling BGP effectively becomes a significant challenge. Two advanced techniques—Route Reflectors (RR) and Confederations—help address these challenges by reducing the number of peer relationships and optimizing route propagation. In this chapter, we will explore the concepts of Route Reflectors and Confederations, their configuration in Junos OS, and their role in scaling BGP networks.

1. The Need for Scaling BGP

In a full-mesh iBGP topology, every BGP router in an autonomous system (AS) must establish a direct peering session with every other router. This requirement results in:

- **Increased Complexity**: The number of connections grows quadratically with the number of routers.
- **High Resource Usage**: Maintaining many sessions consumes CPU and memory.
- **Operational Challenges**: Adding or removing routers disrupts the entire network.

To overcome these challenges, Junos OS supports BGP Route Reflectors and Confederations.

2. BGP Route Reflectors (RR)

a. Overview

A Route Reflector simplifies BGP by allowing a single router (the reflector) to manage routing updates for a group of routers (clients). This eliminates the need for a full-mesh topology.

b. How It Works

1. A Route Reflector receives routes from its clients or non-client peers.
2. It reflects these routes to other clients and non-client peers.
3. This mechanism reduces the number of iBGP connections required.

c. Key Benefits

- Reduces configuration overhead.
- Enhances scalability by minimizing peer connections.
- Centralizes route management.

d. Route Reflection Rules

- **Client to Client**: Routes received from one client are reflected to other clients and non-clients.
- **Non-Client to Client**: Routes received from a non-client are advertised to clients.

3. Configuring a BGP Route Reflector in Junos OS

a. Define the Router as a Route Reflector

To configure a BGP Route Reflector:

```
set protocols bgp group INTERNAL type internal
set protocols bgp group INTERNAL local-address 192.168.1.1
```

```
set protocols bgp group INTERNAL neighbor 192.168.1.2 route-reflector-client
set protocols bgp group INTERNAL neighbor 192.168.1.3 route-reflector-client
commit
```

b. Verify Route Reflection

Use the following command to ensure the routes are being reflected:

```
show bgp neighbor
```

---

4. BGP Confederations

a. Overview

BGP Confederations divide a large AS into multiple smaller sub-ASes, which communicate with each other using eBGP. Internally, these sub-ASes use iBGP, but they appear as a single AS to external peers.

b. Benefits

- Reduces the number of iBGP sessions required.
- Simplifies policy management.
- Provides a hierarchical structure for large networks.

c. Confederation Components

- **Sub-AS**: Each sub-AS operates independently but communicates with other sub-ASes using eBGP.
- **Confederation Identifier**: Externally, all sub-ASes appear as a single AS, represented by a confederation identifier.

---

5. Configuring a BGP Confederation in Junos OS

a. Define the Sub-AS

Assign the sub-AS and confederation identifier:

```
set routing-options autonomous-system 65001
set protocols bgp group EXTERNAL type external
set protocols bgp group EXTERNAL neighbor 192.168.1.4 peer-as 65002
set protocols bgp confederation identifier 65000
set protocols bgp confederation peers 65002
commit
```

b. Verify Confederation Configuration

Check the confederation setup:

```
show bgp summary
```

---

6. Comparing Route Reflectors and Confederations

Aspect	Route Reflectors	Confederations
Use Case	Centralized management of peers	Hierarchical AS segmentation
Configuration	Requires route reflector setup	Involves sub-AS and identifier
Scaling	Reduces iBGP sessions	Divides AS into smaller units
Complexity	Easier to implement	More complex to design initially

7. Best Practices for Route Reflectors and Confederations

For Route Reflectors

- Deploy redundant route reflectors for high availability.
- Limit the number of clients per route reflector to prevent overload.
- Ensure loop prevention using cluster IDs.

For Confederations

- Use consistent policies across sub-ASes to avoid routing loops.
- Reserve distinct AS numbers for sub-ASes.
- Monitor inter-sub-AS communication for performance.

8. Troubleshooting BGP Scalability Solutions

a. Route Reflector Issues

- **Problem**: Missing routes in the client routing table.
  - **Solution**: Verify the route-reflector-client configuration.
  - Command:

```
show bgp neighbor <client-IP> detail
```

b. Confederation Issues

- **Problem**: Routing loops between sub-ASes.
  - **Solution**: Check AS path attributes and ensure no sub-AS is advertising incorrect routes.
  - Command:

```
show route advertising-protocol bgp
```

Conclusion

BGP Route Reflectors and Confederations are essential tools for scaling large networks. While route reflectors centralize route management and simplify configuration, confederations introduce hierarchical AS structures, enhancing scalability. By carefully implementing these solutions in Junos OS, network administrators can optimize BGP performance, reduce operational overhead, and build robust, efficient networks.

Policy-Based Routing (PBR)

Policy-Based Routing (PBR) provides network administrators with a flexible way to dictate the routing behavior of packets based on predefined policies. Unlike traditional routing, which relies on the destination address, PBR enables routing decisions to be based on various attributes such as source address, application type, or other packet characteristics. This approach is particularly useful in scenarios requiring traffic engineering, Quality of Service (QoS), or advanced security implementations.

In this chapter, we will explore the fundamentals of PBR, its use cases, and its implementation in Junos OS.

1. Understanding Policy-Based Routing

a. What is PBR?

Policy-Based Routing (PBR) is a mechanism that overrides the default routing table lookup. Instead of relying solely on the destination IP address, PBR routes packets based on policies defined by administrators. These policies can include:

- Source IP address
- Source or destination port numbers
- Application types
- Protocols (e.g., TCP, UDP)

b. Why Use PBR?

PBR is ideal in situations where traffic needs to be routed based on:

- **Business Policies**: Prioritizing specific applications or users.
- **Traffic Segmentation**: Routing traffic through specific paths for auditing or compliance purposes.
- **Load Balancing**: Distributing traffic across multiple links.
- **Service Chaining**: Sending traffic through specific services like firewalls or intrusion prevention systems.

2. Key Features of Policy-Based Routing in Junos OS

- **Flexible Match Conditions**: Junos OS allows matching packets based on various criteria using firewall filters.
- **Action-Oriented Policies**: Policies can forward, discard, or reroute traffic based on defined actions.
- **Seamless Integration**: PBR works in tandem with other routing protocols and features in Junos OS.
- **Performance**: Efficient packet processing ensures minimal impact on network performance.

3. Configuring Policy-Based Routing in Junos OS

Implementing PBR in Junos OS involves the following steps:

a. Define a Firewall Filter

Create a filter to match specific traffic and define actions:

```
set firewall family inet filter PBR-FILTER term 1 from source-address
192.168.1.0/24
set firewall family inet filter PBR-FILTER term 1 then routing-instance
PBR-INSTANCE
set firewall family inet filter PBR-FILTER term 2 then accept
```

- **Term 1** matches traffic from the source subnet 192.168.1.0/24 and redirects it to a specific routing instance.
- **Term 2** accepts all other traffic.

b. Apply the Firewall Filter to an Interface

Attach the filter to the inbound traffic of an interface:

```
set interfaces ge-0/0/0 unit 0 family inet filter input PBR-FILTER
```

c. Configure the Routing Instance

Define the routing instance to handle the redirected traffic:

```
set routing-instances PBR-INSTANCE instance-type forwarding
set routing-instances PBR-INSTANCE interface ge-0/0/0.0
set routing-instances PBR-INSTANCE routing-options static route 0.0.0.0/0 next-hop
10.1.1.1
```

---

4. Verifying PBR Configuration

To ensure that PBR is functioning as expected, use the following commands:

a. Verify Firewall Filter Statistics

Check the number of packets matched by the filter:

```
show firewall filter PBR-FILTER
```

b. Verify Routing Instance Status

Ensure the routing instance is operational:

```
show routing-instances
```

c. Trace the Packet Flow

Trace the path of a specific packet to confirm policy application:

```
show route forwarding-table family inet
```

---

5. Advanced PBR Use Cases

a. Load Balancing

Use PBR to distribute traffic across multiple uplinks by defining policies based on source or application types.

b. Service Chaining

Direct traffic through specific services like firewalls, proxy servers, or deep packet inspection tools.

c. Bypassing Congested Paths

Reroute traffic dynamically to avoid congested or unreliable links.

d. Traffic Monitoring and Auditing

Route sensitive traffic through monitoring systems for logging and compliance purposes.

---

6. Best Practices for Policy-Based Routing

- **Keep Policies Simple**: Avoid overly complex filters to maintain performance and manageability.
- **Monitor Regularly**: Continuously monitor filter statistics and routing instances to ensure policies are applied correctly.
- **Use Specific Matches**: Define precise match conditions to avoid unintended traffic redirection.
- **Test in a Lab Environment**: Always test PBR configurations in a controlled environment before deploying them in production.

---

7. Troubleshooting Policy-Based Routing

a. Issue: No Traffic Matches the Policy

- **Solution**: Verify the firewall filter configuration and ensure the match criteria are correct.
  - Command:

    ```
    show configuration firewall
    ```

b. Issue: Traffic is Dropped

- **Solution**: Check the routing instance configuration and ensure the next-hop address is reachable.
  - Command:

    ```
    ping <next-hop-IP>
    ```

c. Issue: High CPU Usage

- **Solution**: Optimize filter terms and use specific matches to reduce processing overhead.

Conclusion

Policy-Based Routing offers a powerful mechanism to customize traffic flow based on business needs. By leveraging PBR in Junos OS, network administrators can implement advanced traffic engineering, enhance QoS, and improve overall network efficiency. With proper planning, monitoring, and adherence to best practices, PBR can be a cornerstone of intelligent and dynamic network management.

Route Redistribution Techniques

Route redistribution is a critical concept in modern networking that enables the integration of multiple routing domains or protocols within a network. By facilitating the exchange of routing information between different protocols, route redistribution ensures seamless communication across diverse network environments. Junos OS provides a robust framework for implementing and managing route redistribution, allowing administrators to tailor the process to their network's specific requirements.

In this chapter, we explore the fundamentals of route redistribution, its use cases, configuration methods in Junos OS, and best practices.

1. Understanding Route Redistribution

a. What is Route Redistribution?

Route redistribution refers to the process of sharing routing information between different routing protocols. For example:

- Redistributing OSPF routes into BGP
- Redistributing static routes into OSPF

b. Why is Route Redistribution Important?

Networks often use multiple routing protocols due to diverse requirements or integration with external systems. Redistribution enables:

- **Protocol Interoperability**: Ensures connectivity across domains running different routing protocols.
- **Hybrid Networks**: Facilitates the coexistence of static and dynamic routes.
- **Scalability**: Simplifies route sharing in large, multi-protocol environments.

c. Challenges in Redistribution

While powerful, redistribution can introduce:

- **Routing Loops**: When improperly configured, loops may occur.
- **Suboptimal Routing**: Inconsistent metrics across protocols can lead to inefficient paths.
- **Route Filtering Complexity**: Overlapping policies can complicate troubleshooting.

2. Key Components of Route Redistribution in Junos OS

a. Routing Policy Framework

In Junos OS, redistribution is governed by routing policies. Policies define:

- Which routes are redistributed.
- Protocol-specific attributes such as metrics, tags, or next-hops.

b. Protocol-Specific Options

Each routing protocol in Junos OS supports redistribution with unique configurations:

- OSPF allows external route types.
- BGP supports extended attributes like communities and MED.

- Static routes can be tagged and redistributed selectively.

---

3. Configuring Route Redistribution in Junos OS

To configure route redistribution, follow these steps:

a. Define a Routing Policy

Create a policy to control which routes are redistributed:

```
set policy-options policy-statement REDIST-TO-BGP term 1 from protocol ospf
set policy-options policy-statement REDIST-TO-BGP term 1 then accept
set policy-options policy-statement REDIST-TO-BGP term 2 then reject
```

This policy:

- Matches routes learned via OSPF.
- Accepts them for redistribution into BGP.
- Rejects all other routes.

b. Apply the Policy to the Target Protocol

Attach the policy to the protocol where routes are redistributed:

```
set protocols bgp group EXTERNAL export REDIST-TO-BGP
```

c. Adjust Metrics and Tags (Optional)

Set attributes for redistributed routes:

```
set policy-options policy-statement REDIST-TO-BGP term 1 then metric 10
set policy-options policy-statement REDIST-TO-BGP term 1 then community add
COMMUNITY-1
```

d. Verify the Configuration

Check the policy application and route redistribution:

```
show route advertising-protocol bgp
```

---

4. Verifying Route Redistribution

After configuring redistribution, ensure that routes are propagating correctly:

a. Check the Routing Table

View the redistributed routes in the target protocol:

```
show route protocol bgp
```

b. Inspect the Policy Application

Confirm that the policy is being applied as expected:

```
show policy-options policy-statement REDIST-TO-BGP
```

c. Analyze the Protocol's Advertisements

Verify routes advertised to neighboring devices:

```
show bgp neighbor <neighbor-IP> advertised-routes
```

5. Advanced Route Redistribution Use Cases

a. Multi-Protocol Environments

Redistribute routes between OSPF, BGP, and static routes to unify disparate network domains.

b. Conditional Redistribution

Use match conditions to control redistribution:

- Specific route prefixes
- Tags or metrics
- Next-hop addresses

c. Load Balancing

Combine redistribution with equal-cost multi-path (ECMP) to distribute traffic evenly across multiple links.

d. Traffic Engineering

Leverage redistribution to manipulate traffic flows using metrics or BGP communities.

6. Best Practices for Route Redistribution

- **Use Filters and Policies**: Prevent unwanted routes from being redistributed to avoid routing loops and unnecessary table growth.
- **Monitor Metrics Consistently**: Ensure metrics are properly adjusted to maintain optimal routing.
- **Restrict Redistribution Scope**: Only redistribute routes necessary for specific connectivity requirements.
- **Test in a Lab Environment**: Validate redistribution configurations in a controlled environment before deployment.
- **Document Configurations**: Maintain clear documentation of all redistribution policies for easier troubleshooting.

7. Troubleshooting Route Redistribution

a. Missing Routes

- **Solution**: Check policy conditions and ensure the correct routes are matched.
  - Command:

    ```
    show route extensive
    ```

b. Incorrect Next-Hop

- **Solution**: Verify the next-hop address in the routing table and adjust policies if needed.

c. Routing Loops

- **Solution**: Use route tags or AS path filters to prevent loops.
  - ○ Command:

```
show route as-path
```

d. Suboptimal Routing

- **Solution**: Compare route metrics and adjust policies to prioritize desired paths.

Conclusion

Route redistribution is an essential tool for integrating diverse network environments, enabling seamless communication across different routing protocols. By leveraging the robust policy framework in Junos OS, administrators can implement precise and efficient redistribution strategies while minimizing potential risks. With proper planning, validation, and adherence to best practices, route redistribution can significantly enhance network scalability and flexibility.

Section 7:
Network Automation and Scripting

Introduction to Junos Automation

Automation has become an essential aspect of network management, enabling network administrators to enhance efficiency, reduce manual errors, and optimize operational workflows. Junos OS provides a robust set of tools and frameworks designed specifically for automating repetitive and complex tasks. From simplifying routine configurations to implementing advanced event-driven actions, Junos automation is a cornerstone of modern network operations.

This chapter introduces the core concepts of Junos automation, its benefits, and the tools and technologies it offers.

1. The Importance of Automation in Networking

a. Challenges in Manual Network Management

Traditional network management often involves manual configuration and monitoring, which can lead to:

- **Human Errors**: Incorrect or inconsistent configurations.
- **Time-Consuming Processes**: Prolonged downtime during updates or troubleshooting.
- **Scalability Issues**: Difficulty managing growing and complex networks.

b. Advantages of Network Automation

Junos automation addresses these challenges by:

- **Increasing Efficiency**: Streamlining routine tasks like device configuration and software updates.
- **Improving Accuracy**: Minimizing errors with predefined scripts and policies.
- **Enhancing Scalability**: Enabling centralized management of large-scale networks.
- **Facilitating Innovation**: Allowing engineers to focus on strategic projects rather than repetitive tasks.

2. Automation Capabilities in Junos OS

Junos OS offers several automation features that cater to diverse operational needs:

a. Scripting Support

Junos OS supports scripting languages such as:

- **SLAX (Simple Lightweight XML)**: Designed specifically for Junos automation.
- **XSLT (Extensible Stylesheet Language Transformations)**: Used for XML-based transformations.
- **Python**: Widely used for general-purpose and advanced automation.

b. Event-Driven Automation

Junos OS can automate responses to specific network events using:

- **Event Policies**: Define actions triggered by system or network events.
- **Event Scripts**: Scripts that execute automatically in response to predefined conditions.

c. Configuration Management

Automation simplifies the configuration process with:

- **Configuration Templates**: Standardized templates for device setup.
- **Commit Scripts**: Scripts that validate or modify configurations during the commit process.

d. Network Management Protocols

Junos OS integrates with:

- **NETCONF**: A standardized protocol for managing network devices.
- **REST APIs**: APIs for interacting with Junos devices programmatically.

3. Automation Tools in Junos OS

Junos OS provides several tools to facilitate automation:

a. Junos CLI Automation

The Junos CLI itself supports basic automation with:

- **Command Aliases**: Shortcuts for frequently used commands.
- **Batch Scripts**: Scripts that execute multiple CLI commands sequentially.

b. Junos XML API

The XML API allows developers to:

- Extract detailed system information.
- Modify device configurations programmatically.

c. Junos PyEZ

Junos PyEZ is a Python library designed for network automation, enabling:

- Programmatic access to device configurations and operational data.
- Simplified interactions with Junos devices using high-level APIs.

d. Junos Automation Framework

The framework includes tools for creating and deploying custom scripts:

- **SLAX and XSLT Scripting Support**: For detailed control over network operations.
- **Event Policies and Scripts**: For real-time event handling and automation.

4. Common Use Cases for Junos Automation

Junos automation is versatile and can be applied to various scenarios:

a. Configuration Management

- Automatically apply standardized configurations to new devices.
- Validate configurations during deployment to prevent errors.

b. Monitoring and Troubleshooting

- Use event scripts to monitor network health and generate alerts.
- Automatically collect diagnostic data during outages.

c. Policy Enforcement

- Enforce security policies consistently across devices using commit scripts.
- Automate responses to policy violations.

d. Routine Maintenance

- Automate software upgrades and backup processes.
- Schedule routine health checks across the network.

---

5. Getting Started with Junos Automation

a. Assessing Your Automation Needs

Before implementing automation, identify:

- Tasks that are repetitive or error-prone.
- Processes that require real-time responses.
- Areas where automation can save time or resources.

b. Setting Up the Environment

To begin automating with Junos:

1. **Enable Automation Tools**: Ensure the required automation tools and libraries are installed on your devices.
2. **Access Developer Resources**: Refer to Juniper's developer documentation for APIs and scripting guidelines.
3. **Test in a Lab Environment**: Validate automation scripts in a controlled setting before deploying them in production.

c. Writing Your First Script

Start with simple automation scripts. For example:

- A script to display interface statistics:

```
from jnpr.junos import Device

dev = Device(host='192.168.1.1', user='admin', password='password')
dev.open()
print(dev.rpc.get_interface_information())
dev.close()
```

---

6. Best Practices for Junos Automation

- **Use Version Control**: Maintain scripts in a version control system like Git to track changes.

- **Start Small**: Automate simple tasks first before tackling complex processes.
- **Monitor and Log**: Ensure scripts generate logs for auditing and troubleshooting.
- **Document Everything**: Keep clear documentation of your automation workflows and scripts.
- **Test Rigorously**: Always validate scripts in a lab environment before deploying them to production.

Summary

Junos automation empowers network administrators to optimize workflows, reduce errors, and scale operations effectively. With tools like Junos PyEZ, SLAX scripts, and the XML API, Junos OS provides a comprehensive automation framework tailored to modern networking needs. As you explore the capabilities of Junos automation, you'll unlock new levels of efficiency and reliability in your network operations.

Configuring and Using NETCONF

Network Configuration Protocol (NETCONF) is a standardized protocol designed to manage and configure network devices. It is a core element of network automation, providing a robust framework for programmatically interacting with devices running Junos OS. This chapter explores NETCONF in the context of Juniper Networks, covering its configuration, operational principles, and practical use cases.

1. Introduction to NETCONF

NETCONF is defined by the **IETF (Internet Engineering Task Force)** in **RFC 6241**. It uses an XML-based encoding for data exchange and supports secure communication over SSH.

a. Features of NETCONF

- **Transactional Configuration**: Ensures changes are applied as a single atomic operation.
- **Configuration Validation**: Allows pre-validation of configurations before committing them.
- **Session Management**: Maintains stateful sessions between client and server.
- **Structured Data Models**: Works with XML-based structured data.

b. Benefits of NETCONF

- **Consistency**: Ensures uniform configuration across devices.
- **Efficiency**: Reduces manual efforts in repetitive tasks.
- **Automation-Friendly**: Integrates seamlessly with scripting and orchestration tools.
- **Extensibility**: Compatible with newer data modeling standards like YANG.

2. Configuring NETCONF on Junos OS

a. Prerequisites

Ensure the following conditions are met before enabling NETCONF:

- **Device Compatibility**: Confirm the Junos OS version supports NETCONF.
- **SSH Configuration**: NETCONF relies on SSH for secure communication.

b. Enabling NETCONF

To enable NETCONF over SSH, use the following CLI commands:

```
set system services netconf ssh
commit
```

This configuration allows NETCONF clients to interact with the Junos device over SSH.

c. Configuring Access Control

You can restrict NETCONF access by specifying authorized users and IP ranges. For example:

```
set system login user netconf-user class super-user
set system services ssh root-login deny
set system services netconf ssh-ip-filter 192.168.1.0/24
commit
```

3. Establishing a NETCONF Session

a. Using the `junos-eznc` Python Library

The `junos-eznc` (PyEZ) library simplifies NETCONF interactions. Here's how to establish a connection:

1. **Install the Library**:

```
pip install junos-eznc
```

2. **Connect to a Device**:

```
from jnpr.junos import Device

dev = Device(host='192.168.1.1', user='netconf-user', password='password')
dev.open()
print(dev.facts)
dev.close()
```

b. Using Third-Party NETCONF Clients

You can use tools like **Postman**, **Ansible**, or **ncclient** for NETCONF interactions. For example, using `ncclient`:

1. **Install the Library**:

```
pip install ncclient
```

2. **Connect and Fetch Data**:

```
from ncclient import manager

with manager.connect(
    host="192.168.1.1",
    port=830,
    username="netconf-user",
    password="password",
    hostkey_verify=False
) as m:
    print(m.get_config(source="running").data_xml)
```

---

4. Core NETCONF Operations

NETCONF supports several operations, including:

a. `<get-config>`

Retrieves configuration data from the device. Example:

```
<rpc>
  <get-config>
    <source>
      <running/>
    </source>
  </get-config>
</rpc>
```

b. `<edit-config>`

Applies changes to the device configuration. Example:

```
<rpc>
  <edit-config>
    <target>
      <candidate/>
    </target>
    <config>
      <configuration>
        <interfaces>
          <interface>
            <name>ge-0/0/1</name>
            <unit>
              <name>0</name>
              <family>
                <inet>
                  <address>
                    <name>192.168.2.1/24</name>
                  </address>
                </inet>
              </family>
            </unit>
          </interface>
        </interfaces>
      </configuration>
    </config>
  </edit-config>
</rpc>
```

c. `<commit>`

Commits configuration changes to the device.

d. `<lock>` and `<unlock>`

Locks and unlocks the configuration datastore to prevent simultaneous changes.

e. `<rpc-reply>`

Acknowledges the result of a NETCONF request, including errors if applicable.

---

5. NETCONF Use Cases

NETCONF is versatile and can be used in various scenarios:

a. Bulk Configuration Changes

Automate the application of standardized configurations across multiple devices.

b. Real-Time Monitoring

Retrieve operational data such as interface statistics or system logs.

c. Integration with Orchestration Tools

Combine NETCONF with tools like Ansible or Terraform for scalable network management.

d. Troubleshooting

Automate diagnostic workflows by fetching logs and metrics via NETCONF.

---

6. Troubleshooting NETCONF

a. Common Issues

1. **Authentication Errors**: Ensure correct credentials and SSH access.
2. **Session Timeouts**: Adjust session timers if sessions disconnect prematurely.
3. **Configuration Validation Failures**: Debug configurations using the Junos CLI before applying them via NETCONF.

b. Debugging NETCONF

Enable NETCONF logging to diagnose issues:

```
set system syslog file netconf-log any info
commit
```

Logs are stored in `/var/log/netconf-log`.

---

7. Best Practices for Using NETCONF

- **Secure Access**: Use strong passwords, restrict IP access, and enable SSH only for authorized users.
- **Validate Configurations**: Test configurations in a lab before applying them to production devices.
- **Monitor Sessions**: Track active NETCONF sessions to prevent unauthorized access.
- **Leverage Libraries**: Use libraries like PyEZ or ncclient for efficient automation.
- **Document Workflows**: Maintain clear documentation of NETCONF interactions and scripts.

Summary

NETCONF is a powerful protocol for managing and automating Junos-based networks. With its structured approach to configuration, robust security features, and support for modern scripting tools, NETCONF is an indispensable tool for network administrators. By leveraging NETCONF's capabilities, you can streamline network operations, reduce errors, and enhance overall efficiency.

Writing SLAX Scripts

SLAX (Styled Layered Architecture for XML) is a scripting language developed by Juniper Networks, designed specifically for interacting with Junos OS. It extends the XSLT (Extensible Stylesheet Language Transformations) standard and simplifies automation tasks such as configuration management, monitoring, and troubleshooting. This chapter provides an in-depth guide to understanding and writing SLAX scripts, along with practical examples to enhance network automation.

1. Introduction to SLAX

a. What is SLAX?

SLAX is a domain-specific scripting language tailored for Junos OS. It allows network engineers to write scripts for:

- Automating routine configuration tasks.
- Retrieving operational data.
- Modifying XML-based Junos configurations.

b. Why Use SLAX?

- **Native to Junos**: Directly supported by Junos OS.
- **Simplified Syntax**: Easier to use than raw XSLT.
- **Integration**: Works seamlessly with Junos event policies and scripts.
- **Flexibility**: Enables advanced logic and conditions in scripts.

2. Getting Started with SLAX

a. Script Structure

A SLAX script generally consists of the following components:

1. **Header**: Defines the namespace and version.
2. **Input/Output**: Specifies the data sources.
3. **Templates**: Contains logic and operations.

b. SLAX Script Skeleton

```
version 1.0;

ns junos = "http://xml.juniper.net/junos/*/junos";

template example {
    <output>
        "This is a simple SLAX script."
    </output>
}
```

c. Loading and Running SLAX Scripts

1. **Save the Script**: Save the script with a `.slax` extension.
2. **Transfer to the Device**: Use `scp` or `ftp` to upload the script to the Junos device.
3. **Invoke the Script**: Execute the script using the Junos CLI:

```
op script run <script-name>.slax
```

3. Key Features of SLAX

a. Variables

Define and use variables to store data for reuse:

```
var $interface = "ge-0/0/0";
```

b. Control Structures

SLAX supports loops and conditional statements for logical operations.

If-Else Example:

```
if ($status = "up") {
    <output>"Interface is operational."</output>
} else {
    <output>"Interface is down."</output>
}
```

For Loop Example:

```
for $i in (1 to 5) {
    <output>"Loop iteration: {$i}"</output>
}
```

c. Templates

Templates are reusable blocks of logic:

```
template display-interface($interface) {
    <output>"Details for interface: {$interface}"</output>
}
```

4. Writing Operational SLAX Scripts

a. Fetching Interface Details

This script retrieves the status of a specific interface:

```
version 1.0;

ns junos = "http://xml.juniper.net/junos/*/junos";

template interface-status {
    var $interface = "ge-0/0/0";

    op command "show interfaces {$interface} terse" {
        <output>"Interface: {$interface} Status: {$status}"</output>
    }
}
```

b. Automating Configuration Tasks

SLAX can modify configurations programmatically. For example:

```
version 1.0;

ns junos = "http://xml.juniper.net/junos/*/junos";

template configure-interface {
    var $interface = "ge-0/0/0";
    var $address = "192.168.1.1/24";

    config {
        <interfaces>
            <interface>
                <name>{$interface}</name>
                <unit>
                    <name>0</name>
                    <family>
                        <inet>
                            <address>
                                <name>{$address}</name>
                            </address>
                        </inet>
                    </family>
                </unit>
            </interface>
        </interfaces>
    }
}
```

5. Deploying SLAX Scripts in Junos OS

a. Event Policies

SLAX scripts can be triggered by system events. For example:

1. **Define an Event Policy**:

   ```
   set event-options policy interface-down events interface-down
   set event-options policy interface-down then execute-script
   interface-check.slax
   ```

2. **Link the Script**: Use execute-script to trigger the SLAX script.

b. Operational Mode

Run SLAX scripts interactively:

```
op script run check-ospf-status.slax
```

6. Practical Examples

a. Monitoring OSPF Neighbors

```
version 1.0;
```

```
ns junos = "http://xml.juniper.net/junos/*/junos";

template ospf-neighbors {
    op command "show ospf neighbor" {
        for $neighbor in $output/ospf-neighbor {
            <output>"Neighbor: {$neighbor/interface}"</output>
        }
    }
}
```

b. Bandwidth Usage Report

```
version 1.0;

ns junos = "http://xml.juniper.net/junos/*/junos";

template bandwidth-report {
    op command "show interfaces extensive" {
        for $intf in $output/interface {
            <output>"Interface: {$intf/name}, In: {$intf/statistics/input-bytes},
Out: {$intf/statistics/output-bytes}"</output>
        }
    }
}
```

7. Debugging SLAX Scripts

- **Syntax Errors**: Validate the script using tools like XMLLint.
- **Runtime Logs**: Enable script logging for runtime errors:

  ```
  set system syslog file slax-log any info
  commit
  ```

- **Test in Lab**: Always test scripts in a controlled environment before deploying to production.

8. Best Practices

- **Modular Design**: Break scripts into smaller, reusable templates.
- **Error Handling**: Include checks and fallbacks for potential issues.
- **Documentation**: Comment scripts to explain logic and usage.
- **Version Control**: Maintain scripts in a version control system like Git.

Summary

SLAX scripts are a powerful tool for automating and managing Junos networks. By mastering SLAX, network engineers can streamline repetitive tasks, enhance monitoring capabilities, and reduce operational overhead. This chapter has introduced the basics of SLAX scripting, demonstrated practical examples, and provided best practices to ensure effective use of SLAX in real-world scenarios.

Automating with Python and PyEZ

In modern network environments, automation has become a cornerstone for efficient operations, rapid deployment, and streamlined management. Python, with its simplicity and power, has become a go-to programming language for network automation. When combined with PyEZ—a Python library specifically designed for Junos OS—automation becomes even more accessible and effective for Juniper Networks devices.

This chapter explores the essentials of using Python and PyEZ for automating Junos OS. It covers installation, basic operations, configuration management, and advanced use cases to empower you to automate your network like an expert.

1. What is PyEZ?

PyEZ is a Python library developed by Juniper Networks, designed to simplify interaction with Junos OS. It provides an abstraction layer that eliminates the need for complex device communication protocols, allowing engineers to focus on automation logic.

Key Features of PyEZ

- **Device Connectivity**: Easy connection to Junos devices using NETCONF over SSH.
- **Configuration Management**: View, load, and commit configurations programmatically.
- **Operational Data Retrieval**: Execute operational commands and retrieve system data.
- **Customization**: Extendable with custom Python scripts for advanced use cases.

2. Setting Up Python and PyEZ

a. Prerequisites

1. A workstation with Python installed (preferably version 3.6 or higher).
2. Network connectivity to Junos devices with NETCONF enabled.

b. Installing PyEZ

Install PyEZ using pip, the Python package manager:

```
pip install junos-eznc
```

c. Enabling NETCONF on Junos Devices

To use PyEZ, NETCONF must be enabled on the Junos device:

```
set system services netconf ssh
commit
```

3. Connecting to a Junos Device with PyEZ

Establishing a connection to a Junos device is the first step in automating with PyEZ.

a. Basic Connection Example

```
from jnpr.junos import Device
```

```
# Connect to the Junos device
dev = Device(host='192.168.1.1', user='admin', passwd='password')
dev.open()

print(f"Connected to: {dev.facts['hostname']}")
dev.close()
```

b. Using a Context Manager for Automatic Resource Management

```
from jnpr.junos import Device

with Device(host='192.168.1.1', user='admin', passwd='password') as dev:
    print(f"Device Model: {dev.facts['model']}")
```

4. Retrieving Operational Data

a. Running Show Commands

You can execute operational commands and retrieve structured data:

```
from jnpr.junos import Device
from jnpr.junos.op.ethport import EthPortTable

with Device(host='192.168.1.1', user='admin', passwd='password') as dev:
    eth_ports = EthPortTable(dev)
    eth_ports.get()
    for port in eth_ports:
        print(f"Interface: {port.name}, Status: {port.admin}")
```

b. XML Command Output

For raw XML output:

```
from jnpr.junos.utils.command import Command

with Device(host='192.168.1.1', user='admin', passwd='password') as dev:
    cmd = Command(dev)
    output = cmd.execute('show version', format='xml')
    print(output)
```

5. Managing Configurations

a. Retrieving Configuration

You can retrieve the current configuration:

```
from jnpr.junos.utils.config import Config

with Device(host='192.168.1.1', user='admin', passwd='password') as dev:
    cfg = Config(dev)
    cfg.lock()
    print(cfg.retrieve())
    cfg.unlock()
```

b. Loading and Committing Configuration

PyEZ simplifies configuration changes:

```
from jnpr.junos.utils.config import Config

with Device(host='192.168.1.1', user='admin', passwd='password') as dev:
    cfg = Config(dev)
    cfg.lock()
    cfg.load(path='config.set', format='set')
    cfg.commit()
    cfg.unlock()
```

c. Rolling Back Configuration

```
with Device(host='192.168.1.1', user='admin', passwd='password') as dev:
    cfg = Config(dev)
    cfg.lock()
    cfg.rollback(1)
    cfg.commit()
    cfg.unlock()
```

6. Automating Tasks with PyEZ

a. Interface Configuration

Below is a script to configure multiple interfaces:

```
from jnpr.junos import Device
from jnpr.junos.utils.config import Config

config = """
set interfaces ge-0/0/1 unit 0 family inet address 192.168.1.1/24
set interfaces ge-0/0/2 unit 0 family inet address 192.168.2.1/24
"""

with Device(host='192.168.1.1', user='admin', passwd='password') as dev:
    cfg = Config(dev)
    cfg.lock()
    cfg.load(config, format='set')
    cfg.commit()
    cfg.unlock()
```

b. Automating VLAN Creation

```
from jnpr.junos import Device
from jnpr.junos.utils.config import Config

vlan_config = """
set vlans VLAN10 vlan-id 10
set vlans VLAN20 vlan-id 20
"""

with Device(host='192.168.1.1', user='admin', passwd='password') as dev:
    cfg = Config(dev)
    cfg.lock()
    cfg.load(vlan_config, format='set')
    cfg.commit()
    cfg.unlock()
```

7. Error Handling and Debugging

PyEZ provides robust error handling mechanisms for automation scripts.

a. Try-Except Blocks

```python
from jnpr.junos import Device
from jnpr.junos.exception import ConnectError

try:
    with Device(host='192.168.1.1', user='admin', passwd='password') as dev:
        print(f"Connected to: {dev.facts['hostname']}")
except ConnectError as err:
    print(f"Failed to connect: {err}")
```

b. Logging

Enable logging for debugging:

```python
import logging
from jnpr.junos import Device

logging.basicConfig(level=logging.DEBUG)
with Device(host='192.168.1.1', user='admin', passwd='password') as dev:
    print(dev.facts)
```

8. Best Practices for Python and PyEZ Automation

- **Script Modularity**: Break tasks into reusable functions.
- **Error Handling**: Always handle exceptions to avoid script crashes.
- **Logging**: Use logs to monitor script behavior and identify issues.
- **Configuration Backups**: Take a backup before making changes.
- **Testing**: Test scripts in a lab environment before deploying to production.

Summary

Python and PyEZ empower network engineers to automate Junos OS devices efficiently. With their combination, tasks such as configuration management, operational data retrieval, and troubleshooting can be performed programmatically, saving time and reducing errors. This chapter has provided a foundational guide to automating with Python and PyEZ, including practical examples to get started immediately.

Understanding Event Scripts in Junos OS

Event scripts in Junos OS provide a powerful way to automate actions based on system events or conditions. By leveraging these scripts, network administrators can implement proactive responses to network changes, streamline repetitive tasks, and enhance the operational efficiency of their Juniper devices.

This chapter explores the fundamentals of event scripts in Junos OS, their use cases, configuration methods, and practical examples to demonstrate their application.

1. What Are Event Scripts?

Event scripts are scripts written in Extensible Stylesheet Language Transformations (XSLT) or SLAX that are executed automatically in response to system-generated events. These events can include configuration changes, interface status updates, or log messages.

Key Features of Event Scripts

- **Proactive Automation**: Automate responses to predefined network events.
- **Customizable Actions**: Tailor scripts to meet specific operational requirements.
- **Integration with System Logs**: Trigger scripts based on syslog messages.
- **Real-Time Execution**: Execute scripts immediately when an event occurs.

2. Use Cases for Event Scripts

Event scripts can address various network automation needs, such as:

1. **Interface Monitoring**: Detect when an interface goes down and automatically execute recovery steps.
2. **Dynamic Configuration**: Apply specific configurations based on system conditions.
3. **Log Analysis**: Monitor log files for specific messages and take action, such as sending alerts.
4. **Resource Optimization**: Automate resource adjustments based on usage thresholds.

3. How Event Scripts Work

Event scripts rely on two primary components:

1. **Event Policies**: Define the conditions under which the script is triggered.
2. **Event Scripts**: Contain the logic and actions to be executed.

Execution Flow

1. A system event, such as a log message or interface state change, occurs.
2. Junos OS evaluates the event against configured event policies.
3. If the conditions match, the corresponding event script is executed.

4. Creating and Deploying Event Scripts

a. Writing an Event Script

Event scripts can be written in either SLAX (Structured Language for XML) or XSLT. Below is an example in SLAX:

```
version 1.0;

ns junos = "http://xml.juniper.net/junos/*";

template trigger_event {
    var $event = $junos:trigger-event;
    match $event {
        if ($event/type = "interface-down") {
            op:execute("clear interface statistics ge-0/0/0");
        }
    }
}
```

b. Uploading the Script

Save the script to the /var/db/scripts/event/ directory on the Junos device:

```
scp interface-monitor.slax root@192.168.1.1:/var/db/scripts/event/
```

c. Configuring Event Policies

Define an event policy in the Junos configuration to associate the script with specific events:

```
set event-options policy interface-monitor events "INTERFACE_DOWN"
set event-options policy interface-monitor then execute-script
"interface-monitor.slax"
commit
```

5. Testing Event Scripts

a. Simulating Events

Manually trigger an event to test the script:

```
simulate-event INTERFACE_DOWN interface ge-0/0/0
```

b. Verifying Execution

Check the log file to confirm script execution:

```
show log messages | match interface-monitor
```

6. Advanced Event Script Features

a. Passing Parameters

Parameters can be passed to scripts to customize behavior dynamically:

```
template trigger_event {
    var $parameter = $junos:parameter["custom-parameter"];
    match $parameter {
        if ($parameter = "alert") {
            op:execute("send log message 'Custom Alert Triggered'");
```

```
        }
    }
}
```

b. Conditional Execution

Implement conditional logic for more complex automation:

```
if ($event/type = "high-cpu-usage" and $event/threshold > 80) {
    op:execute("restart process rpd");
}
```

7. Debugging and Troubleshooting

a. Common Errors

1. **Script Syntax Issues**: Validate the script syntax using tools like xmllint for XSLT or SLAX validators.
2. **Execution Failures**: Check for permissions or missing event policy configurations.

b. Logs for Troubleshooting

Enable detailed logs for event scripts:

```
set system scripts traceoptions file script-trace
set system scripts traceoptions level all
commit
```

Review the logs:

```
show log script-trace
```

8. Best Practices for Event Scripts

1. **Start Simple**: Begin with straightforward use cases before implementing complex logic.
2. **Test in a Lab**: Always test scripts in a non-production environment.
3. **Use Descriptive Names**: Name scripts and policies clearly for easier management.
4. **Monitor Performance**: Ensure that scripts do not negatively impact device performance.
5. **Document Scripts**: Maintain documentation for each script, including triggers and expected behavior.

9. Practical Example: Interface Flap Monitoring

Script: Interface Flap Logger

This script logs a message whenever an interface flaps:

```
version 1.0;

template trigger_event {
    var $event = $junos:trigger-event;
    match $event {
        if ($event/type = "interface-flap") {
```

```
            op:execute("send log message 'Interface $event/name flapped at
$event/time'");
        }
    }
}
```

Policy Configuration

```
set event-options policy interface-flap events "INTERFACE_FLAP"
set event-options policy interface-flap then execute-script
"interface-flap-logger.slax"
commit
```

Summary

Event scripts in Junos OS provide a robust framework for automating responses to system events. By understanding how to create, deploy, and test these scripts, you can significantly enhance the efficiency and reliability of your network. Whether it's monitoring interface states, managing resources, or analyzing logs, event scripts empower you to automate operations in real-time.

Section 8:
High Availability and Scalability

Virtual Router Redundancy Protocol (VRRP)

Virtual Router Redundancy Protocol (VRRP) is a robust protocol designed to enhance network availability by enabling seamless failover of routing responsibilities between routers. This chapter delves into the fundamentals of VRRP, its configuration in Junos OS, and practical applications to ensure uninterrupted network connectivity.

1. Introduction to VRRP

What is VRRP?

VRRP is a network protocol that provides automatic assignment of available routers to participate in a virtual router group. It ensures that a backup router can take over when the primary router fails, maintaining network stability and reducing downtime.

How VRRP Works

- **Virtual Router**: VRRP defines a virtual router with a shared IP address.
- **Master and Backup Routers**: One router acts as the master, handling traffic, while others remain in a backup state.
- **Priority-Based Election**: Routers are assigned priorities, with the highest-priority router becoming the master.
- **Heartbeat Messages**: The master sends periodic advertisements to the backups to indicate it is operational.

Key Benefits

1. **High Availability**: Ensures seamless failover to backup routers.
2. **Reduced Downtime**: Minimizes network disruption during router failures.
3. **Load Balancing**: Can distribute traffic across multiple routers using different VRRP groups.

2. VRRP Operation in Junos OS

In Junos OS, VRRP integrates smoothly with routing and interface configurations. Key elements include:

1. **VRRP Group**: A group of routers configured with a shared virtual IP address.
2. **Master Router**: The active router that forwards traffic for the virtual IP.
3. **Backup Router**: A standby router that takes over if the master fails.
4. **Priority Levels**: Determine the master router; higher values indicate higher priority.

3. Configuring VRRP in Junos OS

Follow these steps to configure VRRP on a Junos OS device:

Step 1: Define VRRP on an Interface

Assign a VRRP group and virtual IP address to an interface:

```
set interfaces ge-0/0/0 unit 0 family inet address 192.168.1.1/24 vrrp-group 1
virtual-address 192.168.1.254
```

Step 2: Set the Router Priority

Configure the priority for the router. The default is 100; increase it for the preferred master:

```
set interfaces ge-0/0/0 unit 0 family inet address 192.168.1.1/24 vrrp-group 1
priority 120
```

Step 3: Enable Preemption

Preemption allows a higher-priority router to take over the master role when it becomes available:

```
set interfaces ge-0/0/0 unit 0 family inet address 192.168.1.1/24 vrrp-group 1
preempt
```

Step 4: Configure Advertisement Interval

Set the interval for heartbeat advertisements:

```
set interfaces ge-0/0/0 unit 0 family inet address 192.168.1.1/24 vrrp-group 1
advertisement-interval 1
```

Step 5: Apply and Commit Configuration

Verify and commit the configuration:

```
commit
```

---

4. Monitoring VRRP

Monitor VRRP operation to ensure it is functioning correctly:

View VRRP Status

Check the status of VRRP groups:

```
show vrrp
```

Sample Output

```
Interface        Group  State   Master Address   Priority
ge-0/0/0.0       1      Master  192.168.1.1      120
ge-0/0/1.0       1      Backup  192.168.1.2      100
```

Monitor Advertisements

Verify the VRRP advertisements being sent and received:

```
show log messages | match VRRP
```

---

5. Advanced VRRP Configurations

a. Tracking Interface State

VRRP can track the state of other interfaces to adjust the master router's priority dynamically. If a critical interface goes down, the router lowers its priority:

```
set interfaces ge-0/0/0 unit 0 family inet address 192.168.1.1/24 vrrp-group 1
track ge-0/0/1 priority-cost 20
```

b. Using Multiple VRRP Groups

For load balancing or high availability across subnets, configure multiple VRRP groups on the same interface:

```
set interfaces ge-0/0/0 unit 0 family inet address 192.168.1.1/24 vrrp-group 1
virtual-address 192.168.1.254
set interfaces ge-0/0/0 unit 0 family inet address 192.168.1.1/24 vrrp-group 2
virtual-address 192.168.1.253
```

---

6. Troubleshooting VRRP

a. Common Issues

1. **Priority Conflicts**: Ensure only one router has the highest priority.
2. **Heartbeat Failure**: Check advertisement intervals and ensure network connectivity.
3. **Misconfigured IP**: Verify that virtual IPs do not conflict with physical IPs.

b. Debugging Commands

1. **VRRP Logs**: Check the logs for VRRP-related messages:

   ```
   show log messages | match VRRP
   ```

2. **Interface Details**: Confirm the interface configuration:

   ```
   show configuration interfaces ge-0/0/0
   ```

---

7. Real-World Example: Implementing VRRP for Redundancy

Scenario

An enterprise network requires high availability for its gateway at 192.168.1.254. Two routers are configured in a VRRP group to ensure redundancy.

Configuration for Router 1 (Master)

```
set interfaces ge-0/0/0 unit 0 family inet address 192.168.1.1/24 vrrp-group 1
virtual-address 192.168.1.254
set interfaces ge-0/0/0 unit 0 family inet address 192.168.1.1/24 vrrp-group 1
priority 120
set interfaces ge-0/0/0 unit 0 family inet address 192.168.1.1/24 vrrp-group 1
preempt
```

Configuration for Router 2 (Backup)

```
set interfaces ge-0/0/0 unit 0 family inet address 192.168.1.2/24 vrrp-group 1
virtual-address 192.168.1.254
set interfaces ge-0/0/0 unit 0 family inet address 192.168.1.2/24 vrrp-group 1
priority 100
set interfaces ge-0/0/0 unit 0 family inet address 192.168.1.2/24 vrrp-group 1
preempt
```

Summary

VRRP is an essential protocol for building resilient network infrastructures. By automatically assigning gateway responsibilities and enabling seamless failover, VRRP minimizes downtime and ensures continuous network operation. With its integration into Junos OS, VRRP configuration and management are straightforward, allowing administrators to implement redundancy with ease.

Configuring Graceful Restart and Nonstop Routing

In modern networks, maintaining continuous packet forwarding during control plane disruptions is essential for ensuring high availability and reliability. Junos OS provides advanced mechanisms such as **Graceful Restart** and **Nonstop Routing (NSR)** to achieve this. These features help preserve forwarding states and prevent traffic loss, even during control plane restarts or protocol reconvergence events.

This chapter covers the fundamentals, configuration, and practical applications of these critical high-availability features in Junos OS.

1. Understanding Graceful Restart and Nonstop Routing

What is Graceful Restart?

Graceful Restart is a protocol feature that enables a router to retain its forwarding state while temporarily restarting its control plane. During this process:

- The forwarding plane continues to route traffic.
- Neighboring routers maintain their adjacency with the restarting router, avoiding route flaps.

Supported by protocols like OSPF, BGP, and IS-IS, Graceful Restart ensures minimal impact on network stability during planned or unplanned control plane restarts.

What is Nonstop Routing (NSR)?

NSR is a Junos OS-specific feature designed to maintain routing protocol sessions without relying on neighboring routers to support Graceful Restart. In NSR:

- The router synchronizes routing information between redundant control plane processes.
- Protocol sessions, such as BGP and OSPF, are seamlessly preserved during control plane failures.

Key Differences Between Graceful Restart and NSR

Feature	Graceful Restart	Nonstop Routing
Dependency	Requires support from peers.	Does not require peer support.
Focus	Protocol reconvergence.	Session preservation.
Implementation	Industry-standard protocols.	Junos OS-specific mechanism.

2. Benefits of Graceful Restart and NSR

1. **High Availability**: Ensures continuous packet forwarding during control plane disruptions.
2. **Reduced Downtime**: Minimizes network service interruptions during maintenance or failover.
3. **Protocol Flexibility**: Supports multiple routing protocols such as OSPF, BGP, and IS-IS.
4. **Enhanced Scalability**: Prevents routing protocol session drops, reducing network churn.

3. Configuring Graceful Restart in Junos OS

Graceful Restart is supported by various routing protocols. Below is an example configuration for enabling Graceful Restart in OSPF and BGP.

Step 1: Enable Graceful Restart for OSPF

```
set protocols ospf graceful-restart
```

Step 2: Enable Graceful Restart for BGP

```
set protocols bgp graceful-restart
set protocols bgp graceful-restart restart-time 120
set protocols bgp graceful-restart stalepath-time 300
```

Explanation of Configuration

- `graceful-restart`: Enables the feature for the specified protocol.
- `restart-time`: Specifies the time (in seconds) the router waits for a peer to reestablish after restarting.
- `stalepath-time`: Determines how long stale routes are retained before being removed.

Step 3: Verify Graceful Restart Configuration

After configuring, verify the status using:

```
show ospf neighbor
show bgp summary
```

---

4. Configuring Nonstop Routing (NSR) in Junos OS

Nonstop Routing relies on redundant control plane processes within the same router. Here's how to enable NSR for a seamless routing experience.

Step 1: Enable NSR Globally

```
set routing-options nonstop-routing
```

Step 2: Verify NSR Capability for Protocols

Ensure that the desired protocols support NSR. For instance:

- OSPF:

  ```
  show ospf overview
  ```

- BGP:

  ```
  show bgp summary
  ```

Step 3: Monitor NSR Status

Check the NSR synchronization and state:

```
show task replication
```

---

5. Monitoring and Troubleshooting Graceful Restart and NSR

a. Monitoring Graceful Restart

- View the status of Graceful Restart operations:

```
show ospf neighbor | match graceful
show bgp summary | match GR
```

- Check protocol-specific logs for restart events:

```
show log messages | match "graceful"
```

b. Monitoring NSR

- Verify NSR synchronization status:

```
show task replication
```

- Check for protocol-specific NSR readiness:

```
show ospf overview | match NSR
```

c. Common Issues and Solutions

Issue	Solution
Protocol neighbors not retaining state	Verify that Graceful Restart is enabled on peers.
Stale routes remain too long	Adjust stalepath-time for timely route cleanup.
NSR replication errors	Check task synchronization logs.

6. Real-World Application: High Availability in Data Centers

Scenario

A data center requires high availability for routing services during software upgrades. By enabling Graceful Restart and NSR, the network ensures uninterrupted traffic flow.

Solution Configuration

1. Enable Graceful Restart for OSPF and BGP:

```
set protocols ospf graceful-restart
set protocols bgp graceful-restart
set protocols bgp graceful-restart restart-time 120
set protocols bgp graceful-restart stalepath-time 300
```

2. Enable NSR for seamless control plane failover:

```
set routing-options nonstop-routing
```

3. Monitor operational status during the upgrade:

```
show ospf neighbor
show bgp summary
show task replication
```

Summary

Graceful Restart and Nonstop Routing are indispensable tools for achieving high availability in Junos OS. By preserving forwarding states and protocol sessions, these features prevent traffic loss and ensure network reliability during planned or unplanned control plane interruptions.

Understanding Link Aggregation Groups (LAGs)

As network demand continues to grow, ensuring high availability, scalability, and efficient bandwidth utilization has become critical. **Link Aggregation Groups (LAGs)** address these challenges by allowing multiple physical links to act as a single logical link. This approach enhances bandwidth, provides redundancy, and simplifies network configurations.

This chapter explores the fundamentals of LAGs, their advantages, and how to configure and troubleshoot them in Junos OS.

---

1. What is a Link Aggregation Group (LAG)?

A **Link Aggregation Group (LAG)** is a method of combining multiple physical Ethernet links into a single logical link. LAG is commonly implemented using the **Link Aggregation Control Protocol (LACP)**, defined in IEEE 802.3ad/802.1AX standards. LAGs provide the following benefits:

- **Increased Bandwidth**: Aggregate the bandwidth of multiple links.
- **Redundancy and Fault Tolerance**: If one link fails, traffic is redistributed across the remaining links.
- **Load Balancing**: Traffic is evenly distributed across member links based on hash algorithms.
- **Simplified Management**: Treat multiple links as a single logical interface.

---

2. Key Components of LAG in Junos OS

a. Physical Interfaces

These are the individual Ethernet links that are aggregated to form a LAG.

b. Aggregated Ethernet Interface (ae Interface)

The logical interface that represents the LAG in Junos OS. It is identified as aeX, where X is a number (e.g., ae0, ae1).

c. Link Aggregation Control Protocol (LACP)

An optional protocol used to dynamically manage LAGs. LACP ensures that only active links participate in the LAG and facilitates link negotiation.

---

3. Benefits of LAG in High Availability and Scalability

1. **Enhanced Bandwidth Utilization**: Combine the capacity of multiple physical links to create higher throughput.
2. **Resilience**: Automatically reroutes traffic in case of a link failure without interrupting communication.
3. **Improved Load Balancing**: Balances traffic using parameters such as source/destination MAC addresses, IP addresses, or TCP/UDP ports.
4. **Simplified Configuration**: Reduces the complexity of managing multiple links.

---

4. Configuring LAG in Junos OS

Step 1: Define the Aggregated Ethernet Interface

1. Assign a logical ae interface and set its properties.
2. Add physical interfaces to the LAG.

Step 2: Enable LACP (Optional)

Enable LACP for dynamic negotiation of member links.

Configuration Example

Here's an example of configuring a LAG with LACP enabled:

```
# Create the aggregated Ethernet interface
set interfaces ae0 aggregated-ether-options lacp active
set interfaces ae0 aggregated-ether-options minimum-links 2

# Add member physical interfaces to the LAG
set interfaces ge-0/0/0 gigether-options 802.3ad ae0
set interfaces ge-0/0/1 gigether-options 802.3ad ae0
set interfaces ge-0/0/2 gigether-options 802.3ad ae0

# Assign an IP address to the LAG (Layer 3 example)
set interfaces ae0 unit 0 family inet address 192.168.1.1/24
```

Explanation of Commands

- `lacp active`: Configures the LACP mode as active, enabling the device to send LACP packets.
- `minimum-links`: Specifies the minimum number of active links required for the LAG to remain operational.
- `802.3ad`: Indicates the interface is part of a LAG.

---

5. Verifying and Monitoring LAGs

Use the following commands to ensure the LAG is correctly configured and operational:

Verify LACP Status

```
show lacp interfaces
```

- Displays the LACP state, including the active and standby links.

Check Aggregated Interface Status

```
show interfaces ae0
```

- Provides detailed information about the ae0 interface, including its member links and traffic statistics.

Verify Member Link Status

```
show interfaces ge-0/0/0 detail
show interfaces ge-0/0/1 detail
```

- Confirms the operational status of individual member interfaces.

---

6. Troubleshooting LAG Issues

a. Common Issues

1. **Member Link Not Joining LAG**: Verify LACP configuration and physical connectivity.
2. **Uneven Traffic Distribution**: Check the load-balancing hash algorithm.
3. **LAG Not Operational**: Ensure the minimum required links are active.

b. Troubleshooting Commands

- **Check LACP Configuration**:

```
show configuration interfaces ae0
```

- **Verify LAG Statistics**:

```
show lacp statistics
```

- **Inspect Log Files**:

```
show log messages | match ae0
```

---

7. Best Practices for LAG Deployment

1. **Use Equal Speed Links**: Ensure all member links operate at the same speed (e.g., 1Gbps or 10Gbps).
2. **Enable LACP**: Dynamic negotiation using LACP enhances fault tolerance and simplifies management.
3. **Avoid Loops**: Verify proper VLAN configurations to prevent bridging loops.
4. **Monitor Continuously**: Use monitoring tools to detect and resolve potential link issues promptly.

---

8. Real-World Application: Data Center Redundancy

Scenario

A data center requires high availability and increased throughput for critical server-to-switch communication. LAG is implemented to aggregate four 10Gbps links between the core switch and an access layer switch.

Configuration

1. Define the LAG:

```
set interfaces ae1 aggregated-ether-options lacp active
set interfaces ae1 aggregated-ether-options minimum-links 3
set interfaces ge-1/0/0 gigether-options 802.3ad ae1
set interfaces ge-1/0/1 gigether-options 802.3ad ae1
set interfaces ge-1/0/2 gigether-options 802.3ad ae1
set interfaces ge-1/0/3 gigether-options 802.3ad ae1
```

2. Assign VLANs or IP addresses to ae1 for Layer 2 or Layer 3 connectivity.
3. Verify the operational state:

```
show lacp interfaces ae1
```

Summary

Link Aggregation Groups (LAGs) are a cornerstone of high availability and scalability in modern networks. By aggregating multiple links, LAGs provide increased bandwidth, redundancy, and simplified management. Configuring and maintaining LAGs in Junos OS ensures robust network performance and fault tolerance.

Redundant Routing Engines

High availability is a cornerstone of modern networks, ensuring uninterrupted service even during hardware failures or system upgrades. Juniper Networks achieves this through **Redundant Routing Engines (REs)**, which provide fault tolerance and operational continuity in critical network environments.

This chapter explores the architecture, configuration, and best practices for using redundant routing engines in Junos OS.

---

1. Introduction to Redundant Routing Engines

A **Redundant Routing Engine (RE)** is a high availability feature in Juniper devices, primarily used in MX, EX, and SRX Series devices. These platforms can be equipped with two routing engines:

- **Master RE**: Actively handles control plane tasks, such as routing protocol operations, forwarding table management, and user interface interactions.
- **Backup RE**: Monitors the master RE and takes over seamlessly in case of failure.

Redundant REs ensure that control plane functions remain operational, while data plane forwarding is unaffected during failover.

---

2. Benefits of Redundant Routing Engines

1. **High Availability**: Minimize downtime by quickly switching to the backup RE during hardware or software failures.
2. **Seamless Upgrades**: Perform **In-Service Software Upgrades (ISSU)** with minimal impact on operations.
3. **Enhanced Scalability**: Support larger routing tables and higher processing capabilities.
4. **Operational Redundancy**: Preserve critical configurations and system state across both REs.

---

3. How Redundant REs Work

a. State Synchronization

The master RE continuously synchronizes the following with the backup RE:

- **Routing Tables**: Ensure all routing protocol states are mirrored.
- **Forwarding Information Base (FIB)**: Maintain forwarding entries for data plane continuity.
- **System Configuration**: Propagate configuration changes to the backup RE.

b. Failover Process

Failover occurs in two scenarios:

1. **Planned Failover**: Triggered during maintenance tasks, such as upgrades or testing.
2. **Unplanned Failover**: Triggered automatically upon master RE failure. The backup RE transitions to the master role and resumes control plane operations.

---

4. Configuring Redundant Routing Engines in Junos OS

Redundant REs require proper configuration to ensure smooth operation. Below is a step-by-step guide:

Step 1: Verify Device Compatibility

Ensure your device supports dual routing engines. Platforms like the MX Series typically include this functionality.

Step 2: Configure Routing Engine Redundancy

```
# Enable redundancy and specify priorities
set chassis redundancy graceful-switchover
set routing-options redundancy-group 1 member 0 priority 100
set routing-options redundancy-group 1 member 1 priority 50
```

- **Graceful Switchover**: Ensures state synchronization and minimal disruption during failover.
- **Priority**: Assigns roles to REs (higher priority becomes master).

Step 3: Monitor Synchronization

Ensure routing tables and FIBs are synchronized:

```
show system synchronization
```

Step 4: Test Failover

Test redundancy by simulating a failover:

```
request chassis routing-engine master switch
```

Verify the backup RE takes over as master.

---

5. Verifying and Monitoring Redundant REs

Use the following commands to monitor RE status and ensure redundancy is functional:

Check Routing Engine Status

```
show chassis routing-engine
```

This command provides details about the master and backup REs, including CPU usage, memory utilization, and uptime.

Verify Failover Readiness

```
show system switchover
```

Indicates whether the system is ready for a switchover and lists any potential issues.

Monitor Synchronization

```
show system synchronization status
```

Confirms the state synchronization between the master and backup REs.

---

6. Best Practices for Redundant RE Deployment

1. **Enable Graceful Switchover**: Always configure `graceful-switchover` to ensure minimal service impact during failover.
2. **Use Matching RE Hardware and Software**: Ensure both REs have identical hardware specifications and run the same Junos OS version.
3. **Monitor RE Health Regularly**: Continuously monitor CPU, memory, and synchronization status.
4. **Test Failover Scenarios**: Periodically perform planned failovers to validate redundancy and ensure operators are familiar with the process.
5. **Perform Upgrades During Maintenance Windows**: Use ISSU where possible to minimize impact.

---

7. Troubleshooting Redundant REs

a. Common Issues

1. **Synchronization Errors**: Occur when routing tables or configurations fail to synchronize.
2. **Unresponsive Backup RE**: The backup RE may fail to respond or take over during failover.
3. **Failover Delays**: Long failover times can disrupt critical services.

b. Troubleshooting Commands

- **Check Failover Logs**:

```
show log messages | match switchover
```

- **Verify Synchronization**:

```
show system synchronization
```

- **Inspect Routing Protocol States**:

```
show bgp summary
show ospf neighbor
```

c. Resolution Steps

1. Restart the backup RE if synchronization issues persist:

```
request system reboot other-routing-engine
```

2. Reconfigure synchronization parameters to resolve discrepancies.

---

8. Real-World Example: Enterprise Core Redundancy

Scenario

An enterprise core network uses an MX Series router with dual REs to maintain uninterrupted BGP and OSPF routing during upgrades and unexpected failures.

Configuration

1. Enable graceful switchover:

```
set chassis redundancy graceful-switchover
```

2. Configure redundancy priorities:

```
set routing-options redundancy-group 1 member 0 priority 120
set routing-options redundancy-group 1 member 1 priority 80
```

3. Test failover:

```
request chassis routing-engine master switch
```

Summary

Redundant Routing Engines are a vital feature for high availability in Juniper devices. By enabling smooth failover and ensuring control plane continuity, redundant REs minimize downtime and protect critical network operations. Proper configuration, monitoring, and testing are essential for deploying redundant REs effectively.

Load Balancing in Junos OS

In modern networks, load balancing plays a crucial role in enhancing performance, ensuring availability, and optimizing resource utilization. Junos OS provides robust load-balancing capabilities that allow traffic distribution across multiple links, devices, or servers. This chapter explores the fundamentals of load balancing, its benefits, and the configuration process in Junos OS.

1. Understanding Load Balancing

Load balancing is a technique used to distribute network traffic or processing load evenly across multiple resources. In Junos OS, load balancing is primarily applied in the following contexts:

- **Link Load Balancing**: Distributing traffic across multiple physical or logical interfaces.
- **ECMP (Equal-Cost Multi-Path)**: Balancing traffic across multiple paths with equal routing cost.
- **Server Load Balancing**: Distributing traffic to a pool of servers based on specific criteria.

Key Objectives:

1. **Enhance Network Performance**: Maximize throughput by using all available resources.
2. **Ensure Redundancy**: Provide failover capabilities by redirecting traffic during link or device failures.
3. **Improve Scalability**: Support increased traffic demand by distributing the load efficiently.

2. Load Balancing Techniques in Junos OS

a. Per-Packet Load Balancing

- Splits traffic on a per-packet basis across multiple links.
- Ensures even distribution but may cause packet reordering, which can impact protocols sensitive to sequence.

b. Per-Flow Load Balancing

- Distributes traffic based on flows (e.g., source/destination IP pairs).
- Prevents packet reordering, making it ideal for TCP traffic.

c. Application-Aware Load Balancing

- Directs traffic based on application characteristics.
- Commonly used in server load balancing scenarios.

3. Configuring Load Balancing in Junos OS

Junos OS provides flexible configuration options for implementing load balancing. Below are the typical scenarios and configurations:

a. Link Aggregation with LACP

Load balancing can be achieved by bundling multiple physical links into a single logical interface using Link Aggregation Control Protocol (LACP).

Configuration Example:

```
set interfaces ae0 aggregated-ether-options minimum-links 2
set interfaces ae0 aggregated-ether-options lacp active
set interfaces ae0 unit 0 family inet address 192.168.1.1/24
set interfaces ge-0/0/0 ether-options 802.3ad ae0
set interfaces ge-0/0/1 ether-options 802.3ad ae0
```

- This configuration combines ge-0/0/0 and ge-0/0/1 into a single interface ae0.
- Traffic is distributed across these links.

b. Equal-Cost Multi-Path (ECMP) Routing

ECMP enables load balancing across multiple paths with the same routing cost in the routing table.

Configuration Example:

```
set routing-options forwarding-table export load-balance
set policy-options policy-statement load-balance term 1 then load-balance
per-packet
```

- ECMP ensures even traffic distribution across paths with equal metrics.

c. Server Load Balancing

In scenarios involving multiple servers, load balancing can distribute client requests evenly.

Configuration Example (using NAT pools):

```
set security nat source pool web-servers address 192.168.1.10/32
set security nat source pool web-servers address 192.168.1.11/32
set security nat source rule-set server-lb from zone trust
set security nat source rule-set server-lb to zone untrust
set security nat source rule-set server-lb rule 1 match source-address 0.0.0.0/0
set security nat source rule-set server-lb rule 1 then source-nat pool web-servers
```

- This configuration evenly distributes traffic across 192.168.1.10 and 192.168.1.11.

---

4. Monitoring and Troubleshooting Load Balancing

a. Verifying Load Balancing Status

Use the following commands to check load-balancing operations:

```
show interfaces ae0 extensive
```

Displays traffic statistics and distribution across aggregated links.

```
show route forwarding-table
```

Verifies ECMP routes and traffic distribution.

b. Troubleshooting Commands

- **Check Interface Statistics**:

  ```
  show interfaces statistics
  ```

- **Verify Load Balancing Policies**:

  ```
  show configuration policy-options
  ```

- **Monitor NAT Pools for Server Balancing**:

  ```
  show security nat source-pool
  ```

5. Best Practices for Load Balancing in Junos OS

1. **Use Per-Flow Balancing for TCP Traffic**: To avoid packet reordering, configure per-flow load balancing for applications relying on sequence integrity.
2. **Optimize Link Aggregation**: Ensure uniform link speeds in LACP configurations to prevent traffic congestion on slower links.
3. **Monitor Regularly**: Continuously monitor load distribution and link utilization to identify potential bottlenecks.
4. **Implement Failover Mechanisms**: Combine load balancing with redundancy protocols like VRRP for high availability.
5. **Fine-Tune Hash Algorithms**: Adjust hashing algorithms for specific traffic patterns to improve distribution efficiency.

6. Real-World Example: Load Balancing in a Data Center

Scenario

A data center uses MX Series routers with ECMP to balance traffic across three upstream links to its Internet Service Providers (ISPs). Additionally, server traffic within the data center is load-balanced using LACP.

Configuration Summary

1. **ECMP Routing**:

   ```
   set routing-options forwarding-table export load-balance
   ```

2. **LACP for Internal Traffic**:

   ```
   set interfaces ae0 aggregated-ether-options lacp active
   set interfaces ge-0/0/0 ether-options 802.3ad ae0
   set interfaces ge-0/0/1 ether-options 802.3ad ae0
   ```

Outcome

- Enhanced throughput across multiple paths to ISPs.
- Balanced load on internal server traffic, preventing overutilization of any single link.

Summary

Load balancing in Junos OS is a versatile tool for optimizing network performance and ensuring high availability. Whether through link aggregation, ECMP routing, or server load balancing, Junos OS provides robust solutions tailored to diverse networking environments.

Section 9:
Performance Optimization

Quality of Service (QoS) Fundamentals

Quality of Service (QoS) is a critical aspect of modern network management, enabling administrators to prioritize traffic, optimize bandwidth, and ensure that mission-critical applications maintain their performance under varying network conditions. In Junos OS, QoS is a robust framework offering granular control over traffic flows, ensuring efficient and predictable network behavior.

1. What is Quality of Service (QoS)?

Quality of Service (QoS) refers to the technologies and techniques used to manage network traffic to meet specific performance requirements. By prioritizing certain types of traffic over others, QoS helps prevent congestion, reduce latency, and optimize bandwidth utilization.

Key Objectives of QoS:

- **Traffic Prioritization**: Ensure time-sensitive traffic (e.g., VoIP, video) is delivered promptly.
- **Bandwidth Allocation**: Allocate resources effectively to prevent bottlenecks.
- **Traffic Shaping and Policing**: Control the flow of traffic to ensure compliance with predefined limits.
- **Congestion Management**: Handle network congestion without compromising critical applications.

2. QoS in Junos OS

In Junos OS, QoS is implemented at multiple levels of the network architecture to manage traffic flows effectively. Key components include:

1. **Classification**: Categorizing traffic into classes based on headers, applications, or other attributes.
2. **Policing**: Monitoring and enforcing traffic rate limits.
3. **Shaping**: Smoothing traffic bursts to match the network's capacity.
4. **Scheduling**: Allocating resources based on traffic priority.
5. **Marking**: Assigning traffic with specific CoS (Class of Service) markings for consistent treatment across the network.

3. QoS Traffic Classes in Junos OS

Junos OS supports traffic classification into different service levels, enabling prioritized handling based on business requirements.

Common Traffic Classes:

1. **Real-Time Traffic**: High-priority traffic such as VoIP and video conferencing.
2. **Business-Critical Traffic**: Applications like ERP systems or transactional databases.

3. **Best-Effort Traffic**: General-purpose traffic without specific delivery requirements.
4. **Background Traffic**: Low-priority traffic like backups or updates.

---

4. Configuring QoS in Junos OS

QoS configuration in Junos OS involves defining traffic policies, applying them to interfaces, and monitoring their performance.

a. Traffic Classification

Traffic is classified into forwarding classes based on filters or predefined rules.

Configuration Example:

```
set class-of-service classifiers dscp custom-dscp-classes forwarding-class
expedited-forwarding code-points 101110
set class-of-service classifiers dscp custom-dscp-classes forwarding-class
assured-forwarding code-points 001010
set class-of-service classifiers dscp custom-dscp-classes forwarding-class
best-effort code-points 000000
```

- This configuration maps specific DSCP values to forwarding classes.

b. Traffic Policing

Traffic policing enforces rate limits on inbound or outbound traffic.

Configuration Example:

```
set firewall policer rate-limit if-exceeding bandwidth-limit 10m burst-size-limit
1m
set firewall policer rate-limit then discard
```

- This sets a rate limit of 10 Mbps for a specific traffic stream.

c. Traffic Shaping

Traffic shaping smooths traffic bursts by queuing excess packets.

Configuration Example:

```
set class-of-service traffic-control-profiles profile1 shaping-rate 20m
set class-of-service traffic-control-profiles profile1 burst-size 1m
```

d. Scheduling and Queuing

Scheduling determines how traffic is dequeued from buffers.

Configuration Example:

```
set class-of-service schedulers high-priority-scheduler transmit-rate percent 40
set class-of-service schedulers high-priority-scheduler priority high
set class-of-service forwarding-classes expedited-forwarding queue
high-priority-scheduler
```

- High-priority traffic is allocated 40% of bandwidth.

e. Applying QoS Policies

QoS policies are applied to interfaces to enforce the defined behavior.

Configuration Example:

```
set interfaces ge-0/0/0 unit 0 family inet filter input qos-filter
```

5. Monitoring QoS Performance

Junos OS provides tools to monitor QoS metrics and ensure configurations are working as expected.

Common Commands:

- **Check Interface QoS Statistics**:

  ```
  show interfaces queue ge-0/0/0
  ```

- **Verify Classifier Mapping**:

  ```
  show class-of-service classifiers
  ```

- **Monitor Traffic Rates**:

  ```
  show firewall
  ```

6. Best Practices for QoS Configuration

1. **Identify Traffic Types**: Understand network traffic patterns to define appropriate traffic classes.
2. **Use Traffic Marking**: Consistently mark traffic to ensure end-to-end QoS treatment.
3. **Apply Rate Limiting**: Prevent individual flows from monopolizing bandwidth.
4. **Monitor and Adjust**: Regularly monitor QoS policies and adjust based on evolving network demands.
5. **Balance Resource Allocation**: Allocate sufficient resources for critical traffic without over-allocating.

7. Real-World Example: QoS for a VoIP Network

Scenario

A company deploys VoIP phones alongside general web traffic. QoS is required to prioritize VoIP traffic and ensure call quality during peak hours.

Configuration Summary

1. **Traffic Classification**:

   ```
   set class-of-service classifiers dscp voip forwarding-class
   expedited-forwarding code-points 101110
   ```

2. **Traffic Policing**:

   ```
   set firewall policer voip-rate-limit if-exceeding bandwidth-limit 5m
   burst-size-limit 512k
   ```

3. **Scheduling**:

```
set class-of-service schedulers voip-scheduler transmit-rate percent 50
set class-of-service schedulers voip-scheduler priority high
```

4. **Policy Application**:

```
set interfaces ge-0/0/0 unit 0 family inet filter input voip-filter
```

Outcome

VoIP traffic is prioritized, ensuring smooth and uninterrupted calls, even during high traffic periods.

Summary

Quality of Service in Junos OS is a powerful mechanism to control and optimize network performance. By classifying, policing, shaping, and scheduling traffic, QoS ensures the efficient use of network resources and supports critical business applications. Proper implementation of QoS policies allows networks to adapt dynamically to varying traffic demands, ensuring consistent and reliable service.

Traffic Shaping and Policing

Traffic shaping and policing are critical techniques for managing network traffic and ensuring consistent performance. These methods help control the flow of data, prevent congestion, and enforce policies that align with business objectives. In Junos OS, traffic shaping and policing are implemented using flexible and powerful tools that allow administrators to customize traffic behavior based on application and network requirements.

1. What is Traffic Shaping?

Traffic Shaping is the process of regulating network traffic to conform to a desired bandwidth profile. It involves smoothing out bursts of traffic, reducing packet loss, and ensuring that critical applications receive the necessary bandwidth.

Key Objectives:

- **Optimize Bandwidth Usage**: Ensure efficient use of available bandwidth.
- **Prevent Congestion**: Manage bursty traffic to avoid network overload.
- **Improve Application Performance**: Prioritize critical applications and ensure their performance remains unaffected.

2. What is Traffic Policing?

Traffic Policing is a technique used to monitor and enforce traffic rate limits. Unlike shaping, which delays packets to conform to bandwidth limits, policing drops or re-marks packets that exceed the defined thresholds.

Key Objectives:

- **Enforce Bandwidth Limits**: Prevent specific traffic flows from monopolizing network resources.
- **Provide Fair Usage**: Ensure equitable distribution of bandwidth among users and applications.
- **Enhance Network Security**: Protect against malicious traffic patterns by dropping excessive or abnormal flows.

3. Traffic Shaping and Policing in Junos OS

Junos OS provides comprehensive tools for shaping and policing traffic. These mechanisms are implemented using classifiers, policers, schedulers, and filters.

Key Components:

1. **Classifiers**: Identify and categorize traffic based on attributes like IP address, protocol, or application type.
2. **Policers**: Apply rate limits and enforce compliance with bandwidth policies.
3. **Schedulers**: Manage the queuing and forwarding of traffic, ensuring prioritized handling.
4. **Filters**: Define specific rules for shaping or policing traffic on an interface.

4. Configuring Traffic Shaping in Junos OS

Traffic shaping is achieved using **traffic-control profiles** and schedulers that specify bandwidth limits and queuing behavior.

Example Configuration:

```
set class-of-service traffic-control-profiles shaping-profile shaping-rate 10m
set class-of-service traffic-control-profiles shaping-profile burst-size 1m
set interfaces ge-0/0/0 unit 0 traffic-control-profile shaping-profile
```

- **shaping-rate**: Limits traffic to 10 Mbps.
- **burst-size**: Allows short bursts up to 1 Mbps.

5. Configuring Traffic Policing in Junos OS

Traffic policing is implemented using policers that define bandwidth limits and actions for non-compliant traffic.

Example Configuration:

```
set firewall policer policing-example if-exceeding bandwidth-limit 5m
burst-size-limit 512k
set firewall policer policing-example then discard
set interfaces ge-0/0/0 unit 0 family inet filter input policing-filter
```

- **bandwidth-limit**: Limits traffic to 5 Mbps.
- **burst-size-limit**: Allows bursts up to 512 Kbps.
- **discard**: Drops packets exceeding the defined limits.

6. Combining Traffic Shaping and Policing

In many scenarios, traffic shaping and policing are used together. Shaping smooths traffic bursts, while policing enforces strict rate limits.

Combined Configuration:

1. Apply a shaping profile to control traffic bursts.
2. Use a policer to drop excessive traffic beyond acceptable thresholds.

7. Monitoring and Verifying Configuration

Junos OS offers various commands to monitor and verify traffic shaping and policing.

Commands:

- **View Policer Statistics**:

  ```
  show firewall
  ```

- **Verify Traffic-Control Profiles**:

  ```
  show class-of-service traffic-control-profiles
  ```

- **Check Interface Queue Usage**:

```
show interfaces queue ge-0/0/0
```

8. Real-World Use Case: Traffic Shaping and Policing for Video Streaming

Scenario:

A company wants to ensure smooth video streaming for training sessions while limiting bandwidth usage by non-essential applications.

Configuration:

1. **Classify Traffic**:

```
set class-of-service classifiers dscp video-stream forwarding-class
expedited-forwarding code-points 101110
```

2. **Shape Video Traffic**:

```
set class-of-service traffic-control-profiles video-profile shaping-rate 20m
burst-size 2m
```

3. **Police Non-Essential Traffic**:

```
set firewall policer non-essential-limit if-exceeding bandwidth-limit 5m
burst-size-limit 512k
set firewall policer non-essential-limit then discard
```

Outcome:

- Video traffic flows smoothly, ensuring high-quality streaming.
- Non-essential applications are limited to 5 Mbps, preventing network congestion.

9. Best Practices for Traffic Shaping and Policing

1. **Understand Traffic Patterns**: Analyze traffic flows to identify critical and non-critical applications.
2. **Set Realistic Limits**: Configure bandwidth limits and burst sizes based on available resources.
3. **Prioritize Critical Applications**: Ensure important traffic classes have sufficient bandwidth.
4. **Regular Monitoring**: Continuously monitor traffic and adjust policies as needed.
5. **Test Policies**: Validate shaping and policing configurations in a lab environment before deployment.

Summary

Traffic shaping and policing are essential tools for managing network performance and ensuring fair bandwidth allocation. In Junos OS, these features provide a flexible framework for controlling traffic flows and maintaining consistent application performance. By combining traffic shaping and policing, network administrators can optimize bandwidth usage, prevent congestion, and meet business objectives.

Understanding and Configuring CoS in Junos

Class of Service (CoS) is a critical feature in modern networking, enabling differentiated treatment of network traffic based on priority. In Junos OS, CoS provides a comprehensive framework to classify, queue, and prioritize traffic, ensuring optimal performance for applications and maintaining Quality of Service (QoS) standards.

1. What is Class of Service (CoS)?

Class of Service (CoS) is a network mechanism that differentiates traffic into multiple categories based on predefined criteria. By assigning priorities to traffic flows, CoS ensures that critical applications receive the necessary bandwidth and low-latency treatment, even during network congestion.

Key Objectives of CoS:

- **Traffic Prioritization**: Ensure that high-priority traffic (e.g., voice and video) is served first.
- **Bandwidth Management**: Allocate resources efficiently among different traffic classes.
- **Congestion Management**: Handle traffic surges by queuing and prioritizing data packets.
- **Service-Level Agreements (SLAs)**: Maintain agreed-upon performance standards for critical services.

2. CoS Framework in Junos OS

Junos OS implements CoS through a series of well-defined components:

Key Components:

1. **Classifiers**: Identify traffic and assign it to forwarding classes.
2. **Forwarding Classes**: Categorize traffic into groups with similar QoS requirements.
3. **Schedulers**: Manage queuing, forwarding, and resource allocation for each forwarding class.
4. **Policers**: Enforce rate limits for specific traffic classes.
5. **Rewrite Rules**: Modify traffic markings (e.g., DSCP, EXP) as it traverses the network.

3. Traffic Classification

Traffic classification is the first step in CoS. It involves identifying packets based on attributes like source/destination IP, protocol type, or application. Junos OS uses **classifiers** to map packets to specific forwarding classes.

Example Configuration:

```
set class-of-service classifiers dscp classifier-1 forwarding-class
expedited-forwarding code-points 101110
set class-of-service classifiers dscp classifier-1 forwarding-class best-effort
code-points 000000
```

- **Expedited-forwarding**: Assigns traffic like voice or real-time applications.
- **Best-effort**: Assigns traffic without specific QoS requirements.

4. Forwarding Classes

Forwarding classes group traffic into categories with similar treatment. Each class is associated with specific resources and priority levels.

Common Forwarding Classes:

- **Expedited-Forwarding (EF)**: High-priority, low-latency traffic (e.g., VoIP).
- **Assured-Forwarding (AF)**: Medium-priority traffic with guaranteed delivery.
- **Best-Effort (BE)**: Default class for non-critical traffic.

5. Schedulers and Queuing

Schedulers determine how packets are forwarded from queues. They manage bandwidth allocation, queuing priority, and buffer management.

Example Scheduler Configuration:

```
set class-of-service schedulers scheduler-1 transmit-rate percent 50
set class-of-service schedulers scheduler-1 priority high
set class-of-service schedulers scheduler-1 buffer-size percent 20
```

- **Transmit-rate**: Allocates 50% of interface bandwidth to this scheduler.
- **Priority**: Ensures high-priority treatment.
- **Buffer-size**: Limits queue depth to 20% of total buffer space.

6. Traffic Policing

Policers enforce rate limits on traffic classes to prevent overuse of network resources. Policing can drop or re-mark packets exceeding defined thresholds.

Example Policer Configuration:

```
set firewall policer policer-1 if-exceeding bandwidth-limit 10m burst-size-limit 1m
set firewall policer policer-1 then discard
```

- **Bandwidth-limit**: Limits traffic to 10 Mbps.
- **Burst-size-limit**: Allows short bursts up to 1 Mbps.

7. Rewrite Rules

Rewrite rules adjust traffic markings, such as Differentiated Services Code Point (DSCP) or MPLS EXP bits, ensuring consistent CoS treatment across network boundaries.

Example Rewrite Rule:

```
set class-of-service rewrite-rules dscp rewrite-1 forwarding-class
expedited-forwarding loss-priority low code-point 101110
```

8. Implementing CoS in Junos OS

A complete CoS implementation involves defining classifiers, forwarding classes, schedulers, policers, and rewrite rules. These components are then applied to network interfaces.

Example End-to-End CoS Configuration:

```
set class-of-service classifiers dscp dscp-classifier forwarding-class
expedited-forwarding code-points 101110
set class-of-service schedulers scheduler-ef transmit-rate percent 50
set class-of-service rewrite-rules dscp rewrite-dscp forwarding-class
expedited-forwarding code-point 101110
set interfaces ge-0/0/0 unit 0 family inet address 192.168.1.1/24
set interfaces ge-0/0/0 unit 0 family inet filter input dscp-classifier
set class-of-service interfaces ge-0/0/0 unit 0 shaping-rate 100m
```

9. Monitoring CoS

Junos OS provides tools to monitor CoS configurations and performance.

Useful Commands:

- **View Classifiers**:

  ```
  show class-of-service classifiers
  ```

- **Check Queue Statistics**:

  ```
  show interfaces queue ge-0/0/0
  ```

- **Inspect Policer Statistics**:

  ```
  show firewall
  ```

10. Real-World Application of CoS

Scenario:

A company prioritizes voice and video traffic while ensuring fair bandwidth distribution for other applications.

Solution:

- Classify voice traffic into **expedited-forwarding** and allocate 50% of bandwidth.
- Assign video traffic to **assured-forwarding** with 30% of bandwidth.
- Configure **best-effort** for non-critical traffic.

Outcome:

- Voice and video traffic receive high-priority treatment.
- Non-critical traffic utilizes remaining bandwidth without impacting critical services.

11. Best Practices for CoS in Junos OS

1. **Understand Traffic Needs**: Analyze traffic patterns to identify critical and non-critical flows.
2. **Balance Resources**: Avoid over-allocating bandwidth to high-priority classes at the expense of others.
3. **Validate Configurations**: Test CoS policies in a lab environment before deployment.
4. **Monitor Regularly**: Use monitoring tools to ensure configurations meet performance goals.
5. **Adapt to Changes**: Update CoS policies as network requirements evolve.

Summary

Understanding and configuring CoS in Junos OS is essential for delivering reliable and high-performance networking. By leveraging CoS features like traffic classification, forwarding classes, schedulers, and policing, administrators can meet SLAs, optimize bandwidth, and enhance user experience. Effective CoS implementation ensures a robust and efficient network infrastructure.

Troubleshooting Latency Issues

Latency issues can significantly degrade network performance, affecting application response times and overall user experience. In Junos OS environments, addressing latency involves a systematic approach to identifying, analyzing, and resolving the root causes. This chapter provides a comprehensive guide to understanding latency, its sources, and effective troubleshooting techniques using Junos OS tools.

---

1. Understanding Latency in Networks

Latency is the time it takes for a data packet to travel from its source to its destination and back (round-trip time).

Types of Latency:

1. **Propagation Delay**: The time required for a signal to travel through a medium.
2. **Transmission Delay**: The time to push all packet bits onto the wire.
3. **Processing Delay**: The time taken by routers and switches to process the packet.
4. **Queuing Delay**: The time packets spend in queues waiting to be transmitted.

Common Effects of High Latency:

- Slow application responses.
- Poor VoIP and video quality.
- Timeouts in critical services.

---

2. Identifying Latency Sources

Latency can originate from multiple sources in a network:

1. **Congestion**: High traffic loads on links or interfaces.
2. **Suboptimal Routing**: Inefficient path selection due to routing protocol issues.
3. **Hardware Performance**: Overloaded CPUs or memory constraints in devices.
4. **Faulty Interfaces**: Errors or failures in physical or logical interfaces.
5. **QoS Misconfigurations**: Poor traffic prioritization leading to queuing delays.

---

3. Tools for Diagnosing Latency in Junos OS

Junos OS provides robust tools for latency analysis and troubleshooting:

a. Ping

Measures round-trip time to a specific destination.

```
ping <destination-IP>
```

b. Traceroute

Identifies the path packets take to a destination and measures delays at each hop.

```
traceroute <destination-IP>
```

c. Traffic Monitoring

Captures real-time traffic statistics on interfaces.

```
show interfaces statistics
```

d. Queue Monitoring

Monitors queuing delays caused by congestion.

```
show interfaces queue <interface>
```

e. Firewall Filters

Analyzes packet flows and identifies bottlenecks.

```
show firewall
```

f. JFlow or sFlow

Tracks network flows to detect high-latency paths or traffic surges.

---

4. Common Latency Issues and Solutions

a. Congestion on Interfaces

- **Symptoms**: High utilization and increased queuing delays.
- **Solution**:
    - Verify interface utilization:

        ```
        show interfaces statistics
        ```

    - Apply traffic shaping to prioritize critical traffic:

        ```
        set class-of-service schedulers scheduler-1 transmit-rate percent 50
        ```

b. Routing Loops or Suboptimal Paths

- **Symptoms**: High latency due to inefficient routing paths.
- **Solution**:
    - Check the routing table:

        ```
        show route
        ```

    - Use traceroute to identify loops or inefficient hops:

        ```
        traceroute <destination-IP>
        ```

    - Update routing policies to enforce optimal paths:

        ```
        set policy-options policy-statement optimal-path term 1 then preference 10
        ```

c. Faulty Interfaces

- **Symptoms**: Packet drops or high error rates on specific interfaces.
- **Solution**:
    - Verify interface health:

```
show interfaces extensive
```

   ○ Replace or repair faulty cables or hardware.

d. Insufficient QoS Configuration

- **Symptoms**: High-priority traffic suffers from delays.
- **Solution**:
   ○ Validate QoS configuration:

```
show class-of-service interfaces
```

   ○ Ensure critical traffic is assigned to low-latency queues:

```
set class-of-service schedulers voice-scheduler transmit-rate percent 30
```

---

5. Advanced Troubleshooting Techniques

a. Packet Capture and Analysis

Captures packets for in-depth analysis of latency causes.

```
monitor traffic interface <interface>
```

b. SNMP Monitoring

Tracks latency metrics using SNMP.

- Configure SNMP traps:

```
set snmp trap-group latency-group targets <server-IP>
```

- Use tools like Junos Space for centralized monitoring.

c. Telemetry Streaming

Streams real-time performance metrics to external systems for analysis.

```
set system telemetry-server <server-IP>
```

d. Event Logs

Check system logs for latency-related errors:

```
show log messages
```

---

6. Real-World Example: Latency Diagnosis

Scenario:

A company experiences high latency on VoIP calls during peak hours.

Steps Taken:

1. **Ping and Traceroute**: High round-trip times observed to call server.

2. **Interface Statistics**: Identified congestion on the primary WAN link.
3. **Queue Monitoring**: VoIP traffic stuck in low-priority queues.
4. **Solution**:
    - Adjusted QoS policies to prioritize VoIP traffic.
    - Applied traffic shaping to manage bandwidth usage.

Result:

Significant improvement in call quality and reduced latency.

---

7. Best Practices for Latency Troubleshooting

1. **Baseline Metrics**: Regularly measure network latency under normal conditions.
2. **Proactive Monitoring**: Use telemetry and SNMP to catch issues early.
3. **End-to-End Analysis**: Investigate latency across the entire path, not just one device.
4. **Update Firmware**: Ensure devices run the latest Junos OS version for optimal performance.
5. **Documentation**: Maintain a record of configurations and changes for quick reference.

Summary

Troubleshooting latency issues in Junos OS requires a methodical approach, leveraging the platform's diagnostic tools and best practices. By identifying and addressing root causes like congestion, routing inefficiencies, and QoS misconfigurations, administrators can maintain low latency and ensure high network performance.

Section 10:
Monitoring and Troubleshooting

Using Junos OS Monitoring Tools

Effective network monitoring is essential for maintaining performance, diagnosing issues, and ensuring operational stability. Junos OS offers a range of powerful monitoring tools to observe real-time network performance, analyze data flows, and quickly detect anomalies. This chapter explores the key monitoring tools available in Junos OS and how to use them effectively.

1. Importance of Network Monitoring

Monitoring ensures proactive management and optimization of network resources. Key benefits include:

- **Early Detection of Issues**: Identifying bottlenecks and potential failures before they impact users.
- **Performance Analysis**: Ensuring optimal resource utilization and quality of service.
- **Troubleshooting**: Providing actionable insights for issue resolution.
- **Security**: Detecting suspicious activities or breaches in the network.

2. Overview of Monitoring Tools in Junos OS

Junos OS provides several built-in tools for comprehensive network monitoring. These include:

- **Interface Monitoring**
- **Traffic Statistics**
- **Firewall and Filter Monitoring**
- **System Logs**
- **J-Flow for Network Traffic Analysis**
- **Real-Time Performance Monitoring (RPM)**

3. Monitoring Network Interfaces

Network interfaces are critical points for traffic flow and a primary focus for monitoring.

Key Commands:

1. **View Basic Interface Statistics**:

```
show interfaces terse
```

   - Provides an overview of interface status, including link state and protocol state.

2. **View Detailed Interface Statistics**:

```
show interfaces extensive
```

   - Displays detailed metrics like traffic rates, errors, and queuing information.

3. **Monitor Specific Interface in Real-Time**:

```
monitor interface <interface-name>
```

  ○ Useful for observing real-time changes in traffic and errors.

---

4. Analyzing Traffic Statistics

Traffic statistics help in understanding data flow, bandwidth usage, and identifying congestion points.

Commands:

1. **Traffic Summary**:

```
show interfaces statistics
```

  ○ Provides per-interface statistics on packets and bytes.

2. **Traffic by Protocol**:

```
show interfaces protocols
```

  ○ Breaks down traffic by protocols like TCP, UDP, and ICMP.

3. **Queue Statistics**:

```
show interfaces queue <interface-name>
```

  ○ Useful for monitoring queue usage and ensuring QoS configurations are effective.

---

5. Monitoring System Performance

System performance monitoring ensures that the Junos OS device is operating within capacity limits.

Commands:

1. **CPU and Memory Usage**:

```
show system processes extensive
```

  ○ Displays resource usage by processes.

2. **Disk Space Usage**:

```
show system storage
```

  ○ Helps in identifying storage-related issues.

3. **System Health**:

```
show chassis environment
```

  ○ Monitors temperature, power supplies, and fans for hardware health.

---

6. Using Firewall and Filter Monitoring

Firewall filters in Junos OS can be used to track and analyze packet flows.

Commands:

1. **View Filter Statistics**:

```
show firewall
```

   - Displays hit counts for firewall rules, helping to identify traffic patterns.
2. **Detailed Filter Monitoring**:

```
show firewall filter <filter-name>
```

   - Provides in-depth details about specific filters.

---

7. Real-Time Performance Monitoring (RPM)

RPM in Junos OS helps in testing and verifying network performance by simulating traffic flows.

Steps to Configure RPM:

1. **Define RPM Configuration**:

```
set services rpm probe <probe-name> test <test-name> target address <IP>
```

2. **Start RPM Test**:

```
run show services rpm probe-results
```

   - View latency, loss, and jitter for the probe.

---

8. Using System Logs for Monitoring

System logs provide valuable insights into network events and device operations.

Commands:

1. **View Recent Logs**:

```
show log messages
```

   - Displays the most recent system events.
2. **Filter Logs by Keyword**:

```
show log messages | match <keyword>
```

   - Filters logs for specific events, such as errors or warnings.
3. **Monitor Logs in Real-Time**:

```
monitor start messages
```

   - Displays log entries as they occur.

---

9. Advanced Monitoring with J-Flow

J-Flow is Junos OS's flow monitoring tool for detailed traffic analysis.

Steps to Configure J-Flow:

1. **Enable J-Flow on Interfaces**:

```
set forwarding-options sampling input rate 100
set forwarding-options sampling family inet output flow-server <IP> port
<port>
```

2. **View J-Flow Statistics**:

```
show services accounting flow
```

---

10. Best Practices for Network Monitoring

1. **Baseline Metrics**: Regularly collect baseline data for performance comparison.
2. **Proactive Alerts**: Set up alerts for critical thresholds (e.g., high CPU usage).
3. **Centralized Monitoring**: Use tools like Junos Space for a unified monitoring interface.
4. **Automation**: Automate routine monitoring tasks using scripts or APIs.
5. **Documentation**: Maintain logs and reports for historical analysis.

Summary

Monitoring tools in Junos OS provide network administrators with the visibility needed to maintain performance, diagnose issues, and optimize resource usage. By leveraging commands and features like interface monitoring, traffic analysis, system logs, and J-Flow, administrators can ensure the stability and reliability of their networks.

SNMP Configuration and Management

The Simple Network Management Protocol (SNMP) is a widely used protocol for monitoring and managing devices on a network. It allows network administrators to gather information about network performance, troubleshoot issues, and automate management tasks. In Junos OS, SNMP is a critical component for centralized network management and integration with monitoring tools.

1. What is SNMP?

SNMP is a protocol that enables communication between network devices (agents) and management systems (SNMP managers). Key components of SNMP include:

- **SNMP Agents**: Reside on network devices to provide data about the device.
- **SNMP Managers**: Applications that request and collect information from SNMP agents.
- **MIB (Management Information Base)**: A database of network object identifiers (OIDs) that define what information can be monitored or controlled.

SNMP operates on UDP ports 161 (agents) and 162 (traps).

2. Benefits of Using SNMP in Junos OS

1. **Centralized Monitoring**: Collect data from multiple devices in a unified platform.
2. **Real-Time Alerts**: Receive notifications for critical events via SNMP traps.
3. **Automation**: Automate routine monitoring and management tasks.
4. **Compatibility**: Integrate seamlessly with third-party network monitoring tools like Nagios, SolarWinds, and PRTG.

3. Configuring SNMP in Junos OS

3.1. Enabling SNMP

To enable SNMP on a Junos OS device:

1. Access the configuration mode:

```
configure
```

2. Enable the SNMP service:

```
set snmp community <community-name> authorization <read-only|read-write>
```

3. Example:

```
set snmp community public authorization read-only
```

4. Commit the configuration:

```
commit
```

3.2. Configuring SNMP Traps

SNMP traps are unsolicited messages sent by devices to notify the SNMP manager of specific events.

1. Define SNMP trap targets:

```
set snmp trap-group <group-name> targets <ip-address>
```

2. Example:

```
set snmp trap-group default targets 192.168.1.10
```

3. Specify the types of traps:

```
set snmp trap-group <group-name> categories <category>
```

4. Common categories:
   - link
   - environmental
   - configuration
5. Apply the trap group to SNMP:

```
set snmp trap-group <group-name>
```

4. Monitoring SNMP in Junos OS

4.1. Verifying SNMP Configuration

Use the following command to verify the SNMP configuration:

```
show configuration snmp
```

4.2. Testing SNMP Connectivity

To test connectivity between an SNMP manager and an agent:

```
ping <SNMP-manager-IP>
```

4.3. SNMP Statistics

View SNMP statistics for troubleshooting:

```
show snmp statistics
```

5. Common SNMP Use Cases

5.1. Monitoring Device Health

- Collect metrics such as CPU usage, memory usage, and interface status using OIDs.

5.2. Event Notifications

- Receive real-time notifications for link failures, temperature thresholds, or configuration changes via SNMP traps.

5.3. Integrating with Monitoring Tools

- Use third-party tools to visualize SNMP data for trends and analytics.

---

6. Best Practices for SNMP Configuration

1. **Use Secure SNMP Versions**: Prefer SNMPv3 over SNMPv1/v2c for secure authentication and encryption.

   ```
   set snmp v3 usm local-engine user <username> authentication-sha <password>
   privacy-aes128 <privacy-password>
   ```

2. **Restrict Access**: Limit SNMP access to trusted IPs using access lists.

   ```
   set snmp community <community-name> clients <ip-address>
   ```

3. **Monitor Critical Metrics**: Focus on metrics critical to your network's performance and health.
4. **Regularly Update MIBs**: Ensure your SNMP manager has updated MIBs to interpret device OIDs correctly.
5. **Use Trap Groups**: Organize traps into logical groups for easier management.

---

7. Troubleshooting SNMP Issues

7.1. Common Issues and Solutions

Issue	Cause	Solution
SNMP manager cannot connect	Incorrect community string or IP restrictions	Verify community strings and client access configuration.
No SNMP traps received	Traps not configured or firewall blocking	Verify trap configuration and ensure UDP port 162 is open on firewalls.
MIBs not recognized	Missing or outdated MIB files	Update MIB files on the SNMP manager.

7.2. Debugging Commands

1. **View SNMP Logs**:

   ```
   show log messages | match snmp
   ```

2. **Monitor Real-Time SNMP Activity**:

   ```
   monitor snmp
   ```

Summary

SNMP is an essential tool for monitoring and managing Junos OS devices in any network environment. By enabling SNMP, configuring traps, and integrating with monitoring platforms, administrators can ensure efficient management and quick issue resolution. Following best practices for security and focusing on critical metrics further enhances SNMP's utility in maintaining a robust and high-performing network.

Configuring Telemetry Streaming

Telemetry streaming in Junos OS provides an efficient and scalable way to collect network data in real time. Unlike traditional SNMP-based polling, telemetry streaming continuously pushes structured data to a collector, enabling proactive monitoring and rapid troubleshooting of network devices and performance. This chapter will guide you through understanding telemetry, its benefits, and how to configure telemetry streaming in Junos OS.

1. Understanding Telemetry Streaming

Telemetry streaming involves exporting real-time data from Junos devices to external collectors. The key components of Junos telemetry are:

- **Data Collection Points (Sensors)**: Specify the data to be collected, such as interface statistics, environmental metrics, or routing protocol states.
- **Streaming Protocols**: Formats and transports telemetry data. Commonly used protocols include gRPC, UDP, and HTTP/2.
- **Collectors**: External systems that receive, store, and analyze telemetry data. Tools like Prometheus, Grafana, and Juniper HealthBot are popular for visualizing telemetry data.

2. Benefits of Telemetry Streaming

1. **Real-Time Monitoring**: Provides up-to-the-second updates for faster issue detection.
2. **Scalability**: Reduces the overhead of frequent polling associated with SNMP.
3. **Granularity**: Offers detailed insights into network operations with configurable data intervals.
4. **Proactive Troubleshooting**: Enables anomaly detection and predictive analysis through historical and live data comparison.

3. Configuring Telemetry Streaming in Junos OS

3.1. Basic Telemetry Configuration

1. **Enable Streaming Telemetry**:

```
configure
set system services analytics
commit
```

2. **Configure a Telemetry Sensor**: Define the sensor name, object type, and sampling interval:

```
set services analytics sensor <sensor-name> resource <resource-type>
set services analytics sensor <sensor-name> reporting-rate <seconds>
```

Example:

```
set services analytics sensor interface-stats resource /interfaces
set services analytics sensor interface-stats reporting-rate 10
```

3. **Define a Streaming Destination**: Specify the protocol, destination IP, and port:

```
set services analytics streaming-server <server-name> remote-address
<ip-address>
set services analytics streaming-server <server-name> remote-port <port>
set services analytics streaming-server <server-name> transport <protocol>
```

Example:

```
set services analytics streaming-server telemetry-collector remote-address
192.168.1.10
set services analytics streaming-server telemetry-collector remote-port 5000
set services analytics streaming-server telemetry-collector transport grpc
```

4. **Bind Sensors to the Streaming Server**:

```
set services analytics sensor <sensor-name> server-name <server-name>
```

Example:

```
set services analytics sensor interface-stats server-name telemetry-collector
```

5. **Commit the Configuration**:

```
commit
```

3.2. Advanced Telemetry Features

Configuring Multiple Sensors: You can configure multiple sensors to collect various data points. For example:

```
set services analytics sensor bgp-stats resource /protocols/bgp
set services analytics sensor bgp-stats reporting-rate 5
set services analytics sensor bgp-stats server-name telemetry-collector
```

Using JSON Encoding: For structured data, configure the telemetry output to use JSON:

```
set services analytics sensor <sensor-name> encoding json
```

Compression for Efficiency: Enable compression to reduce bandwidth usage:

```
set services analytics streaming-server <server-name> compression gzip
```

---

4. Monitoring Telemetry Streaming

4.1. Verifying Sensor Configuration

To check the status of telemetry sensors:

```
show services analytics sensors
```

4.2. Monitoring Telemetry Output

View the telemetry data being streamed:

```
show services analytics data-stream
```

4.3. Debugging Streaming Issues

Inspect telemetry logs for troubleshooting:

```
show log messages | match analytics
```

---

5. Integrating Telemetry with Tools

5.1. Using Juniper HealthBot

HealthBot is a Juniper tool designed for real-time telemetry visualization and automation.

1. **Install and Configure HealthBot**: Set up HealthBot on a separate server and configure it to receive telemetry data from Junos devices.
2. **Visualize Data**: Use predefined dashboards or create custom views for telemetry data.

5.2. Third-Party Tools

Integrate Junos telemetry with tools like Grafana and Prometheus using plugins or custom collectors.

---

6. Best Practices for Telemetry Streaming

1. **Optimize Reporting Intervals**: Set intervals based on the criticality of metrics to balance performance and data granularity.
2. **Secure Connections**: Use encrypted protocols like gRPC or HTTPS for secure data transport.
3. **Limit Data Scope**: Configure sensors to collect only necessary data to reduce resource usage.
4. **Centralize Data Management**: Use a centralized system like HealthBot or Prometheus for managing telemetry data from multiple devices.
5. **Test Configurations**: Verify and test telemetry configurations in a lab environment before deployment.

Summary

Telemetry streaming in Junos OS offers a modern, efficient, and real-time approach to network monitoring. By configuring sensors and integrating with analytics tools, administrators can achieve deep insights into their networks. Proper planning and adherence to best practices ensure a scalable and secure telemetry setup.

Packet Capture and Analysis

Packet capture and analysis are critical components of network troubleshooting and performance optimization. They enable administrators to inspect, diagnose, and resolve issues at the packet level, providing insights into network behavior and identifying potential problems. Junos OS offers robust tools for capturing and analyzing packets, making it easier to understand network traffic and resolve issues efficiently.

1. Introduction to Packet Capture in Junos OS

Packet capture involves intercepting and logging packets transmitted across a network. These packets can then be analyzed to determine the root cause of network issues, such as delays, dropped packets, or misconfigured protocols.

Key Uses of Packet Capture

- **Troubleshooting Protocols**: Diagnose issues with routing protocols like OSPF or BGP.
- **Analyzing Performance**: Identify delays or bottlenecks in the network.
- **Security Investigations**: Monitor and analyze suspicious traffic patterns.
- **Compliance and Auditing**: Log network traffic for compliance and audit purposes.

Junos OS provides the **monitor traffic** and **packet capture (pcap)** tools to capture packets for analysis.

2. Capturing Packets Using Junos OS Tools

2.1. The monitor traffic Command

The monitor traffic command is used to capture and display real-time traffic passing through a specific interface. It is a quick and straightforward way to view live traffic on Junos devices.

Syntax:

```
monitor traffic interface <interface-name> [no-resolve] [size <packet-size>]
[matching <filter>]
```

Example:

To capture all traffic on interface ge-0/0/0 without DNS resolution:

```
monitor traffic interface ge-0/0/0 no-resolve
```

Options:

- **no-resolve**: Prevents resolving IP addresses to hostnames, improving performance.
- **size <packet-size>**: Limits the size of captured packets (default is 96 bytes).
- **matching <filter>**: Applies a filter to capture only specific types of traffic (e.g., ICMP, TCP).

Note: The monitor traffic command impacts CPU utilization as it processes traffic in real time. Use it sparingly in production environments.

2.2. Using the Packet Capture Tool (PCAP)

For more detailed analysis, Junos OS supports packet capture in PCAP format, which can be analyzed using external tools like Wireshark or tcpdump.

Steps to Perform a PCAP Capture:

1. **Configure Packet Capture**: Use a firewall filter to define the traffic you want to capture.

```
set firewall family inet filter capture-filter term capture-traffic from
protocol tcp
set firewall family inet filter capture-filter term capture-traffic then
capture
set firewall family inet filter capture-filter term capture-traffic then
accept
```

2. **Apply the Firewall Filter**: Attach the filter to the desired interface.

```
set interfaces ge-0/0/0 unit 0 family inet filter input capture-filter
```

3. **Start Packet Capture**: Use the `monitor traffic` command to capture packets as per the configured filter:

```
monitor traffic interface ge-0/0/0 matching "tcp"
```

4. **Export PCAP File**: Export captured packets to a file for offline analysis.

```
request security capture file create filename <filename> interface
<interface-name>
```

5. **Download the File**: Use SCP or FTP to download the PCAP file to your local system for analysis.

---

3. Analyzing Captured Packets

3.1. Using Wireshark

Wireshark is a powerful open-source tool for analyzing PCAP files. Once you've captured traffic using Junos OS, transfer the PCAP file to your computer and open it in Wireshark.

Key Features of Wireshark:

- **Protocol Decoding**: View detailed information about protocols like TCP, UDP, and HTTP.
- **Filter Traffic**: Use display filters to focus on specific packets.
- **Error Detection**: Identify retransmissions, checksum errors, and malformed packets.

3.2. Analyzing Specific Traffic

To analyze specific traffic types in Wireshark:

- Filter HTTP traffic:

```
http
```

- Filter packets from a specific IP:

```
ip.src == 192.168.1.10
```

- Filter packets to a specific port:

```
tcp.port == 80
```

3.3. Insights from Packet Analysis

Packet analysis can provide insights into:

- Latency issues caused by retransmissions or congestion.
- Packet loss and its potential causes.
- Misconfigured protocols leading to failed connections.

---

4. Advanced Packet Capture Techniques

4.1. Using Custom Filters

Create advanced filters to capture specific types of traffic:

- Capture only ICMP packets:

```
set firewall family inet filter icmp-filter term icmp-only from protocol icmp
set firewall family inet filter icmp-filter term icmp-only then capture
set firewall family inet filter icmp-filter term icmp-only then accept
```

4.2. Sampling Traffic

For high-bandwidth networks, sample traffic instead of capturing every packet to reduce resource usage:

```
set forwarding-options sampling input rate <sampling-rate>
```

4.3. Monitoring Encrypted Traffic

Use Junos OS's decryption capabilities (e.g., for SSL/TLS) to analyze encrypted traffic. Ensure proper permissions and configurations are in place.

---

5. Best Practices for Packet Capture and Analysis

1. **Use Filters**: Narrow down traffic to the most relevant packets to save resources and time.
2. **Minimize Impact**: Avoid using packet capture tools extensively in production to prevent CPU overloading.
3. **Secure Captured Data**: Protect PCAP files as they may contain sensitive information.
4. **Analyze Offsite**: Perform detailed analysis on external tools like Wireshark to reduce the load on the Junos device.
5. **Plan for Storage**: Ensure sufficient storage for captured packets, especially in high-traffic scenarios.

Summary

Packet capture and analysis are indispensable for modern network troubleshooting and optimization. Junos OS provides versatile tools for capturing and exporting network traffic, enabling detailed insights through external tools like Wireshark. By using these techniques effectively, administrators can resolve issues, enhance performance, and maintain robust network security.

Troubleshooting Routing Protocols

Routing protocols are critical to the operation of modern networks, ensuring efficient and reliable communication across devices. However, even well-configured protocols like OSPF, BGP, and IS-IS can encounter issues that disrupt connectivity. Troubleshooting these problems effectively is essential for maintaining network performance and stability. In this chapter, we explore strategies and tools in Junos OS for diagnosing and resolving routing protocol issues.

1. Common Routing Protocol Issues

Routing protocol issues can arise from various sources, such as misconfigurations, hardware failures, or software bugs. Understanding the common problems helps focus troubleshooting efforts.

1.1. Misconfigurations

- Incorrect neighbor relationships (e.g., mismatched authentication settings).
- Misconfigured timers or network statements.
- Incomplete or incorrect route redistribution.

1.2. Network Connectivity Problems

- Physical layer issues preventing protocol adjacencies.
- Packet loss or high latency affecting protocol updates.
- Firewall rules blocking routing protocol traffic.

1.3. Convergence Issues

- Slow convergence times due to suboptimal configurations.
- Stale routes or routing loops.

1.4. Incompatible Configurations

- Protocol-specific incompatibilities (e.g., OSPF area mismatches).
- Multi-vendor environment challenges.

2. Tools for Troubleshooting in Junos OS

Junos OS offers a variety of tools for diagnosing routing protocol issues. These tools provide detailed insights into protocol behavior, making it easier to identify and resolve problems.

2.1. Verifying Configuration

Ensure that the routing protocol configuration is correct and complete.

```
show configuration protocols
```

2.2. Monitoring Protocol Status

Use the following commands to check the status of routing protocols:

- **OSPF**:

  ```
  show ospf neighbor
  show ospf database
  ```

- **BGP**:

```
show bgp neighbor
show bgp summary
```

- **IS-IS**:

```
show isis adjacency
show isis database
```

2.3. Event and System Logs

Review system logs for protocol-specific errors:

```
show log messages | match "<protocol>"
```

2.4. Packet Tracing

Use the `monitor traffic` or `tcpdump` commands to capture routing protocol packets and analyze their contents:

```
monitor traffic interface <interface-name> no-resolve matching "<protocol>"
```

2.5. Route Verification

Ensure that expected routes are present in the routing table:

```
show route
```

---

3. Troubleshooting Steps by Protocol

3.1. OSPF Troubleshooting

OSPF is a widely used link-state routing protocol. Common issues include adjacency formation and database synchronization problems.

Adjacency Issues

Check neighbor states:

```
show ospf neighbor
```

- Ensure interfaces are in the same OSPF area.
- Verify MTU settings and authentication.

Database Issues

Verify LSAs in the database:

```
show ospf database
```

- Check for missing or inconsistent LSAs.
- Look for frequent LSA updates, which may indicate instability.

Debugging OSPF

Use the following command for real-time debugging:

```
set protocols ospf traceoptions file ospf-debug
set protocols ospf traceoptions flag all
```

3.2. BGP Troubleshooting

BGP is a path-vector protocol used for inter-domain routing. Its issues often involve neighbor relationships or policy misconfigurations.

Neighbor Issues

Verify BGP neighbors:

```
show bgp neighbor
```

- Check the state of neighbor sessions (e.g., "Idle" or "Active").
- Ensure TCP connectivity on port 179.

Route Advertisement Issues

Check advertised and received routes:

```
show route advertising-protocol bgp <neighbor-ip>
show route receive-protocol bgp <neighbor-ip>
```

Policy Issues

Review import/export policies for errors:

```
show configuration policy-options
```

Debugging BGP

Enable debugging for BGP session establishment:

```
set protocols bgp traceoptions file bgp-debug
set protocols bgp traceoptions flag state
```

3.3. IS-IS Troubleshooting

IS-IS is a link-state protocol often used in carrier networks.

Adjacency Issues

Check IS-IS adjacencies:

```
show isis adjacency
```

- Verify consistent MTU settings.
- Ensure interfaces are configured in the same IS-IS level.

Database Synchronization

Inspect the IS-IS link-state database:

```
show isis database
```

- Check for missing or inconsistent LSPs.

Debugging IS-IS

Use traceoptions for real-time debugging:

```
set protocols isis traceoptions file isis-debug
set protocols isis traceoptions flag all
```

4. Advanced Troubleshooting Techniques

4.1. Route Redistribution Issues

Routing loops or missing routes can occur during redistribution between protocols. Verify redistribution policies:

```
show policy static-to-bgp
```

Check the routing table for unexpected entries:

```
show route extensive
```

4.2. Graceful Restart and Nonstop Routing

If routing protocols are not recovering after device reboots, verify the graceful restart configuration:

```
show configuration routing-options graceful-restart
```

4.3. High CPU Usage

High CPU usage can disrupt protocol operations. Identify the source:

```
show system processes extensive
```

Optimize protocol timers to reduce overhead:

```
set protocols ospf dead-interval minimal
```

5. Best Practices for Routing Protocol Stability

1. **Use Authentication**: Prevent unauthorized devices from forming adjacencies.

   ```
   set protocols ospf authentication-key <key>
   ```

2. **Monitor Logs Regularly**: Keep an eye on system logs for early signs of issues.
3. **Test Changes in a Lab**: Validate new configurations in a controlled environment.
4. **Implement Graceful Restart**: Minimize downtime during planned maintenance.
5. **Document Configurations**: Maintain an up-to-date record of routing configurations.

Summary

Effective troubleshooting of routing protocols is essential for maintaining a stable and reliable network. By leveraging Junos OS's powerful diagnostic tools and following structured troubleshooting steps, administrators can quickly identify and resolve issues. This chapter provided insights into troubleshooting OSPF, BGP, and IS-IS, along with general strategies for maintaining routing protocol stability.

Debugging Tools in Junos OS

Effective debugging is a critical skill for network administrators working with Junos OS. When issues arise, having the right tools and knowledge can drastically reduce resolution time and improve network performance. This chapter explores the powerful debugging tools available in Junos OS and how to leverage them to troubleshoot and resolve network problems efficiently.

1. Introduction to Debugging in Junos OS

Debugging tools in Junos OS provide detailed insights into the operation of network protocols, interfaces, and devices. They allow administrators to:

- Monitor protocol interactions in real-time.
- Capture and analyze packets.
- Trace and log events for detailed analysis.
- Identify and resolve configuration and operational issues.

2. Key Debugging Tools in Junos OS

2.1. Traceoptions

The `traceoptions` feature in Junos OS allows you to monitor specific protocol activities and events. Trace logs provide detailed information for debugging protocol behavior.

Configuring Traceoptions

To enable `traceoptions`, use the following syntax:

```
set protocols <protocol-name> traceoptions file <filename>
set protocols <protocol-name> traceoptions flag <event-type>
```

For example, to trace OSPF events:

```
set protocols ospf traceoptions file ospf-trace
set protocols ospf traceoptions flag all
```

Viewing Trace Logs

Trace logs are stored in `/var/log/`. Use the `show log` command to view the logs:

```
show log <filename>
```

2.2. Monitor Traffic

The `monitor traffic` command captures packets traversing a specific interface. This is useful for analyzing traffic patterns and diagnosing connectivity issues.

Capturing Traffic

To monitor traffic on an interface:

```
monitor traffic interface <interface-name> no-resolve
```

Filtering Traffic

You can filter captured traffic to focus on specific protocols:

```
monitor traffic interface <interface-name> matching <filter>
```

Example. To capture only OSPF packets:

```
monitor traffic interface ge-0/0/0 matching "proto ospf"
```

2.3. Show Commands

show commands provide real-time information about various system components and operations.

Commonly Used Show Commands

- **Interface Debugging**:

  ```
  show interfaces diagnostics
  ```

- **Routing Protocols**:

  ```
  show route
  show ospf neighbor
  show bgp summary
  ```

- **System Status**:

  ```
  show system processes
  show system memory
  ```

2.4. Log Messages

Junos OS maintains detailed system logs for all operational events, stored in /var/log/messages.
Reviewing these logs is a fundamental step in debugging.

Viewing Log Messages

Use the show log command to review system logs:

```
show log messages
```

Filtering Log Entries

To filter specific events or keywords:

```
show log messages | match "<keyword>"
```

Example: To find all OSPF-related messages:

```
show log messages | match ospf
```

2.5. Ping and Traceroute

Basic tools like ping and traceroute are invaluable for diagnosing connectivity and path-related issues.

Using Ping

Test connectivity to a destination:

```
ping <destination-ip>
```

Example: Verify reachability to a remote router:

```
ping 192.168.1.1
```

Using Traceroute

Trace the path packets take to reach a destination:

```
traceroute <destination-ip>
```

2.6. Packet Capture with `pcap`

Junos OS supports advanced packet capture using the `monitor traffic` command and export to PCAP files for analysis.

Capturing Packets

Use the `monitor traffic` command with output redirection:

```
monitor traffic interface <interface-name> write-file <filename>
```

Exporting PCAP Files

Captured files can be exported for analysis with tools like Wireshark.

3. Debugging Techniques for Common Scenarios

3.1. Interface Issues

If an interface is down or experiencing errors:

1. Check the interface status:

   ```
   show interfaces terse
   ```

2. Verify the physical layer:

   ```
   show interfaces diagnostics
   ```

3. Capture traffic on the interface:

   ```
   monitor traffic interface <interface-name>
   ```

3.2. Routing Problems

If routes are missing or incorrect:

1. Verify routing table entries:

   ```
   show route
   ```

2. Check routing protocol adjacencies:

```
show ospf neighbor
```

3. Enable `traceoptions` for the affected protocol.

3.3. High CPU or Memory Usage

1. Check system processes:

```
show system processes extensive
```

2. Identify protocols or services consuming resources.

---

4. Best Practices for Debugging

1. **Enable Debugging Selectively**: Debugging tools can generate a large amount of data. Enable only the necessary options.
2. **Log and Archive**: Save logs for post-incident analysis and documentation.
3. **Use a Test Environment**: Test changes in a lab environment before applying them to production.
4. **Document Findings**: Keep detailed notes on troubleshooting steps and resolutions for future reference.

Summary

Debugging in Junos OS is a systematic process that relies on a suite of tools and commands to diagnose and resolve network issues. By mastering these tools, network administrators can ensure the reliability and performance of their Juniper networks.

Section 11:
Virtualization and Cloud Integration

Overview of Juniper's Virtualization Capabilities

The rise of cloud computing, virtualized networks, and software-defined infrastructures has transformed the networking landscape. Juniper Networks has embraced these changes by offering robust virtualization capabilities that integrate seamlessly into modern, dynamic environments. This chapter provides an overview of Juniper's virtualization solutions, focusing on their features, benefits, and applications.

1. Introduction to Virtualization in Networking

Virtualization decouples network functions and services from hardware, enabling greater flexibility, scalability, and efficiency. With virtualized networks, organizations can:

- Reduce hardware dependency.
- Optimize resource utilization.
- Accelerate service deployment.
- Enhance network scalability and resiliency.

Juniper's virtualization solutions cater to these needs with high-performance virtual network functions (VNFs) and platforms designed for cloud environments.

2. Key Virtualization Solutions from Juniper Networks

2.1. vMX: The Virtual MX Router

The vMX is Juniper's virtualized version of its MX Series routers, offering carrier-grade routing capabilities in a software-based form factor.

Features:

- Fully functional Junos OS with routing, MPLS, and VPN support.
- Scalable throughput and performance for virtualized environments.
- Compatibility with hypervisors such as KVM, VMware ESXi, and public cloud platforms.

Use Cases:

- Service provider networks requiring agile deployment of routing capabilities.
- Virtualized customer edge (vCE) and data center edge routing.

2.2. vSRX: The Virtual SRX Firewall

The vSRX is a virtualized firewall solution providing advanced security capabilities with Junos OS.

Features:

- Stateful and next-generation firewall (NGFW) capabilities.
- Intrusion prevention, threat intelligence, and content filtering.
- Integration with SD-WAN and secure access service edge (SASE) architectures.

Use Cases:

- Protecting workloads in virtualized and cloud environments.
- Secure branch connectivity with SD-WAN integration.

2.3. Contrail Networking

Contrail is Juniper's software-defined networking (SDN) platform, offering network automation and orchestration for virtualized environments.

Features:

- Seamless integration with multi-cloud environments.
- Network overlays for virtual machine (VM) and container-based workloads.
- Advanced analytics and telemetry for virtualized networks.

Use Cases:

- Simplifying multi-cloud networking.
- Enhancing network visibility and policy management.

---

3. Benefits of Juniper's Virtualization Solutions

3.1. Flexibility and Agility

Virtualized solutions allow organizations to deploy and scale network functions on demand. For example, vMX and vSRX can be spun up or down based on changing network needs.

3.2. Cost Efficiency

By replacing physical hardware with software-based solutions, organizations can reduce capital expenses (CapEx) and operational expenses (OpEx).

3.3. Cloud-Ready Architectures

Juniper's solutions are designed for seamless integration with cloud platforms, including AWS, Azure, and Google Cloud, enabling hybrid and multi-cloud networking.

3.4. Enhanced Security

With tools like vSRX and Contrail Networking, Juniper provides robust security features that adapt to the dynamic nature of virtualized environments.

---

4. Integrating Juniper Virtualization into Existing Networks

4.1. Deployment Models

Juniper's virtualization solutions can be deployed in various models:

- **On-Premises:** Within private data centers using hypervisors or container platforms.
- **Public Cloud:** Leveraging cloud-hosted instances of vMX or vSRX for global reach.
- **Hybrid Cloud:** Combining on-premises and cloud-based deployments for flexibility.

4.2. Orchestration and Automation

With Contrail Networking and integration with third-party orchestration tools like Kubernetes and OpenStack, Juniper simplifies network management in virtualized environments.

---

5. Use Cases and Applications

5.1. Service Providers

- Virtualized customer premises equipment (vCPE) solutions using vMX and vSRX.
- Rapid deployment of new services with SDN orchestration.

5.2. Enterprise Networks

- Secure and scalable branch connectivity with virtualized SD-WAN.
- Enhancing cloud adoption with virtualized firewalls and routers.

5.3. Data Center Modernization

- Efficient traffic management with vMX for virtualized data centers.
- Secure connectivity for multi-cloud applications.

---

6. Challenges and Considerations

While virtualization offers significant benefits, there are challenges to address:

- **Performance:** Ensure virtualized network functions meet performance requirements.
- **Compatibility:** Verify integration with existing physical and virtual infrastructure.
- **Management Complexity:** Simplify management with automation tools like Contrail Networking.

Juniper's solutions address these challenges through high-performance VNFs, broad compatibility, and advanced orchestration capabilities.

Summary

Juniper's virtualization capabilities empower organizations to build agile, secure, and scalable networks that align with the demands of modern IT environments. With solutions like vMX, vSRX, and Contrail Networking, Juniper delivers the tools needed to simplify network operations and accelerate digital transformation.

Configuring vSRX and vMX Instances

Juniper's vSRX and vMX virtual appliances provide robust, software-based implementations of their SRX Series firewalls and MX Series routers, offering flexibility, scalability, and cost efficiency in virtualized and cloud environments. This chapter provides detailed steps for configuring and deploying vSRX and vMX instances to enhance your network infrastructure.

1. Overview of vSRX and vMX

vSRX Overview

The vSRX virtual firewall delivers advanced security services, including stateful and next-generation firewall features, intrusion prevention systems (IPS), and threat intelligence. It is ideal for securing virtualized and cloud-native workloads.

Key Features:

- Advanced security services.
- Scalability for dynamic environments.
- SD-WAN and secure access integration.

vMX Overview

The vMX virtual router provides carrier-grade routing capabilities, leveraging the same Junos OS and feature set as physical MX Series routers. It supports MPLS, VPNs, and advanced routing protocols.

Key Features:

- High-performance routing.
- Full Junos OS feature set.
- Flexible deployment in virtualized or cloud environments.

2. System Requirements

Before deploying vSRX or vMX, ensure that your environment meets the following requirements:

vSRX System Requirements:

- **CPU:** Minimum of 2 virtual CPUs (vCPUs).
- **Memory:** 4 GB RAM (8 GB recommended for advanced features).
- **Disk Space:** 10 GB.
- **Hypervisor Support:** KVM, VMware ESXi, or public cloud platforms (AWS, Azure).

vMX System Requirements:

- **CPU:** Minimum of 2 vCPUs (6 vCPUs for high throughput).
- **Memory:** 4 GB RAM (16 GB recommended for production).
- **Disk Space:** 16 GB.
- **Hypervisor Support:** KVM, VMware ESXi, or public cloud platforms.

3. Deployment Process

The deployment process varies slightly based on the hypervisor or cloud platform you use. Below are generic steps for KVM and VMware environments.

3.1 Deploying vSRX:

1. **Download the vSRX Image:**
   - Obtain the vSRX image from Juniper Networks' support portal.
2. **Create a Virtual Machine:**
   - Open your hypervisor or cloud platform interface.
   - Allocate resources (CPU, RAM, disk) as per system requirements.
3. **Upload the vSRX Image:**
   - Use the hypervisor interface to upload the downloaded image.
   - Select the image as the boot source for the virtual machine.
4. **Network Configuration:**
   - Attach virtual network interfaces to the VM.
   - Map interfaces to appropriate VLANs or network segments.
5. **Initial Configuration:**
   - Access the vSRX CLI via the hypervisor console.
   - Set up the management interface:

```
set system root-authentication plain-text-password
set system services ssh
set interfaces ge-0/0/0 unit 0 family inet address <mgmt-ip>/<subnet>
commit
```

   - Verify connectivity using `ping` and `ssh`.

3.2 Deploying vMX:

1. **Download the vMX Image:**
   - Obtain the vMX package (vFPC and vCP images) from Juniper's support portal.
2. **Create Two Virtual Machines:**
   - One VM for the Virtual Forwarding Plane (vFPC).
   - Another VM for the Virtual Control Plane (vCP).
3. **Configure Resources:**
   - Assign adequate resources to both VMs as per requirements.
4. **Upload and Boot Images:**
   - Use the hypervisor interface to upload and attach the respective images to each VM.
   - Start both VMs.
5. **Initial Configuration:**
   - Access the vCP CLI.
   - Set basic parameters like root password and management IP:

```
set system root-authentication plain-text-password
set interfaces em0 unit 0 family inet address <mgmt-ip>/<subnet>
commit
```

4. Integration and Use Cases

4.1. Integrating with Cloud Platforms

- Deploy vSRX or vMX instances on AWS, Azure, or Google Cloud using their respective VM marketplaces or custom images.

- Leverage public cloud APIs to automate scaling and deployment.

4.2. Hybrid Environments

- Use vSRX to secure hybrid cloud deployments by enforcing consistent security policies across on-premises and cloud environments.
- Deploy vMX as a virtual edge router for seamless interconnectivity between cloud and on-premises data centers.

4.3. SD-WAN Integration

- vSRX instances can act as secure SD-WAN endpoints, enabling encrypted communication and application-aware routing.

---

5. Advanced Configurations

5.1. Clustering vSRX Instances

- Enable active-active or active-passive clustering for high availability:

```
set chassis cluster cluster-id <id> node <node-id>
set interfaces fxp0 unit 0 family inet address <mgmt-ip>/<subnet>
commit
```

5.2. MPLS and VPN on vMX

- Configure MPLS and Layer 3 VPN on vMX to support enterprise WANs:

```
set routing-options router-id <router-id>
set protocols mpls interface <interface>
set policy-options policy-statement <policy-name>
commit
```

---

6. Monitoring and Maintenance

Juniper provides tools for monitoring and troubleshooting virtualized instances:

- **Junos CLI:** Use commands like show interfaces, show system, and show logs.
- **Juniper Contrail:** Integrate with Contrail Networking for centralized management.
- **Telemetry:** Enable telemetry to collect performance metrics.

Summary

The vSRX and vMX instances bring the power of Juniper's SRX firewalls and MX routers to virtualized environments, offering flexibility, scalability, and advanced functionality. Whether you're building secure cloud-native applications or optimizing your network infrastructure, these tools provide the agility and robustness required for modern IT landscapes.

SD-WAN Integration with Juniper Networks

Software-Defined Wide Area Networking (SD-WAN) has become a transformative technology, enabling enterprises to manage their WANs with greater efficiency, agility, and cost-effectiveness. Juniper Networks provides robust SD-WAN solutions that integrate seamlessly with its hardware and software ecosystem, leveraging the power of the Session Smart Router (SSR) and Contrail SD-WAN. In this chapter, we will explore how to deploy and manage SD-WAN with Juniper Networks.

1. Overview of Juniper's SD-WAN Solutions

Juniper's SD-WAN offerings are built to address the challenges of traditional WAN architectures by enhancing performance, simplifying management, and improving security. These solutions leverage Junos OS, SSR, and Contrail SD-WAN to create a seamless, intelligent, and scalable network.

Key Features:

- **Application-Aware Routing:** Dynamically route traffic based on application requirements and network conditions.
- **Integrated Security:** Built-in features like secure tunnels, firewall policies, and intrusion prevention.
- **Centralized Management:** Simplify operations with centralized control via Contrail Service Orchestration (CSO).
- **Cloud-Ready:** Native support for hybrid and multi-cloud environments.

Use Cases:

- Optimizing connectivity for branch offices.
- Enhancing performance for cloud applications.
- Securing WAN traffic with integrated policies.

2. SD-WAN Architecture with Juniper

Core Components:

1. **Session Smart Router (SSR):**
   - Acts as the SD-WAN gateway at branch offices and data centers.
   - Provides dynamic routing, zero-trust security, and application optimization.
2. **Contrail Service Orchestration (CSO):**
   - Centralized management platform for policy creation, network monitoring, and orchestration.
3. **WAN Transport:**
   - Supports multiple WAN transport types (MPLS, broadband, LTE, 5G) for flexibility and resilience.
4. **Cloud Gateways:**
   - Facilitate seamless integration with cloud services like AWS, Azure, and Google Cloud.

3. Deploying SD-WAN with Juniper

Step 1: Planning the Deployment

- Identify branch locations, data centers, and cloud endpoints.
- Define application priorities and performance SLAs.

- Ensure compatibility with existing infrastructure.

Step 2: Configuring Session Smart Routers

1. **Install SSR:**
   - Deploy SSRs at branch offices, data centers, and cloud regions.
   - Use virtual or physical appliances depending on the deployment scenario.
2. **Basic Configuration:**
   - Configure SSR with an initial management IP:

   ```
   set system host-name <hostname>
   set interfaces ge-0/0/0 unit 0 family inet address <mgmt-ip>/<subnet>
   commit
   ```

3. **Application Policies:**
   - Create policies to prioritize business-critical applications and enforce security:

   ```
   set policy-options policy-statement <policy-name>
   set routing-options application-routing application <app-name> priority high
   commit
   ```

Step 3: Setting Up Contrail Service Orchestration

1. **Install and Access CSO:**
   - Deploy the CSO platform on-premises or in the cloud.
   - Log in to the web-based management interface.
2. **Onboarding Devices:**
   - Register SSRs and other network elements with CSO for centralized management.
3. **Policy Configuration:**
   - Use CSO to define and push global policies for routing, security, and QoS.

Step 4: Establishing WAN Links

- Configure multiple WAN links for redundancy and load balancing.
- Use overlay tunnels to ensure secure and efficient data transfer.

---

4. Key SD-WAN Features

4.1. Zero-Trust Security

- Enforce secure communication between endpoints with mutual authentication.
- Leverage integrated firewall capabilities to block unauthorized traffic.

4.2. Application-Aware Routing

- Dynamically adjust routing paths based on application performance needs.
- Prioritize critical applications, such as VoIP and video conferencing.

4.3. Analytics and Monitoring

- Use CSO's real-time dashboards for network performance visibility.
- Monitor SLAs and optimize application delivery.

4.4. Cloud Integration

- Seamlessly connect branch offices to cloud services.
- Use SSRs as secure gateways for hybrid and multi-cloud environments.

5. Advanced Configurations

5.1. High Availability (HA)

- Enable HA for SSRs to ensure service continuity during failures:

```
set chassis cluster cluster-id <id> node <node-id>
set interfaces fxp0 unit 0 family inet address <mgmt-ip>/<subnet>
commit
```

5.2. Traffic Segmentation

- Implement virtual routing and forwarding (VRF) instances to segment traffic securely:

```
set routing-instances <instance-name> instance-type vrf
set routing-instances <instance-name> interface <interface>
commit
```

5.3. WAN Optimization

- Use compression and caching features to enhance WAN performance.

6. Monitoring and Maintenance

6.1. Using CSO for Insights

- Monitor network health and application performance through CSO.
- Set alerts for link degradation and SLA violations.

6.2. Debugging Tools

- Use show sdwan commands on SSR to troubleshoot issues:
```
show sdwan status show sdwan sessions
```

Summary

Juniper's SD-WAN solutions provide a powerful, flexible, and secure platform for modern WAN management. By integrating SSR, CSO, and hybrid cloud connectivity, enterprises can achieve unparalleled agility, performance, and security in their networks.

Cloud-Ready Architectures with Contrail

As organizations transition to hybrid and multi-cloud environments, having a robust cloud-ready architecture is essential. Juniper Networks' Contrail platform provides a comprehensive solution for managing, orchestrating, and securing cloud-native infrastructures. By leveraging Contrail Networking, enterprises can ensure seamless connectivity, policy enforcement, and visibility across their cloud environments.

1. Introduction to Contrail Networking

Contrail Networking is a Software-Defined Networking (SDN) solution designed to automate and orchestrate the network connectivity required for cloud-native workloads. It integrates seamlessly with public, private, and hybrid cloud environments, offering advanced features such as network virtualization, service chaining, and multi-cloud management.

Key Features:

- **Network Virtualization:** Overlay networks that decouple physical infrastructure from logical network configurations.
- **Service Chaining:** Automatic chaining of virtualized network functions (VNFs) such as firewalls and load balancers.
- **Multi-Cloud Support:** Unified management across private and public clouds.
- **Integrated Security:** Microsegmentation and network policy enforcement.

Use Cases:

- Simplifying multi-cloud deployments.
- Automating network provisioning for containerized applications.
- Enhancing security with granular policies and microsegmentation.

2. Core Components of Contrail Architecture

Contrail Networking is built on a modular architecture designed for scalability and integration.

2.1. Control Plane:

- Manages the flow of network data and ensures optimal routing.
- Utilizes BGP and XMPP protocols to distribute routes and policies.

2.2. Data Plane:

- Implements the actual forwarding of packets between virtual and physical networks.
- Supports tunneling protocols like VXLAN and MPLS-over-UDP.

2.3. Orchestration Layer:

- Provides a centralized interface for managing workloads and network policies.
- Integrates with Kubernetes, OpenStack, and VMware environments.

2.4. Analytics and Monitoring:

- Collects telemetry data for real-time visibility into network performance.
- Identifies potential bottlenecks and enforces SLA compliance.

3. Deploying Contrail for Cloud-Ready Architectures

3.1. Planning Your Cloud Environment:

- Define workloads and application requirements.
- Identify integration points with existing infrastructure and public clouds.
- Plan for redundancy and disaster recovery.

3.2. Installation of Contrail Networking:

1. **Hardware/VM Requirements:**
   - Ensure sufficient resources for Contrail control nodes, analytics nodes, and compute nodes.
   - Example:

   ```
   Control Node: 8 vCPUs, 32 GB RAM
   Analytics Node: 4 vCPUs, 16 GB RAM
   ```

2. **Software Installation:**
   - Download and install the Contrail software package.
   - Configure network interfaces for management and data traffic.
3. **Configuring Contrail Nodes:**
   - Set up control, compute, and analytics nodes with appropriate roles.
   - Example commands:

   ```
   contrail-setup --role control
   contrail-setup --role compute
   contrail-setup --role analytics
   ```

3.3. Creating Virtual Networks:

- Use Contrail's UI or CLI to define virtual networks.
- Example CLI command to create a virtual network:

```
contrail-cli virtual-network create --name <network-name>
```

3.4. Integration with Orchestration Platforms:

- Configure Contrail as the networking backend for Kubernetes or OpenStack.
- For Kubernetes, deploy the Contrail CNI plugin:

```
kubectl apply -f contrail-cni-config.yaml
```

4. Advanced Features of Contrail

4.1. Microsegmentation:

- Enforce security policies at the application level.
- Example policy creation:

```
contrail-cli policy create --name <policy-name> --src-net <source> --dst-net
<destination> --action allow
```

4.2. Service Chaining:

- Automate the chaining of services like firewalls, load balancers, and IPS.
- Define the chain using YAML or JSON templates.

4.3. Multi-Cloud Connectivity:

- Seamlessly connect on-premises networks to public clouds.
- Use Contrail's multi-cloud gateway for secure communication.

4.4. Container Networking:

- Enable networking for Kubernetes pods with Contrail's CNI plugin.
- Example pod annotation to apply a network policy:

```
metadata:
  annotations:
    networking.contrail.juniper.net/policy: <policy-name>
```

---

5. Monitoring and Troubleshooting

5.1. Using Contrail's Dashboard:

- Real-time visualization of virtual networks and service chains.
- Monitor bandwidth usage and latency for critical applications.

5.2. CLI and API Debugging:

- Use CLI commands to check network health:

```
contrail-status
contrail-cli virtual-network show --name <network-name>
```

5.3. Analytics for Performance Optimization:

- Leverage Contrail's analytics engine for actionable insights.
- Configure alerts for SLA violations and performance degradation.

---

6. Best Practices for Cloud-Ready Architectures

6.1. Align Network Design with Application Needs:

- Prioritize latency-sensitive applications and ensure adequate bandwidth.

6.2. Automate Configuration Management:

- Use automation tools like Ansible or Terraform for repeatable deployments.

6.3. Secure Your Multi-Cloud Environment:

- Apply microsegmentation to minimize the attack surface.

6.4. Monitor and Optimize Continuously:

- Regularly review analytics data to identify and resolve bottlenecks.

Summary

Juniper Networks' Contrail platform enables organizations to build robust cloud-ready architectures. By automating network provisioning, enhancing security, and simplifying multi-cloud management, Contrail empowers enterprises to scale their operations efficiently and securely.

Section 12:
Case Studies and Best Practices

Designing a Scalable Enterprise Network

Designing a scalable enterprise network is critical to ensuring long-term operational efficiency, adaptability, and reliability. Scalability ensures that as the organization's needs grow—be it through new applications, increased traffic, or expanded geographic reach—the network can adapt without major redesigns or disruptions. This chapter outlines best practices, architectural principles, and considerations for designing enterprise networks that are scalable, secure, and resilient.

1. Importance of Scalability in Enterprise Networks

A scalable network supports business growth and technological advancements without sacrificing performance or requiring costly overhauls. Scalability involves the ability to:

- **Support increased bandwidth:** Handle more users, devices, and applications.
- **Adapt to new technologies:** Integrate with cloud computing, IoT, and AI-based applications.
- **Enable geographic expansion:** Seamlessly connect branch offices and remote users.

Benefits of Scalability:

- Future-proofing infrastructure investments.
- Optimized performance under varying workloads.
- Simplified network management and upgrades.

2. Key Principles of Scalable Network Design

2.1. Hierarchical Network Architecture

Divide the network into layers with distinct roles, typically following the three-layer model:

- **Core Layer:** High-speed backbone for interconnecting distribution layers and data centers.
- **Distribution Layer:** Aggregates access layer traffic and enforces policies.
- **Access Layer:** Connects end-user devices and provides local network access.

This modular approach simplifies troubleshooting, policy application, and future expansions.

2.2. Redundancy and Resilience

- Deploy redundant links, devices, and power supplies to minimize single points of failure.
- Use technologies like **Virtual Router Redundancy Protocol (VRRP)** and **Nonstop Routing (NSR)** to enhance availability.

2.3. Scalability in Addressing and Routing

- Use hierarchical IP addressing schemes to simplify subnetting and route aggregation.
- Deploy **OSPF** and **BGP** for scalable and efficient routing.

2.4. Virtualization and Overlay Networks

- Leverage **Virtual LANs (VLANs)** and **VXLANs** to segment traffic logically.
- Use **SD-WAN** for cost-effective and flexible connectivity across branch offices.

---

3. Designing a Scalable Enterprise Network with Juniper Networks

Juniper Networks provides tools and technologies to build scalable, efficient enterprise networks.

3.1. Core and Distribution Design with Junos OS

- Use high-capacity Juniper routers and switches like the **MX Series** or **QFX Series** at the core layer.
- Implement **Link Aggregation (LACP)** for high-speed, redundant links.
- Enable **MPLS** for efficient traffic engineering and segmentation.

3.2. Automation for Scalability

- Use **Junos Automation** to deploy configurations and updates across devices efficiently.
- Employ tools like **Ansible** or **Python with PyEZ** to streamline network management.

3.3. Implementing SD-WAN for Branch Scalability

- Deploy Juniper's **Session Smart Routers** for SD-WAN connectivity.
- Centralize control and monitoring through **Mist AI** for optimal performance and simplified management.

3.4. Cloud Integration

- Extend scalability to cloud environments with **Contrail Networking**.
- Ensure secure and seamless connectivity between on-premises and cloud infrastructures.

---

4. Case Study: Scalable Network Design for a Growing Enterprise

Scenario: A retail company with 50 branch offices plans to expand to 200 locations within three years. The company needs to ensure seamless connectivity, high availability, and cloud integration.

Solution Implementation:

1. **Core Layer:**
   - Deployed Juniper **MX Series Routers** with redundant links to ensure high availability.
   - Used **BGP Route Reflectors** for scalable route management.
2. **Distribution Layer:**
   - Implemented **QFX Series Switches** with VXLAN support for logical network segmentation.
3. **Access Layer:**
   - Configured **EX Series Switches** with VLANs for end-user and device connectivity.
4. **SD-WAN for Branch Offices:**
   - Used Juniper **Session Smart Routers** to connect branch offices to headquarters and cloud applications.
5. **Cloud Integration:**
   - Leveraged **Contrail Networking** for seamless multi-cloud connectivity.
6. **Automation:**
   - Employed **Junos Automation Scripts** and **Ansible Playbooks** for configuration management across 250 devices.

Results:

- Scalable infrastructure supported 4x growth in users and devices.
- Downtime reduced by 90% due to redundant links and proactive monitoring.

---

5. Best Practices for Scalable Enterprise Networks

5.1. Start with a Modular Design

- Use a building block approach to add capacity as needed.

5.2. Plan for Future Growth

- Overprovision core infrastructure to accommodate future expansions.

5.3. Leverage Automation

- Automate repetitive tasks to ensure consistency and scalability.

5.4. Prioritize Security

- Use **Firewall Filters** and **Microsegmentation** to secure network traffic.

5.5. Monitor Continuously

- Employ tools like **Juniper's HealthBot** to monitor network performance and identify issues proactively.

Conclusion

Designing a scalable enterprise network requires careful planning, the right technologies, and a forward-thinking approach. By leveraging Juniper Networks' robust product portfolio and best practices, enterprises can ensure their networks meet current demands while remaining ready for future challenges.

Best Practices for Configuring Firewalls

Configuring firewalls is a fundamental aspect of securing enterprise networks. Firewalls serve as the first line of defense against unauthorized access, malicious attacks, and data breaches. This chapter explores the best practices for configuring firewalls using Juniper Networks' robust solutions, such as the **SRX Series Services Gateways**, ensuring that enterprise networks remain secure and resilient.

1. Importance of Proper Firewall Configuration

A poorly configured firewall can leave networks vulnerable to attacks, mismanagement, and performance degradation. Key benefits of optimized firewall configurations include:

- Enhanced protection against external and internal threats.
- Better control over network traffic and application access.
- Compliance with regulatory requirements.

2. Key Concepts in Firewall Configuration

2.1. Security Policies

Firewalls rely on security policies to control traffic flow. Security policies in Junos OS define rules for:

- **Source and destination:** Specify the IP ranges or zones.
- **Application or protocol:** Define port numbers and protocols (e.g., HTTP, SSH).
- **Action:** Permit or deny traffic.

2.2. Zones

A zone-based firewall organizes interfaces into zones, such as:

- **Trust Zone:** Internal, trusted network.
- **Untrust Zone:** External or public network.
- **DMZ (Demilitarized Zone):** Hosts public-facing services.

2.3. Stateful Inspection

Stateful firewalls track the state of active connections and apply policies based on context, providing better security than stateless firewalls.

3. Best Practices for Configuring Firewalls

3.1. Define Clear Security Policies

- Use the **principle of least privilege** to minimize access.
- Group similar rules to simplify management and reduce redundancy.
- Regularly audit and refine security policies to align with organizational changes.

3.2. Leverage Juniper's Security Zones

- Assign interfaces to appropriate zones based on their function.
- Enforce inter-zone and intra-zone policies to control traffic flow.

- Use **global security policies** sparingly for broad controls.

3.3. Enable Advanced Security Features

Juniper firewalls offer advanced features to enhance security:

- **Unified Threat Management (UTM):** Enable antivirus, antispam, and content filtering.
- **Intrusion Detection and Prevention (IDP):** Protect against known and emerging threats.
- **Application Layer Gateways (ALGs):** Ensure correct handling of specific protocols like SIP and FTP.

3.4. Optimize Performance

- Use **firewall filters** for fast-path processing of high-priority traffic.
- Configure **session limits** to prevent resource exhaustion during attacks.
- Balance logging granularity to capture necessary data without overwhelming resources.

3.5. Monitor and Update Regularly

- Regularly update the firewall's firmware and signature databases.
- Monitor logs and use **Junos Space Security Director** to analyze trends and identify anomalies.

3.6. Plan for High Availability

- Implement **active/active** or **active/standby** redundancy using clustering.
- Test failover scenarios to ensure seamless transitions during outages.

---

4. Junos Configuration Examples for Firewalls

4.1. Basic Security Policy Configuration

```
set security policies from-zone trust to-zone untrust policy web-access match
source-address any
set security policies from-zone trust to-zone untrust policy web-access match
destination-address any
set security policies from-zone trust to-zone untrust policy web-access match
application junos-http
set security policies from-zone trust to-zone untrust policy web-access then permit
```

4.2. Creating and Assigning Zones

```
set security zones security-zone trust interfaces ge-0/0/1
set security zones security-zone untrust interfaces ge-0/0/2
```

4.3. Enabling Intrusion Prevention

```
set security idp active-policy default
set security idp security-package automatic update
```

---

5. Case Study: Enhancing Firewall Security for a Financial Institution

Scenario: A financial institution required robust firewall configurations to protect sensitive data while enabling secure access for remote employees.

Implementation:

1. Deployed Juniper **SRX Series Firewalls** for perimeter security.
2. Created granular security policies to segment traffic between trust, untrust, and DMZ zones.
3. Enabled IDP and antivirus services to block malware and intrusion attempts.
4. Configured logging to centralize event monitoring and analysis.

Results:

- Reduced unauthorized access attempts by 95%.
- Achieved compliance with financial data security regulations.
- Improved incident response time through centralized monitoring.

---

6. Common Pitfalls to Avoid

- **Over-permissive policies:** Avoid using "allow all" rules, which expose the network to threats.
- **Neglecting updates:** Outdated signatures and firmware can leave vulnerabilities unaddressed.
- **Excessive complexity:** Keep configurations as simple as possible to ensure they are manageable and effective.

Conclusion

Properly configuring firewalls is essential for securing enterprise networks and protecting sensitive data. Juniper Networks' solutions, combined with best practices, provide a comprehensive approach to firewall management, ensuring performance and security. By following these guidelines, organizations can create a resilient and adaptable security infrastructure.

Optimizing Network Performance with QoS

Quality of Service (QoS) is a critical component in ensuring the efficiency and reliability of network performance, especially in modern enterprises where applications have varying bandwidth and latency requirements. In this chapter, we explore best practices and strategies for optimizing network performance using QoS techniques within Juniper Networks' infrastructure.

1. Importance of QoS in Network Performance

With the increasing complexity of enterprise networks, managing traffic effectively is essential to:

- Prioritize mission-critical applications.
- Ensure consistent performance for real-time applications, such as VoIP and video conferencing.
- Minimize latency and jitter in time-sensitive traffic.
- Prevent network congestion and packet loss.

2. Key QoS Concepts

2.1. Traffic Classification

Traffic is classified based on parameters like source, destination, application type, or protocol. Proper classification enables more granular control over traffic.

2.2. Traffic Policing and Shaping

- **Traffic Policing:** Limits the rate of traffic flow by dropping packets that exceed predefined thresholds.
- **Traffic Shaping:** Smooths traffic bursts by queuing packets to conform to a set bandwidth rate.

2.3. Congestion Management

- Implements queueing mechanisms to handle traffic during periods of congestion.
- Common methods include **priority queueing** and **weighted fair queueing (WFQ).**

2.4. Differentiated Services (DiffServ)

DiffServ uses **Differentiated Services Code Points (DSCP)** to mark packets for priority handling across the network.

3. QoS in Junos OS

Juniper Networks provides a robust framework for implementing QoS through:

- **Class of Service (CoS):** Manages network traffic based on classifications and priorities.
- **Hierarchical Scheduling:** Ensures traffic management at multiple levels, such as interfaces and queues.
- **Policy Frameworks:** Combines firewall filters and routing policies with QoS.

4. Best Practices for Optimizing Network Performance

4.1. Identify and Classify Traffic

- Use firewall filters and policies to classify traffic into distinct categories, such as voice, video, and bulk data.
- Leverage application-aware technologies to dynamically classify traffic.

4.2. Design Traffic Queues

- Assign high-priority traffic, such as VoIP and video, to low-latency queues.
- Use weighted queuing to ensure fair allocation of bandwidth for medium and low-priority traffic.

4.3. Implement Traffic Shaping

- Use traffic shaping to smooth traffic flows and reduce congestion on oversubscribed links.
- Configure **token bucket filters** to enforce shaping policies.

4.4. Prioritize Real-Time Applications

- Mark traffic for real-time applications with high-priority tags (e.g., EF for voice).
- Use strict-priority queuing to ensure low-latency traffic is forwarded immediately.

4.5. Monitor and Adjust QoS Policies

- Continuously monitor traffic patterns using Junos OS monitoring tools.
- Adjust QoS configurations based on usage trends and application performance requirements.

---

5. Configuration Example: Implementing QoS in Junos OS

Step 1: Define Forwarding Classes

```
set class-of-service forwarding-classes class voice priority low-latency
set class-of-service forwarding-classes class data priority best-effort
set class-of-service forwarding-classes class bulk priority low
```

Step 2: Configure Schedulers

```
set class-of-service schedulers voice-scheduler priority strict
set class-of-service schedulers voice-scheduler transmit-rate percent 20
set class-of-service schedulers data-scheduler priority low
set class-of-service schedulers data-scheduler transmit-rate percent 70
set class-of-service schedulers bulk-scheduler priority low
set class-of-service schedulers bulk-scheduler transmit-rate percent 10
```

Step 3: Map Traffic to Queues

```
set class-of-service interfaces ge-0/0/0 unit 0 forwarding-class voice queue 0
set class-of-service interfaces ge-0/0/0 unit 0 forwarding-class data queue 1
set class-of-service interfaces ge-0/0/0 unit 0 forwarding-class bulk queue 2
```

---

6. Case Study: Optimizing QoS for a Healthcare Network

Scenario:
A healthcare provider faced issues with VoIP call quality during high-traffic periods, impacting their ability to provide telemedicine services.

Solution:

1. Classified traffic into categories: voice, critical healthcare applications, and bulk data.
2. Configured low-latency queues for voice traffic using Junos OS.
3. Implemented traffic shaping to regulate bulk data transfers.

Results:

- Improved VoIP call quality with near-zero jitter and latency.
- Increased network reliability for healthcare applications.
- Achieved better bandwidth utilization without additional hardware investment.

---

7. Common Pitfalls to Avoid

- **Over-configuring QoS Policies:** Avoid overly complex configurations that are difficult to manage and troubleshoot.
- **Neglecting Monitoring:** Regularly monitor traffic to validate QoS policies and make adjustments.
- **Ignoring Real-Time Traffic Needs:** Ensure priority for time-sensitive applications like voice and video.

Conclusion

Effective QoS implementation ensures that enterprise networks can meet performance demands for critical applications. By following Juniper Networks' best practices and leveraging Junos OS features, organizations can achieve scalable and efficient network performance. The insights shared in this chapter serve as a foundation for designing and managing high-performance networks.

Case Study: Implementing a Hybrid WAN

A **Hybrid WAN** combines the reliability of traditional WAN technologies, such as MPLS, with the flexibility and cost-efficiency of broadband and internet connections. This chapter presents a detailed case study of an enterprise implementing a Hybrid WAN using **Juniper Networks** solutions, focusing on achieving high performance, scalability, and cost optimization.

1. Introduction to the Case

1.1. Business Challenge

A global retail organization faced challenges with its traditional WAN setup:

- Increasing operational costs due to reliance on MPLS circuits.
- Lack of flexibility to accommodate emerging cloud applications.
- Poor performance for branch offices located in remote regions.

1.2. Objectives

- Enhance WAN performance and scalability.
- Reduce costs by integrating broadband and internet links.
- Improve support for cloud-based applications and services.
- Maintain robust security across all network connections.

2. Planning the Hybrid WAN Solution

The organization adopted a **Hybrid WAN** strategy with Juniper Networks, leveraging the following components:

- **MPLS for critical traffic:** Ensuring reliable and low-latency connectivity for mission-critical applications.
- **Broadband/Internet for secondary traffic:** Providing cost-effective connectivity for non-critical and cloud-based services.
- **SD-WAN technology:** For dynamic path selection, performance monitoring, and centralized management.

2.1. Key Design Considerations

- Traffic segmentation based on application criticality.
- Implementation of centralized management for simplified operations.
- High availability with redundant connections at branch sites.
- End-to-end security for all traffic flows.

3. Implementation Steps

3.1. Deployment of Juniper Solutions

- **Branch Devices:** Juniper's SRX Series gateways were deployed at branch offices to enable secure and flexible connectivity.
- **SD-WAN Orchestration:** Juniper's Contrail SD-WAN was used for centralized policy configuration and dynamic path selection.

- **Core Routers:** MX Series routers were integrated at data centers for MPLS termination and traffic aggregation.

3.2. Traffic Segmentation and Policy Configuration

- Mission-critical traffic (e.g., point-of-sale systems) was routed over MPLS links.
- Non-critical and cloud-bound traffic (e.g., video streaming, SaaS) was routed over broadband links.
- Policies were configured to enable dynamic failover in case of a link failure.

3.3. Security Integration

- IPsec VPN tunnels were established for secure communication over broadband and internet links.
- Juniper's Unified Threat Management (UTM) was enabled to inspect traffic for malware and other threats.

3.4. Monitoring and Optimization

- Network analytics tools provided by Junos Space and AppFormix were used to monitor performance.
- Continuous optimization of traffic policies based on real-time analytics.

4. Results and Benefits

4.1. Improved Performance

- Enhanced application performance with dynamic path selection.
- Reduced latency for critical applications due to optimized routing.

4.2. Cost Savings

- Significant reduction in operational costs by offloading non-critical traffic to cost-effective broadband links.

4.3. Scalability

- Simplified addition of new branch offices with plug-and-play configurations.
- Greater flexibility to adapt to changes in traffic patterns and business needs.

4.4. Security and Visibility

- End-to-end encryption ensured robust security for all data flows.
- Comprehensive traffic visibility and analytics enabled proactive troubleshooting.

5. Lessons Learned

5.1. Key Success Factors

- Early identification of traffic requirements and classification.
- Use of SD-WAN for dynamic traffic management and ease of operation.
- Robust integration of security measures, ensuring no trade-off between flexibility and protection.

5.2. Potential Challenges

- Initial complexity in configuring traffic policies across multiple links.
- Need for continuous monitoring and adjustment of policies to ensure optimal performance.

6. Configuration Example: Hybrid WAN with Junos OS

6.1. Configuring MPLS and Broadband Links

```
set interfaces ge-0/0/0 description "MPLS Link"
set interfaces ge-0/0/1 description "Broadband Link"
```

6.2. Policy-Based Routing

```
set policy-options policy-statement Hybrid-WAN term MPLS from source-address
192.168.1.0/24
set policy-options policy-statement Hybrid-WAN term MPLS then next-hop ge-0/0/0
set policy-options policy-statement Hybrid-WAN term Broadband from source-address
192.168.2.0/24
set policy-options policy-statement Hybrid-WAN term Broadband then next-hop
ge-0/0/1
```

6.3. VPN Configuration for Internet Traffic

```
set security ipsec vpn VPN-Branch ike gateway Gateway-Branch
set security ipsec vpn VPN-Branch ike ipsec-policy Policy-Branch
```

Conclusion

This case study highlights how Juniper Networks solutions can help enterprises transition to a **Hybrid WAN** model, delivering improved performance, cost savings, and scalability. By leveraging SD-WAN, robust security, and centralized management, organizations can ensure their networks are future-proof and aligned with evolving business needs.

Lessons from Real-World Network Deployments

Network deployments in the real world often bring unique challenges, such as scaling networks for expanding businesses, adapting to emerging technologies, and maintaining performance amidst rapidly growing traffic. This chapter delves into insights and lessons from **real-world network deployments** using **Juniper Networks** solutions, showcasing strategies and best practices for achieving success in complex networking environments.

1. Importance of Learning from Real-World Deployments

1.1. Adapting to Unique Requirements

No two network deployments are the same. Organizations often face unique challenges related to:

- **Industry-specific needs** (e.g., financial services vs. retail).
- Geographic distribution of network endpoints.
- Integration of legacy infrastructure with modern technologies.

1.2. Leveraging Proven Solutions

Learning from successful deployments enables organizations to:

- Avoid common pitfalls during planning and execution.
- Adopt scalable, flexible, and cost-efficient solutions.
- Ensure seamless integration of advanced technologies.

2. Case Study Summaries

2.1. Enterprise-Wide Network Upgrade

Challenge: A multinational corporation needed to upgrade its aging MPLS-based WAN to support cloud applications and improve connectivity for its branch offices.

Solution:

- Deployed Juniper's Contrail SD-WAN to enable hybrid connectivity using MPLS and broadband links.
- Implemented SRX Series gateways for secure, flexible branch connectivity.
- Centralized network management and orchestration through Junos Space.

Lessons Learned:

- Start with detailed traffic analysis to understand application priorities.
- Adopt SD-WAN to simplify policy management and traffic routing.

2.2. Scaling a Service Provider's Network

Challenge: A regional ISP experienced exponential growth in subscriber numbers and needed to expand its network capacity.

Solution:

- Deployed Juniper MX Series routers to enable scalable high-speed routing.
- Used MPLS to support carrier-grade traffic engineering and high availability.
- Implemented advanced CoS (Class of Service) features to manage bandwidth allocation for premium customers.

Lessons Learned:

- Invest in future-proof solutions to support network growth.
- Prioritize traffic engineering capabilities to manage bandwidth effectively.

2.3. Strengthening Security in a Financial Institution

Challenge: A financial institution faced increasing cybersecurity threats and compliance requirements.

Solution:

- Deployed Juniper SRX Series firewalls for robust network protection.
- Implemented Intrusion Prevention System (IPS) features to detect and block sophisticated attacks.
- Integrated Juniper ATP (Advanced Threat Protection) for proactive threat monitoring.

Lessons Learned:

- Regularly update security policies to address evolving threats.
- Combine firewall protection with real-time threat intelligence for comprehensive security.

---

3. Key Takeaways from Deployment Strategies

3.1. Aligning with Business Objectives

Successful network deployments align closely with the organization's business goals:

- Enhanced performance for critical applications.
- Improved customer experience with reliable and fast connectivity.
- Reduced operational costs through efficient resource utilization.

3.2. The Role of Automation

Automation tools such as **Junos Automation** and **Ansible** simplify complex configurations and ensure consistency across devices:

- Automating routine tasks minimizes errors and speeds up deployment.
- Centralized orchestration enhances scalability.

3.3. The Importance of Testing

Thorough pre-deployment testing helps identify potential issues and validate solutions:

- Simulate real-world traffic scenarios to evaluate performance.
- Test failover mechanisms to ensure high availability.

---

4. Best Practices for Real-World Deployments

4.1. Conduct Comprehensive Planning

- Perform a detailed assessment of current infrastructure and future needs.
- Define clear goals for the deployment, such as improved performance, cost savings, or enhanced security.

4.2. Invest in Scalable Solutions

Choose technologies and solutions that can accommodate future growth without significant redesign or investment:

- Opt for modular hardware such as Juniper's MX Series routers.
- Use SD-WAN for flexible connectivity that scales with demand.

4.3. Focus on Security from the Start

- Design security into the network architecture instead of treating it as an afterthought.
- Use tools like SRX firewalls and IPS to safeguard the network against modern threats.

4.4. Leverage Expertise and Training

- Collaborate with experienced network engineers and Juniper's professional services.
- Train internal teams on the use of Junos OS and associated tools to ensure long-term success.

Summary and Future Outlook

Real-world deployments are a testament to the flexibility and reliability of **Juniper Networks** solutions. Whether scaling networks, integrating cloud technologies, or improving security, organizations can achieve success by adhering to best practices and leveraging Juniper's innovative technologies.

As networks continue to evolve, incorporating **emerging trends** such as AI-driven network optimization and zero-trust security will be essential.

Section 13:
Emerging Trends and Future Directions

AI and Machine Learning in Networking

The evolution of networking is entering a transformative phase where **Artificial Intelligence (AI)** and **Machine Learning (ML)** are becoming pivotal in designing, managing, and optimizing networks. AI and ML have moved beyond buzzwords and are now integral components of modern networking strategies, including **Juniper Networks'** innovative solutions.

This chapter explores the fundamental principles, real-world applications, and the impact of AI and ML in networking, with a focus on how Juniper integrates these technologies to deliver intelligent and adaptive network solutions.

1. The Role of AI and ML in Networking

1.1. Why AI and ML Matter in Networking

As networks become more complex due to the proliferation of IoT devices, cloud integration, and increasing traffic, traditional methods of network management struggle to keep up. AI and ML:

- Enhance **network automation** by identifying patterns and predicting outcomes.
- Provide real-time **insights and analytics** to optimize performance.
- Enable proactive **anomaly detection** and **self-healing** capabilities.

1.2. Key Benefits

- **Improved Efficiency:** AI-driven automation reduces manual interventions, saving time and resources.
- **Enhanced Security:** ML algorithms identify and mitigate security threats in real time.
- **Scalability:** AI helps manage and optimize networks as they scale to meet growing demands.

2. Applications of AI and ML in Networking

2.1. Network Automation

AI enables automated network configuration, monitoring, and troubleshooting. Tools like **Junos OS automation scripts** and **AI-enabled orchestration platforms** simplify management tasks.

Example:

- **Intent-Based Networking (IBN):** AI ensures that network configurations align with business goals by translating high-level intents into specific configurations.

2.2. Predictive Maintenance

ML models analyze historical data to predict potential failures or performance degradation. This proactive approach:

- Prevents downtime by addressing issues before they occur.
- Reduces costs associated with reactive maintenance.

2.3. Enhanced Security

AI and ML improve network security by:

- Identifying unusual patterns that may indicate cyberattacks.
- Adapting security policies dynamically to counter evolving threats.

Juniper's **Advanced Threat Prevention (ATP)** uses AI to detect and respond to malware and phishing attacks in real time.

2.4. Traffic Optimization

AI-driven analytics optimize network traffic by:

- Predicting congestion and rerouting traffic dynamically.
- Allocating bandwidth efficiently based on application priorities.

2.5. User Experience Improvements

AI enables **quality-of-experience (QoE)** monitoring by:

- Analyzing application performance metrics.
- Identifying bottlenecks impacting end-user satisfaction.

---

3. Juniper's AI-Driven Networking Solutions

3.1. Juniper Mist AI

Juniper's **Mist AI** platform leverages AI to deliver seamless network operations and improved user experiences:

- **AI-Powered Insights:** Mist AI collects data from access points, switches, and other devices to provide actionable insights.
- **Proactive Problem Resolution:** AI identifies and resolves issues automatically, often before users are affected.
- **Client-to-Cloud Visibility:** Offers comprehensive visibility into the network, applications, and client behavior.

3.2. Paragon Automation

Juniper's **Paragon Automation** suite integrates AI and ML to ensure service assurance and operational efficiency:

- Ensures SLA (Service Level Agreement) compliance with AI-driven monitoring.
- Automates end-to-end lifecycle management.

3.3. Contrail Insights

Part of the **Contrail Networking** solution, Contrail Insights uses AI and ML to:

- Monitor network health and performance.
- Provide root-cause analysis for troubleshooting.
- Optimize workloads in multi-cloud environments.

4. Challenges in Implementing AI and ML in Networking

While the benefits of AI and ML are substantial, challenges remain:

- **Data Quality:** The effectiveness of AI depends on the quality and quantity of data collected.
- **Integration Complexity:** Integrating AI with legacy systems requires careful planning and investment.
- **Skill Gaps:** Organizations need skilled professionals who can develop, implement, and manage AI-driven solutions.
- **Ethical Considerations:** Privacy concerns arise when analyzing large volumes of user data.

5. Future Trends in AI and ML for Networking

The integration of AI and ML into networking is still in its infancy. Future trends include:

- **Self-Driving Networks:** Networks that can configure, monitor, and troubleshoot themselves with minimal human intervention.
- **AI-Powered Edge Computing:** Deploying AI at the edge for faster decision-making and reduced latency.
- **Federated Learning:** Enabling collaborative ML model training across multiple organizations while preserving data privacy.

Juniper Networks is actively investing in these areas, ensuring its solutions remain at the forefront of innovation.

Summary

AI and ML are reshaping the networking landscape, enabling smarter, faster, and more secure networks. Juniper Networks' AI-driven solutions, such as Mist AI and Paragon Automation, demonstrate how these technologies can be effectively applied to modern networking challenges.

The journey of AI and ML in networking is just beginning, promising a future of networks that are self-healing, self-optimizing, and highly adaptive to evolving needs.

Zero Trust Network Security

The traditional approach to network security relied heavily on the idea of a secure perimeter—often referred to as **"castle-and-moat" security**. However, with the rise of **cloud computing**, **remote work**, and the increasing number of **IoT devices**, this model is no longer sufficient. **Zero Trust Network Security** (ZTNS) has emerged as a robust security framework that assumes no entity, whether inside or outside the network perimeter, can be trusted by default. This chapter explores the principles of Zero Trust, its application in modern networking environments, and how **Juniper Networks** integrates Zero Trust into its solutions to deliver secure and resilient networks.

---

1. Understanding Zero Trust Network Security

1.1. What is Zero Trust?

Zero Trust is a security model based on the principle of **"never trust, always verify."** It emphasizes strict access controls and assumes that threats can exist both outside and inside the network.

Key tenets of Zero Trust include:

- **Least Privilege Access:** Users and devices are granted only the minimum level of access required to perform their tasks.
- **Micro-Segmentation:** Networks are divided into smaller segments to limit lateral movement of threats.
- **Continuous Verification:** Access is continuously monitored and re-evaluated.

1.2. Why Zero Trust is Necessary

- **Evolving Threat Landscape:** Cyberattacks are becoming more sophisticated, targeting internal and external vulnerabilities.
- **Perimeterless Networks:** The rise of mobile devices, cloud services, and remote work has rendered traditional perimeters obsolete.
- **Compliance Requirements:** Zero Trust helps organizations meet regulatory requirements for data protection and security.

---

2. Core Components of Zero Trust Architecture

2.1. Identity and Access Management (IAM)

IAM systems ensure that only authenticated and authorized users or devices can access network resources. Features include:

- **Multi-Factor Authentication (MFA):** Adds an extra layer of security beyond passwords.
- **Role-Based Access Control (RBAC):** Restricts access based on user roles.

2.2. Micro-Segmentation

By segmenting the network into isolated zones, micro-segmentation limits the ability of attackers to move laterally. Juniper's **Advanced Security Director** simplifies the implementation of micro-segmentation.

2.3. Endpoint Security

Endpoints, including mobile devices and IoT, are often the weakest links in network security. Zero Trust ensures:

- Endpoints are continuously monitored.
- Access is contingent on compliance with security policies.

2.4. Data Protection

Zero Trust enforces data encryption both in transit and at rest, ensuring sensitive information remains secure even if accessed by unauthorized parties.

2.5. Threat Detection and Response

AI-driven analytics and continuous monitoring detect anomalies and respond to threats in real time. Solutions like **Juniper ATP (Advanced Threat Protection)** are critical for identifying and mitigating attacks.

---

3. Implementing Zero Trust with Juniper Networks

3.1. Juniper's Zero Trust Framework

Juniper Networks offers a comprehensive suite of tools and platforms to support Zero Trust principles, including:

- **Junos OS:** Provides robust access controls and policy enforcement.
- **Mist AI:** Monitors user and device behavior to detect anomalies and enforce policies.
- **Contrail Networking:** Facilitates micro-segmentation and secure virtual networking.

3.2. Secure Access Service Edge (SASE)

Juniper's SASE framework integrates Zero Trust principles with SD-WAN capabilities, ensuring secure access to cloud and on-premise applications. Key features include:

- Secure web gateways (SWG).
- Cloud-delivered firewalls.
- Identity-driven access policies.

3.3. Enforcing Zero Trust Policies

Juniper solutions enable organizations to implement and enforce Zero Trust policies, such as:

- Real-time policy adjustments based on user behavior.
- Automated blocking of suspicious activities.
- Integration with third-party security tools for a unified approach.

---

4. Real-World Applications of Zero Trust

4.1. Securing Remote Work

Zero Trust ensures secure access for remote employees by:

- Requiring MFA for all connections.
- Encrypting all communications between users and applications.

4.2. Protecting Hybrid Cloud Environments

Zero Trust enables secure interaction between on-premises infrastructure and cloud environments. Tools like **Juniper's Contrail Insights** provide visibility and control across hybrid networks.

4.3. IoT Security

IoT devices often lack robust security measures. Zero Trust mitigates risks by:

- Enforcing strict access controls.
- Monitoring device behavior for anomalies.

5. Challenges in Adopting Zero Trust

5.1. Complexity of Implementation

Transitioning to a Zero Trust model requires:

- A detailed understanding of existing network architecture.
- Deployment of new tools and processes.

5.2. Resistance to Change

Organizations may face resistance from employees or stakeholders due to:

- Perceived disruptions to workflows.
- Initial costs of implementation.

5.3. Integration with Legacy Systems

Zero Trust requires seamless integration with legacy infrastructure, which may lack modern security features.

6. Future Trends in Zero Trust Security

6.1. AI and ML Integration

AI and ML will play a larger role in Zero Trust by:

- Enhancing anomaly detection.
- Automating policy adjustments.

6.2. Edge Computing

As edge computing grows, Zero Trust principles will extend to devices and data processed at the network edge.

6.3. Unified Security Frameworks

The convergence of Zero Trust and SASE frameworks will create more cohesive and scalable security solutions.

Summary

Zero Trust Network Security represents a paradigm shift in how organizations approach security. By enforcing the principles of **"never trust, always verify,"** Zero Trust ensures robust protection against evolving threats in today's perimeterless networks.

Juniper's Role in 5G Deployment

The global shift toward **5G networks** is transforming the telecommunications landscape, promising unprecedented speeds, ultra-low latency, and the capacity to support millions of connected devices. As one of the leading networking innovators, **Juniper Networks** plays a critical role in shaping and enabling the **5G ecosystem**, providing solutions that address the unique challenges and requirements of this next-generation technology.

This chapter delves into Juniper's contributions to 5G, focusing on its technologies, architecture, and solutions designed to enable seamless 5G deployment and operation.

1. Understanding 5G and Its Impact on Networking

1.1. Key Features of 5G

5G is characterized by three primary enhancements over previous generations:

- **Enhanced Mobile Broadband (eMBB):** Delivering faster data speeds and higher capacity for mobile networks.
- **Ultra-Reliable Low Latency Communication (URLLC):** Enabling real-time applications like autonomous vehicles and remote surgery.
- **Massive Machine-Type Communication (mMTC):** Supporting IoT devices and smart cities with scalable connectivity.

1.2. The Challenges of 5G Deployment

Deploying 5G networks involves several challenges, including:

- **Increased Traffic Demands:** 5G generates exponentially more data than its predecessors.
- **Densification of Networks:** The use of small cells and edge computing adds complexity to network management.
- **Security Concerns:** The expanded attack surface requires robust, scalable security solutions.
- **Automation Needs:** Managing 5G's dynamic and complex networks necessitates advanced automation tools.

2. Juniper's Approach to 5G Network Architecture

2.1. Disaggregated and Cloud-Native Infrastructure

Juniper supports the **disaggregation** of traditional network elements, enabling flexible and cost-effective deployment. Key aspects include:

- **Cloud-Native Design:** Juniper's products are optimized for containerized, virtualized environments, ensuring scalability and agility.
- **Separation of Control and User Plane (CUPS):** This approach enhances flexibility and performance in 5G core networks.

2.2. Converged Transport Architecture

Juniper's transport solutions, such as the **MX Series 5G Universal Routing Platform**, provide the scalability and performance needed for 5G networks. Features include:

- Support for **Segment Routing (SR)** and **EVPN** for efficient traffic management.

- Integration with existing 4G/LTE networks for a seamless transition to 5G.

2.3. End-to-End Network Slicing

Network slicing is a core capability of 5G, enabling multiple virtual networks to operate on shared infrastructure. Juniper's solutions enable:

- Dynamic creation and management of slices.
- Quality of Service (QoS) policies tailored to specific applications or services.

---

3. Juniper's 5G-Ready Solutions

3.1. RAN and Edge Optimization

Juniper's **Contrail Edge Cloud** and **Mist AI** platforms optimize performance at the radio access network (RAN) and edge:

- **Contrail Edge Cloud:** Provides orchestration for virtualized RAN and edge workloads.
- **Mist AI:** Uses machine learning to improve performance and troubleshoot edge devices.

3.2. Secure and Scalable Core Networks

The **PTX Series Packet Transport Routers** deliver high-capacity and low-latency connectivity for 5G cores, ensuring secure and scalable data transport.

3.3. AI-Driven Network Automation

Juniper leverages **AI-driven automation** through solutions like **Paragon Automation**, enabling:

- Real-time monitoring and self-healing capabilities.
- Simplified deployment and operation of 5G networks.

3.4. Security for 5G Networks

Security is a critical component of 5G infrastructure. Juniper's **SRX Series Firewalls** and **Advanced Threat Protection (ATP)** solutions provide:

- Comprehensive protection for 5G cores and edge devices.
- Zero Trust principles for securing network access.

---

4. Partnering for 5G Success

Juniper collaborates with leading telecom providers and organizations to accelerate 5G adoption. Examples include:

- Partnerships with major service providers to deploy scalable 5G networks.
- Contributions to standards bodies like the **3GPP** to shape 5G specifications.

---

5. Real-World Use Cases of Juniper's 5G Solutions

5.1. Smart Cities

Juniper's 5G solutions power smart city initiatives by:

- Enabling IoT device connectivity and management.
- Supporting real-time analytics for traffic and infrastructure monitoring.

5.2. Enhanced Mobile Broadband

Service providers leverage Juniper's transport solutions to:

- Deliver faster mobile broadband to users.
- Reduce latency for applications like online gaming and video streaming.

5.3. Industrial Automation

Juniper supports industrial automation by:

- Providing secure, low-latency connectivity for robotic systems.
- Facilitating real-time data exchange in manufacturing environments.

---

6. The Future of Juniper in 5G

6.1. Focus on Open Standards

Juniper is committed to fostering open ecosystems, ensuring its solutions integrate seamlessly with third-party systems.

6.2. Expansion of AI Capabilities

Future enhancements to Juniper's **Mist AI** and **Paragon Automation** platforms will drive further efficiencies in 5G management.

6.3. Sustainability Initiatives

Juniper is focused on reducing the environmental impact of 5G deployments through energy-efficient hardware and software solutions.

Summary

Juniper Networks is at the forefront of the 5G revolution, providing innovative solutions that address the unique challenges of next-generation networks. From secure and scalable infrastructure to AI-driven automation, Juniper's technologies are empowering service providers and enterprises to harness the full potential of 5G.

Future Developments in Junos OS

Juniper Networks' **Junos OS** has consistently evolved to meet the demands of an ever-changing networking landscape. From its inception as a robust operating system for routers to its current role as the foundation of an integrated, versatile networking ecosystem, Junos OS has been a cornerstone of Juniper's success. With the rapid adoption of new technologies like **5G**, **artificial intelligence (AI)**, **cloud computing**, and the **Internet of Things (IoT)**, Juniper Networks continues to innovate and expand Junos OS to address emerging challenges and opportunities.

This chapter explores the future developments and trends shaping Junos OS, highlighting key advancements that will empower networks of tomorrow.

1. The Vision for Next-Generation Junos OS

1.1. Focus on Cloud-Native Architecture

Junos OS is evolving to become fully cloud-native, offering enhanced modularity and flexibility. This approach enables:

- **Microservices Architecture:** Breaking down the OS into independent, scalable components.
- **Containerized Deployment:** Running Junos OS on containers to support dynamic scaling and rapid updates.
- **Seamless Integration:** Enhanced interoperability with public, private, and hybrid cloud environments.

1.2. AI-Driven Networking

As networks become increasingly complex, AI will play a pivotal role in optimizing operations. Junos OS is being enhanced with:

- **Predictive Analytics:** Leveraging AI to anticipate and mitigate network issues before they occur.
- **Autonomous Operations:** Enabling self-healing and self-optimizing network capabilities.
- **Improved User Experiences:** AI-driven insights to simplify configuration and management tasks.

2. Enhancements for Emerging Technologies

2.1. 5G and Beyond

Junos OS is designed to support the **massive bandwidth**, **low-latency requirements**, and **network slicing capabilities** essential for 5G networks and future wireless technologies. Enhancements include:

- **Support for 5G Core Functions:** Enabling ultra-reliable, low-latency communication and massive IoT connectivity.
- **Multi-Access Edge Computing (MEC):** Optimizing performance for applications that require real-time data processing.
- **Dynamic Network Slicing:** Allowing service providers to allocate resources dynamically for diverse use cases.

2.2. IoT and Edge Computing

Junos OS will enable secure, scalable connectivity for IoT devices and edge computing scenarios:

- **Enhanced Scalability:** Supporting billions of connected devices across diverse industries.

- **Edge Intelligence:** Processing data locally for faster decision-making and reduced latency.
- **Zero Trust IoT Security:** Implementing granular access controls and threat detection at the device level.

---

3. Automation and Orchestration Enhancements

3.1. Advanced Automation Capabilities

Building on tools like **PyEZ**, **NETCONF**, and **Event Scripts**, Junos OS will incorporate:

- **Intent-Based Networking (IBN):** Allowing users to define high-level business policies that the network automatically implements.
- **Expanded API Support:** Simplifying integration with third-party tools and platforms.
- **Real-Time Telemetry:** Providing granular, real-time insights for better visibility and control.

3.2. Unified Network Management

Future iterations of Junos OS will streamline management across devices, clouds, and service providers:

- **Single Pane of Glass:** Offering a unified interface for managing diverse network elements.
- **Cross-Domain Orchestration:** Coordinating policies and configurations across WAN, data center, and cloud networks.

---

4. Security Innovations

4.1. Integration with Zero Trust Architectures

Junos OS will advance its alignment with **Zero Trust** principles:

- **Granular Access Controls:** Strengthening security for users, applications, and devices.
- **Dynamic Policy Updates:** Leveraging real-time analytics to adjust security policies proactively.

4.2. AI-Driven Threat Detection

Future iterations will enhance threat detection and response capabilities using AI:

- **Behavioral Analytics:** Identifying anomalous patterns indicative of malicious activity.
- **Automated Mitigation:** Responding to threats in real-time to minimize impact.

---

5. Multi-Vendor and Open-Source Collaboration

5.1. Open Standards and APIs

Juniper is committed to fostering open ecosystems, ensuring Junos OS integrates seamlessly with:

- **Third-Party Tools:** Supporting interoperability across heterogeneous networks.
- **Open Networking Standards:** Collaborating with industry groups to define and implement new standards.

5.2. Open-Source Contributions

Junos OS will continue leveraging and contributing to open-source projects:

- **Linux Integration:** Using Linux-based enhancements to improve modularity and scalability.
- **OpenConfig Support:** Enabling standardized configuration and monitoring across platforms.

6. Sustainability and Green Networking

As environmental concerns grow, Juniper is prioritizing energy efficiency in Junos OS:

- **Dynamic Power Management:** Reducing energy consumption during low network utilization.
- **Optimized Hardware Usage:** Enhancing performance without increasing power requirements.
- **Sustainable Practices:** Supporting carbon-neutral operations through intelligent resource allocation.

7. Real-World Applications and Benefits

7.1. Service Provider Networks

Junos OS innovations will empower service providers to deliver ultra-reliable services while reducing operational costs:

- Improved scalability to handle growing traffic demands.
- Enhanced automation for faster service rollouts.

7.2. Enterprise Networks

Enterprises will benefit from:

- Seamless integration of on-premises and cloud environments.
- AI-driven tools to simplify network management and improve security.

7.3. Government and Critical Infrastructure

Junos OS advancements will enable secure, reliable networks for critical applications, including:

- Defense communications.
- Smart city infrastructure.

Summary

The future of Junos OS is defined by innovation, adaptability, and a commitment to excellence. As the backbone of Juniper Networks' offerings, Junos OS is evolving to address the challenges of modern networking, including 5G, IoT, AI, and beyond. By embracing cutting-edge technologies and fostering open ecosystems, Juniper is ensuring that Junos OS remains a leader in the ever-changing networking landscape.

Appendices

Appendix A: Glossary of Networking Terms

This glossary provides definitions and explanations of key terms and concepts frequently used in networking and Junos OS. It serves as a quick reference for readers to clarify any terminology encountered in this book.

A

- **Access Control List (ACL):** A set of rules used to control network traffic and restrict unauthorized access to devices and data.
- **Aggregate Route:** A single route that represents multiple networks, used to simplify routing tables.
- **Anycast:** A networking method in which the same IP address is assigned to multiple devices, and the nearest one is selected for communication.
- **Autonomous System (AS):** A collection of IP networks and routers under the control of a single organization that presents a common routing policy to the internet.

B

- **Bandwidth:** The maximum amount of data that can be transmitted over a network connection in a given period, usually measured in bits per second.
- **Border Gateway Protocol (BGP):** A dynamic routing protocol used to exchange routing information between autonomous systems.
- **Broadcast:** A method of sending data to all devices on a network simultaneously.

C

- **Class of Service (CoS):** A set of techniques used to manage network traffic by prioritizing certain types of data.
- **Collision Domain:** A network segment where data packets can collide with one another during transmission.
- **Content Delivery Network (CDN):** A system of distributed servers that deliver web content and resources to users based on their geographical location.

D

- **Default Gateway:** The routing device that sends data from a local network to devices on other networks.
- **DHCP (Dynamic Host Configuration Protocol):** A protocol that automatically assigns IP addresses to devices on a network.
- **DNS (Domain Name System):** A system that translates human-readable domain names (e.g., www.example.com) into IP addresses.

E

- **Edge Router:** A router located at the edge of a network that connects internal networks to external networks, such as the internet.
- **Egress Traffic:** Outgoing data traffic leaving a network.
- **Encapsulation:** The process of wrapping data with protocol-specific information for transmission across a network.

F

- **Firewall:** A security system that monitors and controls incoming and outgoing network traffic based on predefined rules.
- **Forwarding Table:** A table in a router or switch that stores information on where to send incoming packets.
- **Frame:** A data packet at the Data Link layer of the OSI model, containing source and destination MAC addresses.

H

- **Hop Count:** The number of intermediate devices (like routers) that a packet passes through to reach its destination.
- **Host:** Any device on a network that has an IP address and can send or receive data.

I

- **Ingress Traffic:** Incoming data traffic entering a network.
- **Interface:** A network connection point on a router, switch, or other networking device.
- **IS-IS (Intermediate System to Intermediate System):** A link-state routing protocol used for moving information efficiently within a network.

J

- **Junos OS:** The operating system used by Juniper Networks devices, designed for reliability, scalability, and programmability.

L

- **LAN (Local Area Network):** A network that connects devices in a limited geographical area, such as an office or building.
- **Link Aggregation (LAG):** The process of combining multiple physical network links into a single logical link for increased bandwidth and redundancy.

M

- **MAC Address:** A unique identifier assigned to a network interface card (NIC) for communication on the physical network.
- **Multicast:** A method of data transmission in which data is sent to multiple devices simultaneously, but only to those that have joined the multicast group.
- **MPLS (Multiprotocol Label Switching):** A routing technique that directs data packets along predefined paths based on labels rather than network addresses.

N

- **NAT (Network Address Translation):** A method of mapping private IP addresses to a single public IP address, enabling devices in a local network to access external networks.
- **NetFlow:** A network protocol used for collecting and monitoring IP traffic data.

O

- **OSPF (Open Shortest Path First):** A dynamic routing protocol that uses link-state information to determine the best path for data transmission.

P

- **Packet:** The basic unit of data transmitted over a network, containing headers and payload.
- **Port:** A logical endpoint in a network connection, identified by a number, used for routing traffic to specific services.

Q

- **QoS (Quality of Service):** A set of techniques used to manage network traffic and ensure optimal performance for critical applications.

R

- **Routing Table:** A database in a router that stores the routes to various network destinations.
- **Routed Protocol:** A protocol that can carry data between different networks (e.g., IP).

S

- **SDN (Software-Defined Networking):** An approach to networking that uses software-based controllers to manage network resources and configurations.
- **Subnet:** A smaller network created by dividing a larger network into segments to improve performance and security.

T

- **Throughput:** The actual amount of data transferred over a network in a given time period.

- **Traceroute:** A diagnostic tool used to track the path that data packets take to a destination.

U

- **Unicast:** A method of data transmission in which data is sent from a single source to a single destination.

V

- **VLAN (Virtual Local Area Network):** A logical grouping of devices in a network to segment traffic and improve management.
- **VPN (Virtual Private Network):** A secure connection over the internet that provides privacy and encryption for data transmission.

W

- **WAN (Wide Area Network):** A network that spans a large geographical area, connecting multiple LANs.

Z

- **Zero Trust:** A security model that assumes no device or user should be trusted by default and enforces strict identity verification and access controls.

This glossary is intended to enhance your understanding of networking concepts as you explore the chapters of this book. For a deeper dive into these terms, refer to the Juniper Networks documentation and additional resources provided in Appendix D.

Appendix B: Juniper Certification Paths

Juniper Networks offers a comprehensive certification program designed to validate the skills and expertise of networking professionals working with Junos OS and other Juniper products. These certifications are highly regarded in the industry and help individuals enhance their career prospects in networking and IT.

Juniper Certification Levels

Juniper certifications are structured across multiple levels to accommodate networking professionals with varying levels of expertise. The certification levels include:

1. Associate Level (JNCIA)

The Juniper Networks Certified Associate (JNCIA) is the entry-level certification and is ideal for those new to networking or Junos OS.

- **Prerequisites:** None
- **Key Focus Areas:**
    - Junos OS fundamentals
    - Basic networking concepts
    - Configuration and monitoring of Junos devices
- **Popular Exam:** JNCIA-Junos (JN0-104)

2. Specialist Level (JNCIS)

The Juniper Networks Certified Specialist (JNCIS) is designed for professionals with intermediate-level knowledge and experience.

- **Prerequisites:** JNCIA certification
- **Specialization Tracks:**
    - **Enterprise Routing and Switching (JNCIS-ENT):** Focuses on advanced networking and enterprise solutions.
    - **Service Provider Routing and Switching (JNCIS-SP):** Geared toward service provider networks.
    - **Security (JNCIS-SEC):** Covers advanced security solutions using Junos OS.
    - **Data Center (JNCIS-DC):** Focuses on Juniper's data center technologies.
    - **DevOps (JNCIS-DevOps):** Centers on automation and DevOps practices.

3. Professional Level (JNCIP)

The Juniper Networks Certified Professional (JNCIP) is a certification for advanced professionals who design and manage complex networks.

- **Prerequisites:** JNCIS certification in the corresponding track
- **Specialization Tracks:**
    - **Enterprise Routing and Switching (JNCIP-ENT)**
    - **Service Provider Routing and Switching (JNCIP-SP)**
    - **Security (JNCIP-SEC)**

- Data Center (JNCIP-DC)
- DevOps (JNCIP-DevOps)

4. Expert Level (JNCIE)

The Juniper Networks Certified Expert (JNCIE) is the highest certification level and is for elite professionals who possess expert-level knowledge of networking.

- **Prerequisites:** JNCIP certification in the corresponding track
- **Specialization Tracks:**
  - **Enterprise Routing and Switching (JNCIE-ENT)**
  - **Service Provider Routing and Switching (JNCIE-SP)**
  - **Security (JNCIE-SEC)**
  - **Data Center (JNCIE-DC)**
  - **Automation and DevOps (JNCIE-DevOps)**
- **Exam Format:** Hands-on lab exam

Specialization Tracks Overview

Each track focuses on specific areas of networking, allowing professionals to specialize in their field of interest:

1. **Enterprise Routing and Switching:**
   Covers LAN/WAN technologies, protocols like OSPF and BGP, and advanced enterprise network configurations.
2. **Service Provider Routing and Switching:**
   Focuses on MPLS, BGP, and service provider technologies for building scalable networks.
3. **Security:**
   Explores firewall configurations, intrusion detection, VPNs, and advanced security measures with Juniper SRX.
4. **Data Center:**
   Centers on technologies like EVPN, VXLAN, and data center architectures.
5. **DevOps:**
   Emphasizes automation tools, scripting with Python, and frameworks like NETCONF and REST APIs.

Certification Benefits

- **Industry Recognition:** Demonstrates expertise in networking and Juniper technologies.
- **Career Advancement:** Opens up opportunities for roles in network engineering, security, and data center management.
- **Practical Knowledge:** Provides hands-on experience in designing and managing real-world networks.
- **Community and Resources:** Certified professionals gain access to exclusive Juniper resources, forums, and learning materials.

How to Prepare

Juniper offers various resources to help candidates prepare for certification exams:

- **Juniper Learning Portal:** Access training courses, study guides, and labs.
- **Practice Exams:** Evaluate your readiness with mock exams.
- **Official Documentation:** Use Juniper's documentation for in-depth technical understanding.
- **Study Groups:** Join community forums and groups to discuss exam topics with peers.

Certification Renewal

Juniper certifications are valid for **three years**. Professionals must renew their certifications by passing the same or a higher-level exam within their specialization track before expiration.

The Juniper Networks certification program provides a structured path for professionals to enhance their skills and validate their expertise. Whether you're a beginner or an experienced professional, pursuing these certifications can significantly boost your career in networking.

Appendix C: Resources for Further Learning

Building a strong foundation in Juniper Networks and its associated technologies requires continuous learning and exploration. This appendix provides a comprehensive list of resources to help you expand your knowledge and stay updated with the latest developments in networking and Junos OS.

1. Official Juniper Networks Resources

Juniper Networks Official Website

- **URL:** [www.juniper.net] (https://www.juniper.net)
- The official website of Juniper Networks is the best place to start. It provides access to product documentation, whitepapers, and company updates.

Juniper TechLibrary

- **URL:** [www.juniper.net/documentation] (https://www.juniper.net/documentation)
- A comprehensive repository of technical documentation, configuration examples, and best practices for all Juniper products.

Juniper Learning Portal

- **URL:** [www.juniper.net/learningportal] (https://learningportal.juniper.net)
- Offers a range of online training courses, certification preparation materials, and hands-on lab exercises.

Juniper Support Portal

- **URL:** [support.juniper.net] (https://support.juniper.net)
- Provides access to software downloads, product release notes, and technical support articles.

2. Certification and Training Resources

Juniper Certification Program

- Juniper's certification program includes JNCIA, JNCIS, JNCIP, and JNCIE tracks. Visit the official certification page for details:
    - **URL:** [www.juniper.net/certification] (https://www.juniper.net/certification)

Juniper Networks Training and Webinars

- Juniper regularly offers free webinars and paid training sessions to help professionals enhance their skills.

Juniper Open Learning

- **URL:** [learningportal.juniper.net/openlearning] (https://learningportal.juniper.net/openlearning)
- A free learning initiative providing video tutorials and practice quizzes for Juniper certifications.

3. Online Communities and Forums

Juniper Elevate Community

- **URL:** [community.juniper.net] (https://community.juniper.net)
- Join discussions with Juniper experts and peers to share knowledge, ask questions, and explore use cases.

Stack Overflow

- **URL:** [stackoverflow.com] (https://stackoverflow.com)
- A platform to ask and answer technical questions related to Junos OS and networking.

Reddit - Networking and Juniper Subreddits

- Explore relevant discussions and insights on networking topics:
  - **/r/networking:** [reddit.com/r/networking] (https://www.reddit.com/r/networking)
  - **/r/juniper:** [reddit.com/r/juniper] (https://www.reddit.com/r/juniper)

4. Books and Publications

Books on Junos OS and Networking

- *Juniper MX Series* by Douglas Richard Hanks Jr.
- *JUNOS Cookbook* by Aviva Garrett
- *Network Automation with Python and Junos OS* by Jonathan Looney

Networking Fundamentals

- *Computer Networking: A Top-Down Approach* by James Kurose and Keith Ross
- *Network Warrior* by Gary A. Donahue

5. Online Learning Platforms

Udemy

- Offers paid courses on Junos OS, automation, and general networking.
- **URL:** [www.udemy.com] (https://www.udemy.com)

Pluralsight

- A subscription-based platform offering comprehensive courses on networking and Juniper technologies.
- **URL:** [www.pluralsight.com] (https://www.pluralsight.com)

Coursera

- Explore networking fundamentals and advanced topics through university-led courses.
- **URL:** [www.coursera.org] (https://www.coursera.org)

6. Hands-On Lab Environments

Juniper vLabs

- **URL:** [jlabs.juniper.net] (https://jlabs.juniper.net)
- Access free virtual labs to practice Junos OS configurations and test network setups.

EVE-NG (Emulated Virtual Environment Next Generation)

- **URL:** [www.eve-ng.net] (https://www.eve-ng.net)
- Use EVE-NG to simulate complex networks, including Juniper devices.

GNS3 (Graphical Network Simulator)

- **URL:** [www.gns3.com] (https://www.gns3.com)
- A powerful open-source network simulation tool for learning and practicing networking.

7. Blogs and Technical Articles

Official Juniper Blogs

- **URL:** [blogs.juniper.net] (https://blogs.juniper.net)
- Features insights from Juniper engineers, product updates, and technical discussions.

Packet Pushers

- **URL:** [packetpushers.net] (https://packetpushers.net)
- A popular blog and podcast focusing on networking trends and technologies.

Network Computing

- **URL:** [networkcomputing.com] (https://www.networkcomputing.com)
- Covers a wide range of networking topics, including Juniper-related content.

8. YouTube Channels and Video Tutorials

Juniper Networks Official Channel

- **URL:** [www.youtube.com/JuniperNetworks] (https://www.youtube.com/JuniperNetworks)
- Watch product demos, tutorials, and recorded webinars.

David Bombal

- **URL:** [www.youtube.com/DavidBombal] (https://www.youtube.com/DavidBombal)
- Features practical networking tutorials and Junos OS walkthroughs.

NetworkChuck

- **URL:** [www.youtube.com/NetworkChuck] (https://www.youtube.com/NetworkChuck)
- Covers a mix of networking, automation, and IT-related topics.

9. Networking Conferences and Events

Juniper NXTWORK

- Juniper's annual conference featuring keynotes, technical sessions, and networking labs.
- **URL:** [www.juniper.net/nxtwork] (https://www.juniper.net/nxtwork)

Cisco Live

- While Cisco-centric, it often covers networking fundamentals applicable to Juniper as well.
- **URL:** [www.ciscolive.com] (https://www.ciscolive.com)

These resources provide a wealth of knowledge for professionals seeking to deepen their expertise in Juniper technologies and networking in general. Whether you're preparing for certifications, enhancing your technical skills, or staying updated with industry trends, leveraging these resources will ensure continuous growth in your networking career.

Conclusion

As we reach the conclusion of **"Juniper Networks Unveiled: A Guide to Junos OS and Network Implementation,"** it is important to reflect on the journey you've undertaken through the intricate world of Juniper Networks and its technologies. This book was crafted to serve as a comprehensive resource, guiding you through the core concepts, configurations, and advanced practices needed to excel in managing Juniper-based networks.

A Holistic View of Networking Excellence

From understanding the foundational aspects of Juniper Networks to diving deep into the configurations of Junos OS, each chapter has been designed to empower you with practical knowledge and strategic insights. Whether it's mastering routing protocols, implementing high-availability solutions, or leveraging automation, this book equips you with the tools to design, deploy, and manage robust and scalable networks.

Key Takeaways

Here are some essential learnings from the book:

- **Mastery of Junos OS**: From navigating the CLI to configuring routing and switching, you've gained a solid foundation in using Junos OS effectively.
- **Advanced Networking Practices**: The chapters on high availability, performance optimization, and network automation provide you with skills to manage complex network environments with confidence.
- **Security and Virtualization**: With a deeper understanding of Juniper's approach to security and cloud integration, you're prepared to tackle modern networking challenges.
- **Emerging Trends**: Insights into AI, machine learning, and zero trust security ensure that you stay ahead in the rapidly evolving networking landscape.

Next Steps on Your Networking Journey

The knowledge gained from this book is just the beginning. Networking is a dynamic field, constantly evolving with new technologies and challenges. To stay competitive and innovative, consider the following:

- **Continuous Learning**: Utilize the resources provided in the appendices, including Juniper's training programs and certifications, to deepen your expertise.
- **Hands-On Practice**: Leverage tools like Juniper's vLabs and network simulation platforms to refine your skills.
- **Networking Communities**: Engage with peers through forums and industry events to exchange ideas and learn from real-world scenarios.

Gratitude and Closing Thoughts

Thank you for choosing this book as your guide to Juniper Networks. Whether you are a networking professional, a system administrator, or a student aspiring to break into the field, this book aims to support your career growth and technical mastery. The world of networking is vast and full of opportunities, and with the knowledge you've gained, you are better equipped to navigate and excel in this exciting domain.

Juniper Networks stands as a beacon of innovation, and as you continue to explore its ecosystem, remember that every challenge you encounter is an opportunity to grow. Embrace new technologies, keep refining your skills, and continue to contribute to building the networks of tomorrow.

Here's to your success in networking and beyond!

www.ingramcontent.com/pod-product-compliance
Lightning Source LLC
LaVergne TN
LVHW081753050326
832903LV00027B/1928